"A terrific read! The real-life story compels, the warmth and humor of the voice appeals. This memoir reminds us of the value of an open heart, and how happenstance and chosen acts of generosity can make the circle of those we love as family grow larger in surprising and oh-so-welcome ways."

—Margaret Hasse, adoptive mother and author of *Milk and Tides*, Minnesota Book Award finalist

"In this memoir, Kate rides the emotional roller coaster of her relationships with her birthmother and other members of her birth family with great honesty and generosity of spirit. As she thoughtfully explores the efforts of balancing fate, faith, family and motherhood, we discover that this isn't just Kate's story—it's the story that many of us live, every day."

—Linda Back McKay, birthmother, adopted mother and author of *Shadow Mothers: Stories of Adoption and Reunion* and creative consultant for the play *Watermelon Hill*

"Engaging, funny and often moving, this memoir tenderly reveals Ms. Vogl's inner turmoil and confusion when her birthmother unexpectedly arrives on the scene. A must read for anyone touched by adoption."

—Jan Schwartz, Licensed Psychologist, MA, LP, LICSW

Lost and Found: A Memoir of Mothers

Lost & Found

A Memoir of Mothers

Kate St. Vincent Vogl

NORTH STAR PRESS OF ST. CLOUD, INC.
St. Cloud, Minnesota

ISBN: 0-87839-331-5
ISBN-13: 978-0-87839-331-2

First Edition, April 15, 2009

Printed in the United States of America

Published by
North Star Press of St. Cloud, Inc.
P.O. Box 451
St. Cloud, Minnesota 56302

northstarpress.com

Dedication

"for Jen and Juls,
so they may know
and never doubt
and never forget
a mother's love"

Kate, Jim, and girls.

Acknowledgments

If I haven't made it clear enough already, I would like to acknowledge the enormous debt of gratitude I owe to Mom and Val and Nor and Aunt Mary and Teresa, without whom I would not have a complete understanding of what it means to be a mother. For that matter, I must add Jen and Julia, without whom I would not have a complete understanding of what it takes to be a mother.

It's all good.

And I'd like to thank my husband, Jim, for everything, but most of all for taking me by the hand when I was about to turn away from the path to my dream. He was the one who led me back. I'm so thankful and so lucky to have found in love and marriage a partner who has given me his all and shown me a strength in family and in faith greater than I'd dreamed possible when I first said, "Yes."

To Jim's family and to mine—expecially to Dad—because who else loves kids and stories as much as I do? To Aimee and Allisyn and Chris, for their generosity, warmth of spirit and willingness to share our story.

To Lorian Hemingway, for clearing the way for me, so I would know once and for all that what I've believed is my calling is something someone else in the world would believe in, too.

To Patricia Weaver Francisco, who saw hope in an early draft and gave me a vision to get me past what I didn't want to see.

To the late great Carol Bly, who saw what I did to fiction and said I should write nonfiction instead.

To Margaret Hasse, who caught a few things we hadn't already, and Linda Back McKay, for giving me the spark to make this book a reality. To Corinne and Seal at North Star, for making it happen.

To my dearest, most wonderful and most patient friend, Christin Walth, who taught me friends can make the best doting mothers, especially when helping out at conferences. Thanks for walking this red carpet with me. Here's hoping to even more!

To my friends Michele and Leslie, too, who willingly shared so much with me. To Sherri, who understood I couldn't visit because of a Pumpkin Fest I needed to do instead.

To my writer's group—particularly Jan Schwartz, Rod Nelsestuen, Ed Clark, Peter Arnstein, Aimee Loiselle, Christopher Davis, and Ben Mulhern. They endured the early chapters and still told me this was important.

To all the ladies in my book club, for plowing through not one of my books but two. And for being honest about what they liked (and didn't). This is a better story for it.

To Amy Jo Hyde, my daughter's superb French teacher, whose book club explored this author's need to be a professional mother. This author is still thinking about that one. You may be right.

To mothers and birthmothers and mothers-in-law and aunts-who-are-not-aunts and aunts who are. And for all kinds of mothers everywhere: This one's for you.

so • ca

Your Call

You should know what to do when the stranger on the phone tells you the name of your husband, your child, and where you live—and then has the name of your father and his hometown and knows your mother just died. You should know that this woman will next tell you your birth date, but you cannot believe all the facts she has at her fingertips, the weight of all she knows. She even knows the hospital you were born in—something you were never quite sure of—but just in case you don't believe everything she has on you, she tells you details about your parents. Details no one would know unless they've sat down with them for a cup of coffee and a slice of pound cake. Characteristics only old friends have earned the right to tease them about, and you hear this stranger rattling them off, from your father's good-natured disorganization to your mother's Swedish practicalities, all in a that's-the-facts list recorded with clinical observation.

And if you didn't know it before, you do now, that you are deep in the midst of an identity theft. Not yours because the life you've lived was never yours to begin with.

Because a lifetime ago, you belonged to this woman—before she signed her name to the stack of papers she's reading from, back when she'd held the sole right for you to call her *Mother*.

⁓ 1 ⁕

Found

We are among the first in the gym for the Grandparents' Lunch. To anyone else, I suppose, we seem a natural trio: mother, daughter, granddaughter. But we're not—not in so many words. Val is my birthmother, Julia's grandmother by blood. And today, Val will be meeting people not in my family. People who don't know our story.

I have no idea how to introduce her.

I can't just say: This is Val, she's my birthmother. That hardly seems fair, to recount her sexual history first thing. I could talk instead about how she's director of a program for troubled teens. But that's not why she's here.

I swear if I'd thought this through more, I might not have invited her.

That's so not true, it's not fair to even think that as my eleven-year-old rushes from one round table to the next, checking paper flower centerpieces for her class photos.

"Over here," my daughter says, waving us over to the table closest to the makeshift stage. "Here's my class." She holds one of the flowers gently in her hand, her student picture as the center pistil. Photo squares of her classmates adorn the rest of the construction paper bouquet.

Val bends over to take it all in. "I love it," she says. She is sincere in her compliment, not the bored parental, "That's nice," I'll admit I sometimes dole out.

I should be more like Val. Be in this moment. This time together is what she's dreamed of. More than anything, I am glad—so glad—to make that real for her.

There's guilt, though, too, for me. That it's not Dad and my stepmom Jackie who are here, though they're too far away to come for a Wednesday luncheon. They're still working. As for my husband Jim's folks, they're older and it's better if one of his sisters would drive them up from Iowa, but that's too complicated for the middle of the week. It's complicated for Val, too, but we both knew there'd be no way she'd miss this when I finally offered.

Years past, I couldn't bring myself to ask, even though I knew how much it would mean to my girls. Even though it's meant my older daughter has missed out on Grandparents' Day completely. It's been that hard to let go of my childhood promise to my mother, made long before she died. But with time comes rationalization, if not peace, and now I've found mine.

A rail thin blonde pulls her grandmother to our table. I recognize the older woman from all the times she'd picked up the girl from Brownies.

"Hey guys," Julia says. So Midwest, to use that collective for girls. "I want you to meet my Nana Val."

Maybe I'm not smarter than my fifth grader, who just made that seem so easy. But that simple line of introduction has gotten me into trouble once before.

The older women reach across the table to shake hands, careful not to let their silk jackets drag across our box lunches.

Val seems to be floating, she's so happy to be a part of this moment. That's when I notice the mole near her eye, a flaw on a face sparkling glad. That mole, it's just like mine. For a moment, I am taken aback by such tangible evidence of our connection. It's there, if only I'd look.

"You're lucky," I say to Julia's friend. "You get to see your grandma all the time. Julia's Nana had to come all the way from Cleveland."

"So, that's where you grew up?" the grandmother nods.

As if, in my early years, Val must have been more to me than a grocery clerk I didn't know (or didn't remember?) in the town where my dad went to work.

Val and I exchange looks.

"Yes," I say, unsure if that counts as a lie during these Catholic school hours. Yes, I grew up in Ohio. But Val didn't raise me. She's not my mother, I want to say, but that would take away from the truth of what she is.

She's a grandmother to my girls, a grandmother my mother could never be. That's what I tell people, when they ask how I feel about my birthmother finding me. It's true, but it's not enough—not for either of us.

Not for Val, who will wait until the next time she sees me to confess she still struggles with the decision made forty years ago to give me up for adoption.

Not for me, either. I am torn I can't give her more. All I can offer Val now, all the love and connection with me and my girls, and I can't give what I'm sure she's still looking for.

I can't bring myself to call her my mother.

THE IRONY IS, OF COURSE, that Val is more real to my girls than my mom will ever be. Val has driven thirteen hours to listen to Jen play Für Elise in a nursing home lobby, and another time she came for Julia tap-dancing all of three minutes as we watched from the back rows of an auditorium. We've met in Chicago to walk with the dinosaurs in the Field Museum and to sip tea at the American Girl Restaurant. We shuffled the husbands off to a bar while we cooed over Jen and Julia as they served their Samantha and Kaya dolls from a three-tiered tray. Triangle-cut peanut butter and jelly sandwiches never tasted so good.

These are memories my girls and I will cherish. It's like what I remember of lunches with my mother. Tea, especially: four cubes of sugar in hot amber water at the Chinese restaurant at Summit Mall. And at Higbee's downtown, I'd have the children's box lunch: shaped like a house, with secret compartments—chicken pot pie when I opened the sliding door, mashed potatoes hiding in the upstairs dormer.

But Mom's gone, dead of cancer when my firstborn was a baby. Some circle of life: Mom had lost her father just after adopting my older sister. Funny, I never could bring myself to call Jim Stewart my grandpa. I never really knew him that way—only as a Washington lawyer, as my parents were always proud to point out.

For my girls, I'm hoping it's different. When I talk about Mom to them, she's Grandma Peri. My girls know what she was to me, of that I'm sure. Just this week my older daughter shared with me her new favorite story, where one of the characters revisits his dead mother's favorite haunts, hoping to connect with her once more.

I know too well what she means.

Val and I have come together—and we'll stay together—for our different reasons. She's connected with a child she thought she'd lost forever. And I welcomed her into my life at first to give thanks, but it's hard to stave off what's been sent from the netherworld. Because the way Val found me was through my mother's obituary.

TO BE FAIR, UNTIL I WAS ALMOST THIRTY, I hadn't considered what it would be like for the woman who'd given birth to me. What it was like to carry a baby she knew she couldn't keep. What it was like to protect me from her father, whose hands knew how to hurt. To be banished to a Home for Unwed Mothers, a sorority my mother had never told me of. To know the gentle man who was her baby's father would do the right thing and marry her if only she'd ask. To be strong enough not to ask.

No, I'd never thought what it was like on the other side.

Not until I'd read Merry Bloch Jones' book about birthmothers just a couple of months before Val first contacted me. I wouldn't have known to pull it off the library shelf, but the title had caught my eye in an alumni newsletter. For the first time, I'd considered how hard it must be to let go of something you're biologically programmed to protect. Most, I learned, never recover. There were no happy endings, not in those pages.

I can't say I'm used to that concept. It's just as jarring to me now as it was the first time I read a book in which something bad happened to a

4

main character. I could not believe Louisa May Alcott let Beth die in Little Women. Death, I'd thought, was the worst thing to grieve about. But in this book on birthmothers, these were all real women, whose lives all derailed after losing a child who'd lived. It was a story without hope, a tale of unrelenting sorrows, in this world where I'd always been taught there would be hope whenever you tried your best, even if you'd messed up a bit in the beginning.

Some mistakes, I guess, don't ever go away. They just grow up.

THIS IS THE STORY. VAL CALLED out of the blue on a Saturday night. Almost ten o'clock. You can imagine her working up the courage until she realizes it'd be too late to call unless she does it now, just does it.

My husband Jim and I on the other end, each with a glass of chardonnay and watching a video that for once wasn't so horrible we'd just shut it off. A date night. Jen was just a baby; our expectations for a good Saturday night had changed.

That's when our phone rang.

We already knew nothing good came from calls that time of night. We'd grown past friends calling from pay phones at bars. We learned that tenet just a few years before, when the phone shrilled after we'd already shut off the lights. It was Dad's mother who'd died; eighty-six and she'd been out shoveling the walk for the paperboy.

So, what godforsaken news would this call bring? Jim and I exchanged dark looks and he pulled himself out of the green armchair.

"Hello?" he said before handing the receiver to me, his face unreadable. My lips formed the word "Who?" but he shrugged. No one he knew.

I got up and went into the darkness of the kitchen. "This is Kate," I said, using my professional, don't bother me voice, but she asked me the obvious again, confirming my full name, my street, that I lived in Charlotte, North Carolina.

"Yes," I said, cautiously now, aware this was some sort of verification she was making.

"And are you the daughter of James St. Vincent of Medina, Ohio?" And was she notifying next of kin? Ever since Mom had died three months before, I'd been worrying whether Dad had lost his will for living—like a Clydesdale he once had, Marie, who died of a broken heart not long after her mate collapsed.

"Yes, Jim St. Vincent is my dad," I said. My husband Jim was hovering on the other side of the kitchen island, his face whitened with worry. Next of kin. Of course. I cradled the phone tight against my shoulder, pulled my feet up onto the top rung of my oak stool.

She launched into her next question, taking a tack I'd never expected. Next of kin, indeed. "I gave birth to a baby girl," she said then, naming the month, the day, the year I was born, the hospital I was born in. "Would that be you?"

Training is meant to prepare you for the worst. When it happens, then, your reaction is immediate, as if a natural response. Before I'd gone to law school, I'd been a trusting soul, never questioning anyone, even if they assured me the sky was green. But now my guard was up instantly, and words came out of my mouth before I'd had any time to think. "Well, I was born in that hospital then, but I don't know how many girls were born there on that date."

Then again, maybe it wasn't something I'd needed training for. Like I told my sister when she said we were adopted: maybe you are, but I'm not.

"I have some background information about the couple who adopted that baby girl. Would you like me to read it to you?"

So I could hear and be convinced she was looking for someone else. "That would be fine," I said. And so she began.

Imagine having someone write two or three pages describing your parents without giving any physical description, just how they act, how they live, how they love. What hobbies they followed, before they had you. What their family life was like when they were kids. Imagine someone telling you all the stories you'd heard growing up, and maybe ones you hadn't, but everything else is there and so tangible you are afraid to speak, this spell might be broken, and you would lose this lens you have to the past and the present and the future and you have nothing to say, it's all so perfect, the life you had and the life you could have had intersecting in this one moment, and you are glad you are there on that stool, with your husband across the counter from you, worry in his eyes, mouthing the words, "Who is it?" and him understanding when you scrawl across a notepad in suddenly uneven handwriting these words, of which you are certain: "My birthmother."

And you will know, there and then, there'll be things this woman you've never met will do for you, little things you shouldn't have to worry about but you do because you can't help but think about your mom, and because you don't want to have to retrace any steps along this path just opened up for you. And later, when you've had her in your home and shared the stories of your childhood no one else would care to listen to but a mom (or someone who would have liked to have been one), then you will have the reluctant audacity to ask this stranger to do something that will break her heart all over again.

Like wait for you to make the next move.

And she knows, she knows, that could be never.

∽ 2 ≈

A Silent Vow

It's inevitable when I tell people I know my birthmother. "Oh, you found her," they say. Drives me crazy, that assumption. It comes with an eyebrow raised, a knowing smile. They've read P.D. Eastman's story about the baby bird who doesn't know better than to ask a cow, a dog, a cat, a steam shovel: "Are you my mother?" And the poor thing keeps repeating, page after page, "I have to find her. I will! I WILL!"

But I never had that driving desire. Maybe I would have if I'd found out a different way that I was adopted. Maybe if I didn't have my mother's easy smile, my dad's Italian eyes. Maybe if we all weren't such a perfect match, or maybe if I was a different person—like my sister.

We found out we were both adopted late in the morning one summer. My sister, Aimee, was maybe ten, which would make me eight. I'd just finished breakfast, stuffing cereal turned too soggy down the drain and finishing it off with a good round of disposal. I stood back from the sink and flipped the switch, knowing to keep my distance from those jaws of death. Usually at that point, Mom would come down the half flight of stairs and tell me I needed breakfast more than the disposal did, but today she was busy.

Aimee was yelling about something, the sound muffled. Maybe they were back in Mom's closet.

What I needed was something to occupy me while those words were being exchanged upstairs. I wanted to get dressed for the day, but Aimee had apparently moved the argument to our room. I'd no idea what they were arguing about. I just knew I needed to steer clear. When Aimee yelled like that, Mom's voice took an edge even Aimee rarely dared touch. This time, though, Mom answered with tears of her own. Mom crying—that was something to keep away from.

Fortunately, there was plenty for me to do down in the kitchen. Especially with the cat there. On the ledge of the bay window crouched Tigger, the tip of her tail twitching, her eye on a blue jay guarding the feeder. I slid onto the ledge, my back against the window, and I stretched my pink flannel nightgown over my knees and drew the bottom edge underneath my feet. I stroked the cat, even though she didn't want me to, as Aimee and Mom slammed doors and cried upstairs. I made up a story, a quiet place I could go to hide from an anguish I didn't wish to discover.

Aimee's footsteps pounded down the stairs. I had to be busy, I had to be—

I whipped my toes out from under my pajamas and studied how I could stretch them apart. How long would I have to pretend to be absorbed with this? Here, this was interesting: no matter how hard I strained, each toe was still bound with the others at their base. I could not separate them further.

"*Katie*." My sister pounded into the kitchen, her face screwed up in tears like the baby pictures of her up in the hall. "I've got something awful to tell you. Just awful," she said, her breath in hiccupping sobs as she pulled me off the window seat and dragged Mom's chair away from the table. She sat me down, then crouched in front of me.

This was serious. This would be worse than anything I'd ever heard before, I could tell. What could she possibly have to say? Gramma had died? We were moving?

"I hate to break this to you," she said, her voice close to shattering.

No way were we due for another visit from Robby, my cousin with hands as big as my head, so big I'd hidden under the reading cot in my room, hoping he'd go away.

"Katie," my sister said, so close now I could smell Peanuts, the stuffed dog she tucked under her face to fall asleep. "I've got to tell you: we're adopted."

We're adopted. What did she mean, we?

Her hands locked onto the arms of my chair, blocking me in. We'd had our share of fights. I'd known since I could read that a carefree afternoon would be lost if I took her side when she was in the middle of a row with Mom. Besides, I'd seen *Sesame Street*. I knew which one just didn't belong. Mom and Dad and I—we all had brown eyes, brown hair. Aimee, on the other hand, was truly blonde, with heavily hooded blue eyes. Everything finally made sense.

"Maybe you are, but I'm not."

Oh, I still cringe at how easy that was for me to say.

"Ma!" Aimee turned to leave the kitchen, bawling again, but Mom was already there. She was crying like Aimee, her eyes screwed up tight and words garbled through yawing sobs.

"It's true," she got out. "It's true." And she bent down and took us both in her arms and buried her head in our little shoulders, so the yoke of my nightgown dampened with her tears. She held us tight, like she might lose us again, these children who were not hers to begin with, children she'd made hers with love. She and Aimee cried together, but not me. I was too young to cry at something like that.

"I didn't know when to tell you," Mom said. "When you were babies you were too young to understand. And then I couldn't tell Aimee without telling you, and you weren't ready yet, and then I didn't know how to bring it up." She tried so hard to stop her tears with the edge of her hand, along the side of her Estée Lauder nose. "I just didn't know," she said, and she squeezed us again, like she did when she told me she loved me more than anything else in the whole wide world.

But I'd read enough Nancy Drews. I knew when something didn't make sense. I had to pull myself away. "If you didn't tell," I said, "how did Aimee find out?"

Aimee, poor Aimee, had a confession of her own. She stared down into the nubby green kitchen carpet until I had to look too, and then miserably she said, as if it could be her fault, "The Bebba."

"Ohhh."

The Bebba had what I would learn to call "issues of his own." Nobody liked him around, and yet he'd come knocking, asking to play. Mom would make us because it wasn't nice to tell him what we really thought of him. I don't think he did anything horrible enough to earn that nickname. Maybe his clothes weren't as nice, maybe he didn't wash his hair as often, maybe he just had the dumb bad luck to irk a kid in the neighborhood with more friends and thus more clout, enough anyway to get everyone to call him the Bebba.

Then again, maybe there was good reason I could never call him friend, and I was about to find out. "What did he say?" I asked.

Apparently he and Aimee had a fight. Words were exchanged until the Bebba hit the end of his sparring ability and pulled out all he had left. "Yeah, well, you're adopted," he'd said, wounding more deeply than with any stick or stone. Maybe his parents had spoken the words in hushed tones over their dinner table. Enough for him to understand that he wasn't supposed to know, that it was something to be ashamed of in his world.

That I've never understood, and maybe it's because I learned of it by the fireplace in our kitchen, not in the midst of a fight with the neighborhood bully. There is something wonderful, absolutely marvelous, about being adopted, after all. Something that makes it better than just being born.

It means, more than anything, that you are wanted, really wanted. That you are meant to be loved, more than anything else in the whole wide world.

I DON'T REMEMBER BEING BUGGED by the news. Maybe it's just my nature, that I don't need to be close—at least if it's not on my terms. Drove Mom crazy that I didn't want to be held as a baby. I'd cry for her to come by my side, but if she'd try to scoop me up, I'd point back to my crib. Put me down.

11

Maybe I just didn't understand what kind of mess could be made by words strewn in the morning chill of our kitchen. Or maybe I bore no wound since I wasn't the one bearing the brunt of the word "adopted" when it was first thrown about. The way the Bebba said it. The way Mom's face changed when asked if it was true, how could it possibly be true?

But I had no sense of betrayal. Whatever confession Mom made that morning, it did not seem to apply to me or what was important in my world. I understood without asking that Mom would still walk us out to the bus in the morning in her Eddie Bauer quilted bathrobe, and I'd still get to sleep in my twin bed with Michigan State bumper stickers carefully applied to the headboard, my cat would—whether I liked it or not—still lay out dead squirrels upon my pink shag carpeting, and whenever I wanted I could still hide under my green corduroy reading cot. None of this would change.

Aimee must have thought otherwise. I tracked her down in Mom's dressing room. She'd pulled the phone down off the vanity and sat frog-legged in the doorway, the phone between her legs as she dialed all her friends, one by one, to solemnly inform them she was adopted. Like it was a terminal illness, like it was contagious. Intent on her duty, she barely had time to toss me a line. "I'm almost done," she said over her shoulder, as if to assure me I could make all my calls shortly as well. I'd made myself comfortable on the blue shag behind her, cross-legged and curious at her urgency.

What did she have to confess? In my child's mind, the issue was over long ago, and it had nothing to do with us. If there was a problem, it belonged to those strangers. I wasn't sure how they'd ended up with babies belonging to our family. "God has different ways of bringing families together," is how a friend of mine explained to her children they were adopted.

When we first were figuring out who was family (and how and why), Aimee seemed to want me beside her. So as she made her calls, I stayed for moral support—as much as an eight-year-old can give. It wasn't long before I started tracing my finger along the decorative columns in Mom's new wallpaper, alternating blue velvet and foil in all its mid-seventies elegance. Only vaguely was I listening to Aimee's telephone confessions when Mom came into the room with an armful of laundry. Aimee lowered her voice, curved her back away from Mom, and whispered news to Carrie of her diagnosis.

"What are you doing?" Mom cried, dropping the basket onto the bed. "Don't do that. Don't call and tell everyone," she said, her voice tight, still trying to rein in her long-held secret.

I don't remember what happened next. Aimee probably slammed the phone down, pretending she'd never called. I'm sure I wanted to disappear. Confrontations made me nervous; they still do. I spent most of my time back then with my nose in a book, flipping past even the most fictitious conflicts. Maybe I backed up against the doorframe and buried my head into my knees. Maybe Mom got down on the floor next to me and enveloped me in her arms.

Strange I would make myself remember her hugging me, not my sister.

"It's not that it's bad, honey," she told us. That I remember. "It's just not their business."

I was young enough to be more concerned with imaginary friends than gossiping neighbors. But even then—even before I realized that Dad wouldn't acknowledge for years what I'd learned down in our kitchen—I knew we were keeping an elephant in our house.

I WAS A CHILD FULL OF STORIES TO TELL, and having the blank slate of unknown parentage allowed for so many possibilities. I was the daughter of a princess who'd fallen in love with a pauper and gave up her rights to the kingdom for love. I was the daughter of a Nobel laureate who had to escape the country and leave me behind. One thing I knew for sure about the girl who had me: she was famous, her reason tragic.

Only once did I dare ask what was known. Maybe a whole year had passed since I'd started looking for faces like mine on the street and in the news, maybe it only seemed that long. Mom was cleaning, and I tracked her down in the living room. She didn't know any more than what she'd already shared, she told me. Either she'd forgotten (as she said) or she was only will-

Iceskating with Mom and Aimee.

ing to offer a mundane cover for the truth: "It was just some college kids who got into trouble," Mom said, before I understood what "trouble" meant.

I could work with the idea, though. Princesses went to college. Then again, maybe she was a genie. If Barbara Eden could live with an astronaut, another could certainly get in trouble. The next time I went in for a physical, I dreaded when the doctor would notice something strange about me. "We'll have to run tests," he'd say. There would be no explanation for the erratic results, but I would know. It would be because I had genie blood in me. I was made of magic.

OF COURSE, I KNEW BETTER THAN TO TELL anybody that. I couldn't even tell my sister; she'd make fun of me for making up stories. I was still smarting from the time at the grocery store when she laughed at me for singing about the yellow-slickered fisherman on the fish sticks box.

But even my imagination had its limits. At the end of the day, all I wanted was to curl up in my pink Holly Hobby bed with my cat, Tigger, at my feet. I knew there was a difference between what went on in my head and what was real. Real to me was Mom and Dad and Aimee. The thought of someone out there who'd had me first? I couldn't begin to fathom that. No, my family was who was there for me. They were tangible, they were all I needed.

But Aimee needed more. She figured I did, too, and pulled me upstairs to the attic to sift through all the baby shower cards Mom had saved.

Aimee settled in, frog-legged and businesslike in her review, directing me to set aside all the questionable cards, those with phrasing that suggested the giver might have been "the one."

I sat down on that plywood floor and helped my big sister look, even though I felt guilty going behind Mom's back to spot clues, even though I'd no burning desire to see my own search through. I helped my big sister look, even though I did not understand why Aimee would want to find her heartache.

She'd been born a preemie; her birthmother had likely been using and abusing substances during the pregnancy. Back then, Mom's delicate phrasing overlay that sharp truth, and still I could not imagine a happy ending for my sister underneath it all—even if I was young and couldn't articulate the worst of what that could be. No way would I want to hear that story told, but Aimee has always wanted so badly to better understand her beginning.

Though my arrival in this world was just "regular," as Mom had put it, I had no desire to find out more. I'd seen the way Mom's smile turned thin and her answers flat when I'd asked what regular trouble meant for college students. I'd seen how much it hurt to admit she hadn't been able to bear us on her own. I had no need to put Mom through that again, if only to find out more about a woman neither of us knew at all.

Years later, Val would be appalled at what little Mom had known. "But the agency had all my information," she said. "I sat through all those interviews."

Somewhere along the way, along the years and after the finalization of my adoption, the papers had been filed away in the drawer and compartmentalized in my parents' minds. And then forever lost to time. I finally sent away for a copy to share with Val after she sent me all she had on my parents. The details concerning my birthmother were blandly regular. A medium brunette, nineteen, from a large family of Italian, Irish and German heritage, had wanted her baby to have a two-parent home. She'd been editor of her high school paper. She'd been "in good health." As for the birthfather, he, too, was of English and German heritage and "in good health," except he had one ear larger than the other: An exception a nineteen-year-old girl had once noted, now forever a part of Catholic Services' records.

When the agency forwarded me the background information—the non-identifying information—of my birthparents, they asked if I wished to place my name on a register to indicate I was willing to be contacted if the other party was, too.

No need, I said, as I read what I already knew about Val and what little they'd had about my birthfather, David. Strange how the summary was written as if meant to be forgotten. Blanked names for blank faces, bland and forgettable so families could move on, become whole, leaving any trouble behind. Better that way, it was believed at the time, to just forget about the women who'd given us up. Relinquished us, as the professionals say now. Open adoption was not even an option through Catholic Services in the 1960s. No, those records had been sealed tight, and looking held a danger of its own.

DINNERTIME, MAYBE FIVE YEARS AFTER we first found out, and the darkness of winter filled the bay window that arced behind my father. Mom and Aimee on either side, discussion brittling into tears. Maybe it was a party my sister wasn't allowed to go to. Maybe her grades needed improvement, or maybe it was just her teenaged attitude. Voices were raised, so it could have been any of that. But Aimee then said the forbidden.

Dad wouldn't believe she used those god-awful words. I swore she did, though, because that's when I took my silent vow. Dad told me, "Boy, if I'd heard that, I would have—" but I didn't hear the rest. All this time, and it was still a hot button for him. I knew what he would have done: he'd stand by Mom's side, he'd straighten Aimee out. Because that was the time he grabbed Aimee by her shirt collar and dragged her out of her chair and across the table until all the cups and plates between them had been scraped out of the way by her body. I should clarify—that was not by any means our typical dinner.

Then again, it was not a typical thing for a daughter to say.

"I'm going to find my real mom," Aimee said that night, her voice harsh and loud, though I tried not to hear it as I pushed creamed corn around on my plate in my feeble attempt at anonymity. "She'll let me," my sister said.

In another house, a teen might be saying, "I hate you." In another generation, she might have taken issue with the Establishment. A mere device children use, a means to achieve an end. As parents we are warned not to take such words seriously, yet how can we not, when our children so uncannily cut to the quick of what we care most about?

My mother, I should tell you, was not typically swayed by her children's threats. She was, after all, a Swede. She would not take any emotional rollercoaster rides, not even when my sister threatened to run away a couple years later. "Leave your credit card on the counter before you go," she said, without turning away from the stove, knowing Aimee would return before nightfall.

We knew we were loved. We did. Mom had made sure my velvet dress was hanging in my closet on Sunday mornings, and she'd ladle heaps of ham and scalloped potatoes on my plate for my birthday. When I was older and needed heaps of other kinds of helpings, she would hug my boyfriend hello when I brought him home from school even though I knew she didn't think he was right for me.

All that and yet, that night, Aimee dared suggest the myriad patchwork repairs made for her stuffed Peanuts dog never counted, that she never asked for escargot snuck into the hospital when her tonsils came out. No, none of what Mom did mattered because of a biological technicality.

"But I changed your diapers," Mom had said, her voice quavering.

So quickly unsettled by those words of my sister.

"I stayed up when you had the mumps, your cheeks out to here."

The fear she must have lived with, to have at the ready this litany of proof of her motherhood for some unnamed person or worse, for us. Maybe she'd practiced at night while sleepless and worried over the impossible possibility: a strange woman at our door, looking for something precious she'd left behind when she didn't know any better, couldn't do anything more.

Aimee didn't push the issue further, not after Dad reached over with a discipline of his own. By then I knew what to do in the face of such raw emotion, such swift justice—keep my head down, mouth shut, and maybe it would just go away.

But this time even the Swede needed some acknowledgement, someone to tell her what she'd offered was enough. She said, "I was the one who pulled all that gravel out of your knee when you fell off your bike."

I remembered, too: Aimee sitting on the edge of the sink down in Gramma Verne's bathroom, Mom digging out one nit of rock after another, cleansing away the blood each time to see what else had dug its way into my sister's flesh.

"You can't go back," Mom said, her tears now undeniable.

I won't go back, I wanted to tell her, not even when I'm grown and can search without telling, but I dared not speak aloud. Not then. I waited until the dishes were cleared, the tears dried.

"Oh, Katie," she said, when I hugged her.

I thought I understood all that was left unsaid, but I was only a child. Mom had tried to tell us, but Aimee wasn't listening. And, like so many others who never listened to the prophets, I never thought the words were meant for me.

What's Up and What's Under

I don't have it in me to be good at card games. "Got a good hand, hon?" my husband will ask, whenever I'm this close to laying down my hand for Gin Rummy. So you can imagine right after my birthmother Val first contacted me, I had the hardest time talking to my father.

"What's new?" he'd ask.

Don't say anything about Val, nothing about Val. "Oh, nothing," I said. If it wasn't for Jen and her first steps, first words, I don't know how I would have filled our conversation.

It's not like I could tell him about Val over the phone. That would be like calling your spouse to say your ex wants to visit and you can hardly wait, is that okay?

I'd tell him when we visited him next. That would be four forever months away. Sixteen phone calls.

Good Lord.

I had to tell someone, someone other than Jim. I was bursting. I called friends I grew up with. No reason, I'd say, just wanted to catch up. "You'll never believe who called," I said as soon as my best friend answered.

19

There was a delay as my words carried across the Atlantic, to Stockholm where she lived. It seemed I told my story into nothingness, but the words caught hold on the other side, and my friend did not let go.

I was not prepared for her answer.

"Just who does this Egg Woman think she is?" Christin asked.

I should have known the soft spot Christin kept in her heart for my folks, for all they did as her parents worked through their divorce and against each other. Even my dad, who couldn't remember my birthday, still remembers how her father, Larry, ditched us during Cotillion breaks to call his new girlfriend. More than twenty years later, Larry would lose that wife, too—this time to cancer. But we had no way of knowing what was to come when Dad told Christin she could count on him, whenever. Now it was Christin's turn to protect Dad against some other woman.

I didn't dare tell her Val had considered talking to Dad first. How weird would that have been? Better to have the initial contact directly between birthparent and child, I thought. Using a third party, even if it were a disinterested one, risked distorting the message. And words spoken that first conversation were too precious to be lost in translation.

Since Val had called, my head had been filled of possibilities, roads not taken, a life not lived. She'd considered having her sister raise me as her own, a sister who'd almost shown up on my doorstep when Val told her she'd found me.

"Doesn't it freak you out to think how she tracked you down?" Christin was not about to let up. "I mean, what kind of information about you is out there?" This was 1995. Google was years from becoming a verb.

Christin knew I hadn't done any looking on my own, knew I had never even called to put my name on the register linking birthmothers and the children they'd had once both had signed on.

I hadn't thought to ask how Val had found me. As cautious as I was on that initial call, you'd think I would have. Clearly, this woman had some sort of public record beyond the background information she'd originally been given. She was reading our names, our towns, from somewhere. This call had been something I'd been expecting, ever since I found out I'd been adopted. Maybe that's why I'd always been at peace not looking for her. And once she was on the line, there were other, more important things I needed to know, needed to tell her. Because as far as I knew, this could be the only chance I'd have to say it.

Thank you, I'd said.

"I just needed to know you were safe," Val explained.

I was more than safe. I was home.

There was another family down the street, she said. They'd adopted a baby. When word got out the child was being abused, Val was tortured with the thought of what she'd done, putting me into a home with strangers.

But they weren't strangers, they were my parents. We had an apple-pie house, dinner parties and vacations on Mackinac, a grandma who'd visit for months at a time.

She wondered if I had any sisters in my adoptive family. She said, "I have eight," as if that was perfectly natural.

God, who else in the world would have that many sisters? That's more siblings than Jan Brady even. But there are strange coincidences in this world. "That's how many my husband has, too," I said. And she had two brothers, just like in Jim's family as well.

She grew up near where my dad worked, she knew the round restaurant we frequented for lunch. Her dad was a mechanical engineer, like mine. From Michigan, like mine. Grandparents from Britain and Italy.

No one from Sweden.

"I've been to Wales," Val offered. "And it seemed like home. The landscape, the thatched-roof cottages."

I knew exactly what she meant. That need to connect with those who made us who we were.

"I should ask about your medical history," I said. The things you find yourself asking a complete stranger. Hello, do you or anyone close to you have a morbid disease?

"We're in pretty good shape, that way," she said. "My mom just passed away, but she was in her eighties. Dad's still around."

"What about—" and how could I put this?

"You probably want to know about David."

A name. Yes, tell me.

She was careful then, her words delicate but softly dancing around the fact that this was a boy she'd loved once, and I was living proof of that. A love unresolved. What would have been the sum of them, if I hadn't been injected into the equation?

"He died a few years ago. I'm sorry," she said. A motorcycle accident. He'd been living out west, married a second time. She didn't think he had any other children. "He was from a successful East Coast family. I was kind of intimidated by them, they were so accomplished. His dad was with an oil company. His mom spent some time in China."

There, the basis for truth in my childhood fantasy. A modern prince who could have swept me away.

"I can give you their number," Val said.

"Oh, I don't think I could make that call." What was I supposed to say? Hello, I'm living proof your son couldn't keep it in his pants?

"I can contact them, if you like."

I turned on my stool, my back to the counter. Before me, the light under the cabinet glowed bright and sure while the rest of the kitchen hid in darkness. "If you want," I said.

MY EAR THROBBED FROM TALKING ON THE PHONE. Hours had passed. I'd no idea we'd talked so long. Jim had shut off the TV, shut down the lights. I crawled upstairs and into bed. I tried being quiet, gently pulling back the covers. But Jim reached out to me, still awake. "Her name is Val," I said, not realizing until then how relieved I was that he'd waited for me. He listened for as long as I talked, as late into the night as I dared, knowing I had an alarm clock I couldn't shut off the next morning.

Thank God for routine, for the comforts of home. When Jenny woke up and called for me as the sky lightened, I hurried down the hall to scoop her out of her crib and hold her tight. Her little body fit next to mine, and I would not let her go. I made her toast with bread I'd made earlier that week, the only kind she'd eat those first spoiled years. I fed her cereal with the Swedish baby spoon Christin had found in Stockholm. And when I put my baby down for a nap, I sat with her in the rocker the Amish had made from alder culled from my parent's woods. I rested my cheek against Jen's fine, fine hair.

A Beatrix Potter border evenly divided the top and bottom halves of her room, Squirrel Nutkin and Peter Rabbit scuttering along just above the bars of her crib. I felt around the corner of the bookshelf for a small, soft fabric book about a snowman. This was the book for me to read to Jen today. And so I read about a boy dreaming about a snowman coming to life. On each page, I pointed to the primary words and the pastel colors. I wanted her to know this book, to love it, but she was reaching for *One Fish, Two Fish*, for her daily dose of Seuss.

"This book," I said. "This one." I caught her fingers and touched her dimpled hand onto the page, onto the picture of the snowman flying with the boy, but she would have none of it. She arched her back over the arm of the chair, a branch that had been bent into a curve and nailed together to hold it forever in place. "Oh, peanut, come on," I pleaded. I lifted her back up and tried to hold her close. "Just one more page," I said. She would love this book, she would, even though on that next page the snowman melted. My voice broke over his words, over his promise he would always be there for the boy, in each falling snowflake. I held Jen close until the tears passed, pushing back on that Amish rocker until Jen was asleep, until I was calmed.

Light shone through the half-closed blinds behind me, and the blue of the room, a shade away from purple, greyed as the sun descended in the sky. The book still lay open on that last page, the book that was the last present my mother ever gave my daughter.

I dug the heels of my hands against my eyes to stop the last of my tears before I lifted her up off my lap and into her crib. I had to stop doing this, I thought. And I'd been so sure I was past the worst of it.

MY MOTHER WAS ALL AROUND ME, and nowhere close. She was in the rattle she'd given Jen, she was in the blanket I curled up in while Jenny napped.

She was in the recipe for Banana Split Delite I made for company ("Elegant and Delicious!" she'd written in evenly spaced script).

She was six feet under.

When Dad asked me to pick out something for her to wear for her funeral, I'd lifted out of her closet the periwinkle chiffon dress she'd worn to my wedding, knowing even then I'd regret it every time I'd look at pictures of that special day.

I should have picked that Eddie Bauer bathrobe she still had.

She and her mother had matching ones for when Gramma came for her marathon visits. I'd come down for breakfast to find them at the kitchen table, quietly sipping coffee, Mom in powder-blue and Gramma Verne in her spring-green quilted robe. By junior high the bus stop was a mile away and Mom would warm up the big brown Caddy and drive me and Aimee down, and she'd be wearing that quilted robe for anyone at the bus stop to see. I was early if I could help it, just so no one else would be there yet to catch sight of that dumb robe. If it was nice, she made us walk home, but one sunny day she was there anyway. Normally, I'd race my sister to the car and bang on the front wooden panel, calling shotgun. But something told me not to. I settled into the back seat quietly and was not surprised when Mom turned to me and said, "Gramma died today."

We'd been expecting it. When her cancer came back and the doctors finally said there was nothing more they could do, we set her up in a hospital bed down in our family room. Dad sent our plane up to Michigan to get Gramma's friend Bernice, to keep her company and help care for her during the day. I'd come home from school to find Bernice sitting in a captain's chair next to Gramma, talking, talking. They'd laugh their hoarse smoker's laughs, and the sound would carry upstairs, where I'd be trying to figure out my Algebra, my books sprawled across the kitchen table. As days passed into weeks, their conversations quieted. Somewhere along the way, Gramma slipped into a coma, whether from pain or from the morphine, I don't know, but the most Bernice could do then was sit, head bowed, her hand upon Gramma's bed. Bernice flew back home, and so Dad brought from work a Motorola walkie-talkie he used to buzz back to the shop. He duct-taped down the "on" button so Gramma Verne could call for us, but in her final days, all we heard were her ragged breaths echoing through the rooms. I'd been afraid to go downstairs, afraid I'd be there when she turned dead, and now she was.

"Is she still there?" I had to ask.

Mom looked at me peculiarly. "No," she said after a moment. "No, she's gone." She shifted the yellow woody station wagon into gear and began the slow drive up the hill.

I was quiet, trying to figure out what it meant for my Gramma to be dead.

"The undertaker insisted she had to have something to wear," Mom said. "So I gave him her bathrobe."

"You would've let her be naked?" I asked. "For all eternity?"

"It'll be a closed casket," Mom said. She held tight to the wheel, high up and close to her heart, though her voice was even and controlled. "Someone else could've used it more."

Fifteen years later, I left Mom's robe hanging on its hook when the same undertaker called to ask what we wanted her to wear. I dug through her drawers to find matching hose and shoes and a slip. She would be as elegant and as beautiful and vibrant as she was at my wedding, when I thought we'd all live happily ever after.

No way I could be practical, even when it counted most. There is no Swede in me.

Not by blood.

❧ 4 ❧

A Fine Way to Say Thanks

oy, did I have the mother of all thank you notes to write. And so, while Jenny napped and Jim called on customers, I tapped words out onto the screen and moved and shaped them until I was ready to stuff the pages into a large manila envelope and ship my life's confession off to a woman I didn't know, but who by all rights should be told everything about me.

March 26, 1995

Dear Valerie:

Let me begin again by saying thank you. Thank you for bringing me into the world. Thank you for being brave enough and strong enough to give your newborn to a family you did not know, to the family that has been so wonderful and so good to me.

I am glad you called.

I did not ask you directly, but I gather your husband also knows who I am and has been supportive of your search for me. That is how I had hoped it would be.

As for David, I hope you understand that, although I would love to know what you can tell me about him, I would feel uncomfortable contacting his family. If he were still alive and wished to contact me, I'd be happy to share with him as I am with you. But such is not the case, and that is fine.

You asked, and so I've enclosed as many representative pictures as I could from my life. All my photo albums from growing up are back at home so I only have a few to pass along. But I do have these memories to share:

My sister Aimee would read to me before I knew how. My Mom took me along to her bridge parties when I was little, and I would sit by her side and read the whole time. My Dad traveled a lot at first when we were little, and so every Friday night we would all go out to the Oaks (at Chippewa Lake), and we'd have dinner there, and afterwards, while Mom and Dad talked, Aimee would sleep under the table and I would read a book—also under the table. Where we sat is called the Family Table now. (I worked there as a bus girl in college so I can attest to that fact.)

I read so much when I was little my mother worried I wasn't playing outside enough. So I'd take my book outside and sit in the tire swing while I read. My teachers (second grade maybe?) said I was too serious. People laugh when I tell them that now.

Mom taught me how to make Dad's mom's homemade ravioli. And we made pasties (it's a meat-pie sandwich) and we baked Christmas cookies. And when I was little, Mom and Aimee and I would "bake" Oreos. We'd pull out a cupcake tray and put a dollop of butter inside, and they would send me outside to play while it baked. Mom would call me inside to see if the cookies were done yet, and sure enough, the Oreos they had put in while I was outside were always ready to come out of the oven when I checked! Mom never did share that recipe.

As I told you (I think), I studied history at Cornell, and then met my husband after law school. I'm glad you called if nothing else to allay my fears he and I were somehow related—I look an awful lot like some of his sisters! He is exactly five weeks younger than I am, and when we told my dad when Jim's birthday was, he said that was the day they brought me home. Which we decided was a lovely coincidence.

Jenny just turned one. She is a wonderful baby. She looks more like Jim than me, with her hazel eyes. And that dimple on her chin—do you know where that comes from?

Enough about me. If you can, I would like to know more about you, about David. I gathered from what you said that your family (whole family?) knew of your pregnancy, that you were no longer with David when you had me. Is that right? Did he know you had a baby girl? Did you have a name you called me in your mind over the years?

I should close by saying I am glad you contacted me now rather than at any other time in my life. I am glad I have a child of my own so I can appreciate (even if it is just to the remotest degree) what you must have gone through when you gave me up for adoption. I am glad to be old enough to appreciate there are and will be many ramifications from you contacting me, even if I don't know what all they will be and whether I will like them all. I must be honest and tell you I am not sure what role, if any, I am prepared for you to play in my life in the future. I am sure I will come to know the right thing to do as time passes. And so, until I hear from you again, I am

Very truly yours,

Kate

I convinced myself I was being poetic, using words like "allay" and "lovely" in what I'd hoped would be a stream of consciousness letter. I was as honest as I could be, telling a life story to someone I did not know.

So, okay, maybe I fudged some of it. Some of my life she didn't need to know. How my sister and I never really got along. How ripped apart we'd all been with Mom's passing. How this was a way to let go of my grief, to share what my mom did for me with Val. As honest as I'd like to think I am, I guess we can only tell what truths we can bear. Val, too, maybe, only shared the parts it didn't hurt to tell.

"Your mother had a hand in this," my best friend from junior high told me. Michele had gone all New Age hippie on me, believing in reincarnation and signs from the dead. "Her spirit is guiding you. Have you seen any butterflies lately?"

No, no butterflies. But still I like to believe Michele was right.

I TORE OPEN VAL'S LETTER AS SOON AS I GOT IT. This was the woman I'd been looking for on the street. The one when people said, "I know your twin," I'd wondered about. I left her letter in the envelope. First I needed to see the pictures. She sent four.

One, with her towering above three other women. I could not have picked her out from among her sisters, if she hadn't listed their names on the back. "She's wearing a cowboy hat," I said to no one in particular. "A cowboy hat."

Two, with her husband. Blond, smiling, glasses. Not related, not my blood.

Three, with her children. Blond, like their father.

Four, by herself, smiling and happy and looking nothing like me, I didn't think, not at all.

Something I'd never considered.

VAL CALLED ME RIGHT AWAY when she got my letter. "I love all these pictures," she said, in a way that I knew she meant it.

"Turned out I still had all the ones of me growing up from the video Jim's sisters made for our wedding," I said. "Those are the ones my mom picked out, the ones she thought were important to share with others."

I swear I could hear Val sorting through the photos again. The first one of me, six months old already, an Easter corsage on my white knit sweater. Did Mom and Dad wait to take my picture until the adoption was final? First grade-school photo, when I'd twirled a comb into my hair until it stuck while I waited in line. When I got my glasses and my Spanish Madame Alexander doll on the same day. My sister and I, bareback on a Clydesdale.

"That—that makes it all the more special," Val said, her voice wavering from the effort of having passed so quickly through the years, presented as my mother would have her see it.

"So would you ever like to come visit?" I asked, but I already knew the answer.

NOW I'D DONE IT. I'D GONE AHEAD and arranged for Val to visit before even telling my dad about her. What kind of a daughter was I?

Apparently one who needed a deadline. I'd planned on telling him when we visited for his Fourth of July birthday. I'd have to for sure now. Didn't matter it'd only been six months since Mom had died, and Dad probably still had food from her wake molding in the fridge. Time to clear my conscience and clean out Mom's closet at the big house.

We always called it that, though Mom wanted us to call it Deer Run. It was that big, the kind of house that could have its own name. She had stationary made, a logo and everything. Three leaping deer, different shades of green. Very 1980s. My parents had built their dream house on a bluff overlooking the brook my sister and I waded through in summers spent on our farm. The barns were on the other tract, connected through the back forty acres and bordered by the railroad to the west. Dad set the house almost a mile back in the hundred-acre woods, and rigged a buzzer to go off inside when cars passed through a pair of brick pillars. The driveway curved in front of the house, encircling an English garden before joining itself back by the pillars. Brick steps led up to French doors, and Dad would greet us by flinging open the leaded-glass door, a martini in his hand.

At least that's what it was like before my mother died.

This trip, the fields lining the beginning of the drive lay fallow.

"It's mid-summer already," I said to Jim.

"Looks like your dad didn't have the energy this year."

We didn't know the half of it. Dad had strung a rusted chain between the brick pillars. He'd tied a yellow cloth in the middle so he wouldn't plow through it when coming home at night.

"This is the gate he installed?" Jim asked, clicking the spare garage door opener Dad had sent us. The chain dropped slowly to the ground. We drove over the links and closed the jerry-rigged gate behind us.

We parked by the brick steps. Last year's geraniums lay dead in pots half the size of my first car. No one came to greet us at the door. I backed out of the Altima, pulling Jen out with her car seat, carefully, gently, so as not to wake her. Jim held the front door open, and I climbed steps lined with thigh-high weeds instead of begonias.

"Dad?" I asked, afraid what I should find inside that cavernous house.

"In here, Kate."

I followed the pungent smell of garlic into the kitchen. Dad worked the stove, his glasses pushed up on his forehead as he stirred a bubbling sauté pan on one burner and fussed with a Dutch oven on another. A wet tea towel draped over his left shoulder. "Can I get you a drink?" he asked, as I set Jenny down.

"I'll get it," I said.

"I might need your help while you're here," he confessed. Grocery bags lined the counter and trailed out the door, all $400 worth for our three day stay. "We've got to get this put away before the raccoons come back." They'd discovered the pet door as well as the cat food. Last night they'd even figured out where the bread drawer was. "It took forever to clean up," he said.

I swung the closest bag onto my hip like a baby and carried it back to the pantry. "Dad, here's your problem." The door to the garage was open, and a twenty-pound bag of cat food spilled across the mudroom floor.

"Leave that there," Dad yelled from the kitchen. "When I travel, Shadow needs that food."

There were new rules in the house, with Mom gone. I still didn't feel old enough yet to tell him he was wrong—at least not outright. I set the bag upright and secured it shut, even found a big bowl to put the food in. It's what a mom would do, though I sorely missed Mom's direction. I did what I could and fretted over what little I accomplished.

Back in the kitchen, Dad kept checking a little notebook.

"Taking notes?" Jim joked. He would be working overtime that weekend, trying to bring levity to our lives.

"No, you know what this is?" Dad showed us a scratchpad no bigger than his palm, flipped it open to his mother's cramped writing. She'd written down all her weekday standards for his father if she'd died first. "It's like having my mom here all over again," he said, and I knew what it was to want that.

All the next day I didn't dare broach the subject of Val, not with what Dad still needed help with. "You've got to tell him before we leave," Jim told me in the darkness when we fell into bed, our palms sore from grasping and pulling the weeds out front. "It'll kill you if you don't, you know."

"I know," I said. I'd laid there, awake for two more hours, stretching out my sore hand and rubbing my palm with my other thumb, all the while thinking about how it wouldn't be fair for me to bring Val up now.

And yet it wouldn't be fair not to, either. That's what I'd decided when I was up with Jen in the middle of the night, walking the halls to get her back to sleep.

In the daylight hours, Jim pulled foot-tall plants out of Dad's gutters, and I vacuumed bees off the carpet. I kept Jen in a playpen all day with a stack of books, hours of play for that easygoing child. Not ideal, but okay for a weekend, and certainly safer than eating a horde of dead bees.

Not until after lunch did I find the bee source: a hole eaten through the ceiling of the apartment above the garage. I made a mental note to tell Dad. I should have stepped up and called the exterminator, should have patched the hole myself. But somehow that seemed worse than telling him this house, the house he and Mom spent years planning for and dreaming of, was too big for him alone.

After we cleaned up, we had drinks by the bar while Dad started the grill and I fed Jen in the wooden high chair I'd used as a baby. I brought along an adapter strap to tie her to the chair and keep her from sliding under the tray. How I didn't die a thousand deaths as a child I'll never know.

Dad put some steaks on, then pulled the sliding door shut behind him and stood ready to make a pronouncement. He was holding the tongs up with one hand, like a medical instrument, and the setting sun shone through the wall of windows behind him, casting him in evening shadow. "I can't stay in this house forever, I know," he said. "But I'm not going to make any other changes in my life this year. Next year, for sure I'll reassess. In the meantime I've got an ad in the paper for a couple to stay in the apartment, to be caretakers of the place."

That's what it was, then, just too much for one person to do. I grinned dopily at my dad, relieved. He was doing just fine after all.

Jen took a hunk of baked potato and stuffed it in her mouth.

"Before you bring anyone in, you'll want to fix that hole in the apartment ceiling," I said. "Looks like that might be where the bees are coming in."

"Yep, I'm on that," Dad said, as if it were taken care of already.

I finished feeding Jen, barely listening now to what Dad and Jim were saying. Since Dad was better, truly better, I could concentrate instead on finding the chance to throw in a line about Val. I found it as I was clearing the dishes before dessert.

"There is something I need to tell you," I began. I told Dad the story, about her call and the pictures we exchanged. "We've only talked three times on the phone," I said, needing to come entirely and finally clean. I was giddy with relief, with the story. Dad's eyes welled up, but that didn't stop me from telling more. Getting teary was part of my everyday, too, now. All it took was a stupid children's book about snowmen, for goodness' sake. I put my hand on his arm. "Mom will always be my mom, you know," I said, but I couldn't say her name without my voice breaking. I held on tight to him. "That doesn't change."

"Well, I'm glad it happened," Dad said, his eyes red-rimmed, no tears yet broken upon his cheek. "Because what I've got, she can't take away. I got my baby, I got your childhood, I got to put you through school, even." He grinned, a wet, happy grin. "I got it all. I got you. I can share it all now."

I hugged him on that stool until we cried, shoulders shaking, sorry for our loss and uncertain of my gain. When I let him go, he leaned back in his stool for only a moment.

Then he put his elbows up on the counter and leaned forward conspiratorially. "I'm going to tell you, though," he warned, "I'm not sharing holidays. It's bad enough, I gotta share with Vogl here."

I thought he meant it, he didn't mind, but now I know he was just playing the hand he was dealt. This was the guy who'd hustled his ten-year-old daughter playing checkers, trying to teach her some people will let you believe you are winning, just to have the chance to take it all away. The same guy who rolled his car out the driveway in neutral so he wouldn't wake Aimee when she was just a baby. He wanted us to be aware of the ways of the world, and yet he wanted to protect us. So he did. He's a player, after all, a salesman who sold heavy equipment for more than fifty years. So even though the fields lay fallow and raccoons roamed his house at night, I was the one who'd laid out my hand, and my father was the one who'd decided to fold. For his birthday, he gave me all I wanted, he gave me all he had.

∽ 5 ∽

Guess Who's Coming to Dinner?

For sixth-grade slumber parties we'd play Mystery Date on the gold shag carpet in my rec room. Whenever I opened the door in the middle of that board, I'd pray to the game gods for the blue-eyed skier—or really, for anyone but the dork with the high-waisted pants. Because no one wanted her sleeping bag next to the girl who'd had the dud show up behind that white plastic door.

Didn't matter how much I prayed or how I turned the knob to my front door, though, when Val stood on the other side. The Fates had made me a part of her life and brought her to my door. All this time, I'd only been fantasizing about opening the door, about finding out who she was. I'd never imagined what would happen afterwards. And as an adult I felt sore out of practice on imagining possibilities now. Would she be like another mother-in-law, 'til death did we part? Though Val of course would be a mother-in-blood.

Crazy what you think about at times like these.

Alone on my stoop, my birthmother stood. Joe, her husband, hovered down below on the sidewalk. She was supposed to be my height, but she

35

looked so small there—and tired. How many nights had she lain awake wondering what it'd be like when we met?

"Val," I said, letting go of the door and opening my arms to a woman I was sure looked nothing like me. "I'm so glad you're here." And her face unwound all the worry spun during that eight-hour car ride, dreaming up the worst that could happen.

She stepped up to me and into my home, and her arms held me tight, arms that had last held me almost thirty years before when I was not yet someone else's child.

VAL CAME BEARING GIFTS, one for the child she'd let go and one for the toddler she could now hold in her lap. We three sat on a sofa the color of blank pages, and our husbands sat in chairs on the other side of the room. As Val handed over a brightly wrapped package, Jenny clapped her palms together, fingers spread wide.

"I didn't get you anything," I said.

"Oh, yes you did," Val said, holding her hand up for Jenny to pat it. "You did." Val helped Jenny open the box, pulling away tissue paper to reveal a school girl's plaid jumper with a short sleeved navy mock turtleneck.

Jenny checked under the tissue paper again, as if looking for a toy inside. No luck. She turned over in Val's lap to climb down to the ground.

I put a hand out to stop her. "What do you say?" I asked.

Jenny grinned. "Panks," she said, toddler speak, and she slid down to the floor.

We sat in awkward silence as Jen tippy-toed over to a basket by the fireplace. She dug through a pile of cardboard covered books for one with a torn cover. Lifting it high over her head, she dropped her bottom down to the floor and curled her legs around the tall pages, oblivious to Val's complete absorption with her and my utter embarrassment that she'd abandoned her gift.

We sat mesmerized by a little girl flipping pages.

"So, Joe," Jim said, "what did you say you did for a living?"

Joe talked of being a buyer for a local grocery store, but I couldn't focus on what he said. Val was sitting next to me, and at that moment I had more questions for her than I had for him.

Val was not, I'd already decided, someone who I would have wondered about if I'd passed her randomly on the street. And maybe I had, when I'd worked downtown Cleveland that summer in law school. Or maybe we'd lunched the next table over at Christmas in Higbee's. I would not have guessed I was hers by blood. Her brown eyes were lighter than mine. Her eyebrows were different.

"How did you know what size to get?" I had nothing but inane questions to ask, not what I really wanted to know. I was still picking apart her features. Our features. I had her nose. Her chin. But that wasn't enough for me to pick her out of a crowd, surely?

"Lots of little kids in my family, you know," she said.

"Sure," I said. But I didn't. I might have had eighteen nieces and nephews from marrying Jim four years earlier, but I'd just learned what 2T meant. I pulled a leg up onto the couch and wrapped my arms around it. I needed something to hold onto.

Val handed me a wrapped box from a bag next to her. "For you," she said, her eyes shining.

The men quieted, as sounds of paper tearing filled the room. My hands covered the package, as if to hush the ripping. I tried to pry open the seams. Jim brought over a pair of scissors to cut through the packing tape.

"I didn't want it to break on the way here," Val said to everyone in the room but me.

With the flaps open, the packing unfurled like a flower. I dug inside.

"Careful," she said as I pulled out a ceramic pumpkin, perfectly shaped with a stem tightly coiled on top.

"The top opens," she said, gesturing. "There's a notch it fits into."

"It's perfect," I said, turning it in my hands. Why would she pick this one, with its curious undertones of gray and brown? There was a chip inside the lid, but I pretended not to notice.

"I made it myself," she said, pantomiming how she shaped it. "Years ago when I took a ceramics class."

I tried not to stare at her hands. She moved them as I did. Could that be inherited, too? I'd never known to look for something like that. I held what she'd formed with hands that moved like mine. "I love it," I said, though I'd never felt like my hands were trespassing another's before.

"You know, David was a sculptor."

"I know," I said, unable to not look at Joe, but he was studying the bottom of his shoe as his wife spoke another man's name.

I pulled the pumpkin in close, deciding what to make of it. Something for me to hang onto, something to link Val and David and me. Did the transitive property cross time as well as equations? I held what she'd held, and he'd once held her. The confluence of touch in the palms of my hands. This, too, was real, as real as my family growing up. I got up and walked between them to set the pumpkin in the center of my kitchen table, so anyone walking in the door could see it. "I'd been looking for something special to go right there," I said.

Val ran her fingers through her hair and smiled comfortably for the first time. It was how she sat, leg tucked under and her hair just pushed back from her face. There, I saw, that's me in twenty years. We even had the same haircut, though I hadn't realized it until then.

"It's just what I needed," I said, still reeling from all I'd touched. "Don't you think?"

JIM PULLED OUT THE WINE AND I pulled out some albums. "Baby pictures anyone?"

Val and I hovered over pages and pages of babies lulled by stroller walks, of poses with relatives loved more than seen, of Jen's birthday cake-smeared face. As I showed the pictures, I found myself talking with my hands, making shapes out of thin air as Val had been.

And then she was watching my hands more than the pictures. Deliberately, I put my hands on the page, forcing myself to not gesture anymore, but her eyes stayed on my hands, now unnaturally still. And in that stillness, I noticed for the first time how thin my wrists were, thin as this woman next to me, in a captain's chair that may well have been the one in which I'd learned I first belonged to someone else.

She'd seen it, too, the parts of me I could not deny were hers.

"I have something else for you," Val said, pulling some books out of a bag. Pictures of her in high school and college. A girl with sleek long hair worn like a veil. She'd been facing away from the camera, but then leaned back and flashed a smile I would see and remember a lifetime later.

"This is Arlene," Val said, pointing to another girl in the picture, the one facing the picture taker. "That's my sister who would have raised you if I'd kept you." And she turned the page. But I wasn't quite ready to look at other albums yet, years recorded by pictures taken out west in wine cellars filled with oaken barrels, others taken of the craggy hills of Wales, others of people I didn't know but in another life I would have. My mind remained frozen on that moment in time, when Val had been facing away from the camera's eye, when she'd straddled the fence deciding whether to place her baby in the arms of a stranger or a sister. How close I was to calling a different woman mother, a woman with wide eyes and arching eyebrows and a definitively stiff bouffant.

"Excuse me," I said. "I need to get dinner on the table."

My mom, not this one, would just comb her hair after washing it. In the winter it lay almost straight, but during the sticky days of August, soft curls danced around her head. Only once do I remember mom having her hair done. At Higbee's downtown. I could only squirm in that hard plastic chair, not play underneath it, while a stylist coaxed my mother's short hair back, smooth against her head, then affixed a matching braided bun. Mom used it for formals that 1971 year, but that smooth cup of hair hid on the upper shelf of her closet until they moved fourteen years later.

How would a hug feel, I wondered, against hair freshly stiffened at a weekly shampoo appointment?

Val stood. "Let me help," she said. "I'm a good helper."

But I couldn't think what to ask of her, and so she hovered on the other end of the kitchen island, the side I'd sat on when she'd first called.

Maybe I didn't ask because I couldn't remember Mom ever asking her friends to pitch in, though they did. Years of having parties together, they knew each other and what to do. Maybe it wasn't that easy, maybe I was busy playing and never paid attention to how Mom ordered the kitchen.

"You need a glass of wine," Val said. "You're not having a glass of wine?" She sounded hurt, as if I'd made clear her being there was not reason to celebrate.

I couldn't drink that first visit, but it wasn't something I'd wanted to tell her, at least not yet. Too soon, too soon, as my mother had said when I'd told her Jim and I were talking marriage three months after we'd met.

"I can't," I told Val. "I'm pregnant."

"You are?" she said, her arms thrown out in disbelief. If she'd known me better, she would have hugged me, but she was careful then not to cross any lines.

Thirteen years later, and she still won't call me, not just to talk. I am embarrassed at times how long has passed between calls. Weeks, a month, once.

"You're not showing," she said, disbelieving my still flat stomach.

I was not yet two months along, either. The last time I hadn't told anyone for several more weeks. Last time we'd found out, it'd been Mom's birthday. We put the test strip on the kitchen counter, plus side up, with a bow on it the same color as the bandana covering her chemo hairdo.

Jim and I had waited on the bar stools for Mom to come over and see. "Don't turn it over," Jim said, but she already had. Until then, she'd no need of home pregnancy kits.

Mom didn't hug me either when she found out she'd soon have a grandchild. Damn Swede. She just picked up the phone and called Dad. "Your daughter has something to tell you," she said, and handed the phone over to me.

I can't remember if I told Dad before Val that I was expecting again. Probably. I still call him first when I have news about the girls.

I'm sure Val never imagined she'd be a part of that time in my life, and I'd never imagined all I'd be sharing. That night I remember cutting up

Jen's ravioli on her divided Winnie the Pooh plate, with A.A. Milne's words sauntering along the edge:

> *I sometimes wonder if it's true*
> *That who is what and what is who.*

    Indeed, what is a mother and a mother is who? Was being a mother as simple as calling one—calling both—by name? And could I?

    We worked through what we could, dividing our time that evening between what Val lost and who she'd gained, between who I'd lost and what I'd gained. We sat down to a ritual of grace and other niceties, and then I went first.

    I had to ask what Christin had bugged me about. "So, Val," I began. "How did you say you found me?"

    She swallowed, hard. It'd only been her first bite. "The obituaries," she said. It'd been Joe's idea. She'd told Chris and Allisyn—"my other kids," she called them—and they'd helped her search through the Highland yearbooks, but couldn't find me.

    And no wonder. Mom had complained that all Aimee had learned in kindergarten was how to slide on her knees, so Dad arranged with a school board member to grandfather us in to go to Medina.

    But that sent Val down a dead end. After all that time in counseling with the Adoption Triad Network, after her long wait until her "other kids" would be old enough to understand, she was left with nothing. That's when Joe suggested checking what for so many was genealogical fodder.

    I could picture them descending the steps to the new addition of the old brick library, where for story hours I sat upon a Charlie Chip can decorated as a sit-upon. Had I gone to school with the librarian working the desk that day? Were the old *Gazettes* still hanging on wooden dowels, like laundry set out to dry?

    "That was in January," Val said.

    That was when I'd told Jen's doctor not to bother using the inert polio vaccine anymore. I'd tried to make the point without saying why, without having to say that my mother was dead. Anything to make those first raw months easier. I'd finally understood why my friend from law school would tell acquaintances her mom was fine, just to avoid having to tell the story of death again.

Butterflies, my friend Michele had told me, were signs of our dear departed, but with Val in my own kitchen I had a flesh-and-blood incarnation my mother had willed for me through her own obituary.

So real, so present I wouldn't think to ask until much later how Val found my name in the first place. Through a detective, is all Val knew, after she'd gone through the requisite two years of counseling. Jen's godmother was adopted through the same agency, and this was what the detective told her: In the mid-1960s, when we were born, all the illegitimate births were kept in the back of the vital records book. At the time of adoption, the record was moved up to the front. The original number would be kept, the first entry blacked out. You just hold the pages up to the light to match the numbers.

That's just the beginning of the search. The hard part is finding whatever happened to the child—or the birthmom. I'd done some genealogy, tracing back four generations on each side of Mom and Dad's family trees. I knew all the hoops to jump through, the microfiche reels to spin through in order to document each step. I knew the joy of finding a connection in black and white. But I couldn't imagine everything that went through Val's mind as she'd huddled in front of a microfiche as the obituary for Perianne St. Vincent spun onto the viewer.

Silverware clicked against the plates and glasses lifted and set against the table.

"This is delicious," Val said, mouth full.

"It's all homemade, you know," Jim offered.

Ravioli is one of those family recipes: takes forever to make but winter meals wouldn't be complete without it. And really, if you think about it, making it was so much easier for me than it was for my father's grandmother. She'd been wed on Christmas Day in Turin on the eve of a new century—I'd found her records out of the Mormon's Torino collection. To make the dish every Sunday, the great-grandmother for whom I am named stuffed meat through a grinder, culled eggs from under the chickens, rolled dough out to just the right thickness on floured towels. I bought everything from a store a half mile from my house and cut up the cabbage with a Cuisinart. A part of me wished I still had to use Mom's old meat grinder, though. She had an ease in the kitchen I've never found, maybe because I was never as good a chemist. "To taste," she'd put on a recipe card. "As needed." But I needed exact numbers, going so far as to count and record the number of turns made with the pepper grinder. (Twenty-eight turns equal "to taste," if you double the recipe.) The dough rolled out evenly through my pasta machine, and the noodles when stuffed cut neatly on a form my mother had bought for me the Christmas before she died. Once frozen on a cookie tray, ravioli pillows can jumble together in a Ziploc in the freezer, to be used in a pinch or when planning ahead.

"You know, we ate Italian," Val said. "But nothing like this."

You can get to a mother's heart, it seems, through her stomach. To get to a cook's all you need is a compliment.

JENNY ASKED VAL TO READ HER A STORY that night. Val looked at me as if asking for permission, but what was she here for, if not to do for my daughter what she could not do for me? I watched from the door as Val settled in the Amish rocking chair. Jen wore footie pajamas and stood between Val and a bookcase filled with books by Seuss and Eastman and Brown. Just like I used to hang onto my blankie, Jen held her Sesame Street receiving blanket—her nummie—bunched up over one arm.

"What should I read?" Val asked.

"This one," Jen said, pulling a board book off the shelf.

"All right then," Val said, gathering up Jen and the book and the nummie blanket. Snuggled on Val's lap, Jenny arranged her nummie across her legs and pointed to the page for Val to begin the story about the baby bunny who wanted to run away, about the mother who would follow him to the hills or the sea to help. "Oh, I love this story," Val said, to my surprise.

43

Val's first visit.

I'd never known it as a child. What other stories would I have learned in that other house with those other children?

Jen pointed to the words again, her fist covered with the blanket.

"I think she wants you to start," I said. All the time Val had spent with children, but with this one Val would question herself. Maybe I get that from her, too, that fear that everything we know won't count when we need it most.

Val pulled Jen close, and as she began, Jen lifted the nummie to her chin, just as she would for me. I slipped out the door to let them have that quiet moment alone. A memory for Val to savor when she returned home and we went our separate ways.

When she came down the stairs, she seemed to be floating in happiness. She smiled quietly at Joe. He smoothed the seat next to him on the couch for her to sit.

"Thank you," she said to me.

The rules I'd set up for this visit suddenly seemed so arbitrary, appropriate for a stranger, but not with Val. "If you want," I said, "just stay here tonight. You don't have to go to a hotel."

"Oh, Katie, no," she said. And then at the door, when I repeated the offer, she hugged me first—spontaneous, grateful, and said, "You've given me enough already tonight."

All but a Walk in the Park

In the morning, Jen posed in her new outfit for her newest number-one fans. In front of the fireplace, hands on bent knees, Mary Janes tapping on the hearthstones. But what to do once the photo shoot was a wrap? Where do you take an out-of-town guest in Charlotte, anyway? I offered up museums and shops and restaurants.

Val said, "I want to do what you normally do. Your normal day. Whatever that is, let's do it."

I looked at Val's penny loafers. "Um, we'd start with a walk."

"So, let's go."

The men decided to stay behind while I changed and Val dug a pair of tennis shoes out of their trunk. I tucked Jen into her stroller and waved good-bye to the boys, wondering what in the world they would have to talk about.

I led Val to a little park I liked to go to with Jen. To get there we had to walk past two neighborhoods and cross over a bridge onto a gravel path lined with leaves already fallen. Val had questions for me, all in the present, as if the past were too much to dig up all at once. Mostly, her questions had to do with my routine, with my new pregnancy. With being a mom, I guess.

Me, I'd wanted to know how she and my birthfather had met, but even now, off on our own, I wasn't quite ready to ask. I was too aware of how my questions would reveal how I'd thought of her—this suddenly all too real person—as I'd grown and she'd grayed. I'd only ever considered finding out about that snapshot in time, when I'd entered the picture. But Val was asking mostly about now. Did this mean she'd want to know about my future, then, too?

As I pushed the stroller onto the dried grass by the playground, Jen was straining against her seat belt. "Ready to play?" I asked as I unsnapped the straps and the safety bar. She ran up to the slide, and Val and I followed. Jen climbed the stairs and stood at the top of the platform. She bounced up and down, her eyes on Val.

"I think she wants you to catch her."

"I can do that," Val said, bending down at the bottom of the slide, her arms outstretched, and Jen slid right into Val's welcoming hug.

"I can take a picture of that if you like," I said. I'm not much for taking pictures, but every precious moment of that weekend I wanted to record, for me and for Jen. As much to record the times Grandma Peri would have loved to have had, the times not possible if she hadn't been dead and gone to bring us together. I'd say Jen pointed out a Monarch as she stood atop the slide, but that would be pure confabulation.

Jen played until Val's camera ran out of film. I lifted her back into her stroller and led Val along the path, past houses to admire as Jen napped on the way back.

A chance now for me to ask Val some questions, but she had another one for me first. "Did you ever hear from David's family?"

"I did," I said, wishing I could keep this part private—at least until I could sort out in my mind what it meant to be in contact with them, too.

She'd written them a letter, hoping they'd reach out to me. What she didn't realize was that they'd long ago moved from their Jersey town. Their semi-retired mail carrier had subbed his old route the day her letter arrived. In an act of postal kindness, he'd forwarded Val's letter to their

47

Vermont address, where they'd summered for years. Homer and Carrell Hall received the note on the fourth anniversary of their son's death.

"His sister called me," I confessed. Her name was Nor, short for Eleanor. She called just as my husband and a friend were leaving for golf. Just one conversation and I could tell what Val had meant when she said she'd been intimidated by his family. As an artist, David had been somewhat of a black sheep in the family. His father was a nationally recognized chemist, several patents under his belt. The sister who called was a Jungian psychotherapist, a playwright in her spare time. Another sister was an educator specializing in oceanography. The youngest, a professor of international law, and his brother was director of information systems at Harvard. A formidable group, particularly when framed by the awe and respect David always held for them.

"I got the feeling they all were looking for some way to reconnect with him again," I said. But I was sure I was a poor substitute. I had only half his DNA and who knew what part of his personality? Certainly not much of his talent. I was decent in art, but I'd been reluctant to take any past ninth grade, worried my GPA would suffer. I was a nerdball.

Mom had encouraged my artistic talents when I was little, sending me to YMCA camps for painting. "It's in your blood," Mom said. "The father." I was young, but did not miss it was an article, not a pronoun she used. Genes granted a predisposition, my mother the scientist had to allow. But not pronouns of belonging, of relationship.

My predisposition then, if I can call it that, showed up in preschool. My teacher once pulled me aside to question something I'd drawn. First I thought I'd let her down—the picture hadn't turned out how I wanted. I'd put so much effort put into that outline of an Irish setter's head. Long snout, ears—but that long distance gaze was hard to capture. I lost energy and drew the rest as a stick figure.

My teacher asked, "How'd you do this?" As if I'd been cheating.

In preschool.

I was four, trying to explain my creative process. I just drew what I saw, I told her. I had no idea stick figures were de rigeur through kindergarten, that I wasn't supposed to know how to read at age two.

When I talked for the first time with my birthfather's sister and she asked about my childhood, I had the same preschool panic: could I be in trouble for this? I couldn't think of any childhood stories to share and forgot everything I'd learned at Cornell. In that first conversation, my birthfather's sister told me he was metaphysical, as if she were hoping I was, too.

Metaphysical?

Whatever I'd learned about philosophy was gone in that instant. Not ghosts, not ghosts, surely she didn't mean ghosts. I fudged an answer. Couldn't help but imply ghosts.

I don't know if I can tell you why I was so unsure of myself those first years in contact with David's family. Maybe because I'd always imagined a birthmother wanting to be back in touch. After all, Aimee had made it clear: her Real Mother would take her back. But I'd never considered the birthfather, never considered there'd be a vested interest there—even though my dad's approval meant so much to me throughout school. Still does.

A birthfather though? He was someone different. He could, after all, walk away from what would be cleaved to a birthmother for some time. Maybe because of that, I felt the need to prove myself worthy of any interest his family would have. Not knowing them well yet, I was sure I'd never stack up.

"You ever see that movie *Quiz Show*?" I asked Val on our walk that day. "You know how Ralph Fiennes's family played trivia for fun at picnics? I get the feeling David's family was like that."

Val laughed, maybe because of how I'd told the story. Now, there's nothing like having someone laugh at your stories to make you feel close to them. But this is the part I'd kept at first from Val: I'd made the connection jealously, wishing I could have been a part of that cinematic scene, wishing I'd have been part of that reality.

Later, much later, when I finally could laugh at my own shortcomings with my birthfather's sister as well, I told Nor I'd seen something of her family in that movie. "Oh, isn't that ironic," she laughed. "Father used to quiz us on Latin and Greek at dinner, and I'd freeze up all the time," she said. The boys, though, they could handle it, she said.

I couldn't help but think: and yet David had chosen art over academics in grad school. More comfortable with expression than any hard science. Did he not want to have to compete with his father, his family? On some level, maybe. But more than that, I think, he loved art and the brilliance of creation, just as much as I love writing, love shaping words upon a page. His raw talent was there, already, at eight, when he drew shading and depth and movement in a floatplane drawn in a note home from camp. And his talent was there in the expressions captured of a Pilgrim man and wife. Was it drawn special for the holiday? Or a doodle while waiting for grownups to finish talking? Did he ever know what he'd done would be tucked away for a future generation to measure herself against?

I don't know whether David ever panicked over whether others considered him worthy, but I do know about Val and myself. So strange that it's the very moments we should not question ourselves, whether tucking in children at night or talking metaphysics over the phone, that we feel most vulnerable. Perhaps self-doubt, like hand gestures, can be passed down as well.

There was so much I didn't know about David, and what I wanted most to find out was what Val saw of him in me. So I waited (procrastinated?) on our walk until Jen was asleep, head drooped to the side for me to ask what David was like. "For real," I said, feeling so very unreal, unnatural, finally being in a position to ask.

"What do you mean?" Val said. "What do you want to know?"

Everything I should? There were so many things to know. This was, as far as I knew, my only chance to find out. I'd only ever thought there'd only be one meeting with whoever my birthmother would be. Once I had her story, that's all I needed. I couldn't imagine who'd want a lifetime of a relationship to follow.

So I had to fit it all in. I was soaking up all I could about Val, but I knew next to nothing still about David. I wanted to ask: what made him laugh? Did he ever see her cry? Was it just a one night stand, or something more? How much more? And how in the world could I ask all that of someone I barely knew? "I guess I was wondering how you guys met. Were you in a class together or something?"

"No, nothing like that," Val said. "He was a grad student—in art. He'd been dating a friend." Val laughed, embarrassed. "And she stood him up."

The friend was a nymphomaniac, she explained, as if that made it okay to hook up with a friend's boyfriend.

But it was more complicated than that. Tina was a friend of Val's roommate. And Tina was seeing someone behind David's back. David called Val's room, looking to see if her roommate knew where Tina was. The only one there, Val answered, knowing full well Tina was out on a date with another guy.

"I have no idea where she could be," she told him.

"You want to grab a drink?" he asked. She couldn't say no.

They were just friends, she insisted. She was only a freshman. He didn't try to kiss her until they'd been out on a few dates. And Tina was okay with it after she'd found out, she said. She was seeing someone else by that point.

Val would hang out with David at his studio, go through his canvasses lining the wall as he worked on a sculpture—a shapeless form, then a woman becoming whole under the touch of his hands.

He was a romantic. He took her to dinner and to plays. To the art museum, even.

This was what she'd told me that first time I'd asked. It's a lot to take in, the story of how you came to be. It's a story parents pass on to their children, the oral histories of the family. But how often do you get the other side to the story when you are adopted?

Writing this, I had the chance to ask again, to get it right. Val knew I'd started writing about being adopted, about how she came to be a part of my life. "Share everything," she said, when I asked whether I could or should explore how she lived with the shadows cast upon her life, her guilt over abandoning her firstborn to strangers.

For that reason, I tell you this. It's Val's story, but in it I heard David's, too. The weight of words of those too young to bear them. A reluctance to ask for more, a later realization of what more could have been given.

Thirteen years after my long walk with Val, I'd sit huddled on concrete steps near a gym where Jen was running drills, shooting baskets. With a cell phone clutched to my ear, I asked Val to tell me once again the story I first heard that day. She hadn't told me all this that first time. Whether it was because of the years we'd since shared or the solitary intimacy a phone can offer, she finally told me this:

He hadn't yet said he loved her when she told him she was pregnant. But he said, "Do you want me to marry you?" He said, "Because I can."

"No," she told him. "I can take care of things." Was that relief she saw on his face? Or was that just what she'd feared she'd see?

"What's that supposed to mean?" he asked. It was 1965, eight years before a woman dubbed Roe would take her case to the Supreme Court, but back alley abortions could be arranged.

Not for a Catholic girl, though. "I'll give the baby up," she said.

He said he had an aunt who could help. He could give her a call.

"No," Val said. "I can take care of it."

"Do you need money?" he asked. "I can give you money."

"No," she said, the thought turning her stomach worse than morning sickness. Money for a baby? "No, I'll take care of it."

David was quiet a moment, staring off into the emptiness of the night. "Well, that's good, I guess," he said. "I really don't have any money right now."

So much emotion there, but words seem stark when one side is afraid to ask for anything, and the other doesn't know what to give.

Val was barely pregnant when she went home from her freshman year that May, but her mother, having had ten other children herself, knew right away. And her mother had insisted Val tell her father.

It didn't seem to go any better.

"What do you mean he won't marry you?" her father had asked.

"He's not going to marry me, Dad."

"What do you mean he's not going to pay for this?" Louder now, his voice filling the living room, her head. Would he hit her now, too?

"He's just not going to, Dad, okay?" She could fill the room, too, with her voice.

"What's that supposed to mean?"

"It means," Val yelled, standing, then starting up the stairs, "that I. Will. Take. Care. Of. It!" Forty years later, she'd be telling me this over the phone and her voice still filled with frustration and anger and independence.

And she could remember what her father said then, after she'd slammed her door shut: "What's that supposed to mean?"

They sent her to a home, one for unwed mothers. David called while she was there, came out to see her even, when he was back from New Jersey for school. According to the non-identifying information Catholic Services sent me on them, they continued seeing each other after I was born, "despite her parents' disapproval."

"He would have married me if I'd wanted it," Val told me. "But I knew it wasn't right. It wasn't meant to be." It sounded as if it were a mantra she'd used, something to repeat quietly to herself when the weight of the emptiness in her arms was too much to bear.

"You were such a beautiful baby," she told me. "I held you as much as I could those first few days. But once I made that decision—" She stopped for a moment, and I remembered she'd said the same thing when she first shared the story all those years ago, on a walk through the park. "I just wanted you to get placed right away."

I remember how she said it the first time, not looking at me but looking at some point in the distance—beyond where the leafless trees before us converged, their misshapen, empty branches straining to reach the sky.

"I just wanted someone to hold you," she'd said.

I DON'T REMEMBER THE REST of that emotion-filled day that followed our walk. But that night for bed I undressed slowly, deliberately, pulling back the layers I'd worn that day. "I'm glad I had the chance to meet her," I said to Jim in the darkness. "To talk with her about everything." I was glad she was leaving in the morning, glad to get back to being the family I knew ours to be.

"Joe and I had a chance to talk today while you two were gone on that marathon walk."

"You did?" Poor Jim. Stuck making small talk while I was out pulling skeletons from closets.

"I guess it's been something of an obsession of hers, finding you," Jim said. "It's become a major strain on their marriage."

Some other woman I was.

"He didn't even know about you when they were married. She didn't tell him until after their son was born."

Until it was safe. Until she regained something of what was lost: not just love, not just a child—but happiness. The ceiling looked blue in the darkness. Without my contacts in, the rough popcorn surface looked smooth and forgiving. "God, what a secret to have to live with."

"What a sense of betrayal for him," Jim said, sliding his arms around me.

"She wasn't who he thought she was," I said, nestling into the crook of his neck.

"She was supposed to have been this nice Catholic girl."

I looked up at him, in the dark. "Well, so was I."

"You've got something to tell me?"

"Nothing you don't know already."

And we curled within that womb of darkness, other people's secrets laying heavily upon us.

ജ 7 ര

In the Flesh

I t's not often you get the chance to meet the object of your imagination. So, if offered of course you take it. But would you choose to live with it always? It'd be like having Christmas every day. It would dim the magic, wouldn't it? There'd been good reason I'd promised my mother I wouldn't go looking for my birthmother. So I'd met Val, but I didn't need to do anything more with her. I wouldn't go back. I didn't need to.

But I worried—because that's what I do—I worried that though I couldn't offer Val that next step, she'd want it anyway, wouldn't she? Worse, she'd ask for it. She'd make the presumptive close, that sales lingo I'd heard from both my father and my husband.

And I'd have to say no.

So this was my dilemma the morning Val and Joe were leaving. Val and I sat at the table from Mom and Dad, the one that had been in my kitchen growing up. Jen was making Joe watch *Barney* with her in the family room.

"Do you know when you'll be in Cleveland next?" Val asked as I got out a mug. Right at the beginning of our morning, much more boldly than I could ever be. And I was sure she meant: When you're visiting your dad, we should get together.

I didn't answer at first, just finished pouring her a coffee. I turned my back to her, put the pot back in the coffeemaker. "Well," I said, "we've been spending so much time there the past couple years," I began slowly, "with Mom being sick. We need to focus on Jim's folks now. They're older, you know." I sat down and studied the pattern on my Diet Coke can, as though I had to memorize it before I could drink any more.

"But you'll be down for the holidays, won't you?" Hopeful and expectant. Certainly I knew where I got that, now.

"We're doing Thanksgiving in Iowa," I said, spinning the can around with short, tight twists. I couldn't bring myself to look at her. "And Dad wanted to do Christmas in Key Largo this year."

"Oh." A quiet syllable. "Okay."

I would not share holidays. I couldn't, not after what Dad had said after I first told him. Why would I want to, anyway? She was, after all, still a stranger to me. Not until then had I imagined she'd have feelings that could be hurt if I didn't take into account what she'd been dreaming of, too.

She said, "How do you feel about that?" For a moment, I panicked she'd read my thoughts. But no, all she'd done was put aside her worries for mine, like Dad. "Will it be weird having Christmas down there?"

Could she not tell what I was saying or could she really be so empathetic after I'd just as well slapped her?

"It won't be as hard," I said. "Besides, we've had Christmases down there before." Aloe slathered on skin burnt taut and red, ice sculptures presiding over seafood buffets. Dolphins leaping through hula hoops, Dad letting me steer the boat through mangrove-lined canals. The years marked off by which plane we had. The Baron, with black tread on the wing to climb in through the co-pilot's window. The 421, with the door that flipped down forming steps to the ground. The Com-Air, with a stewardess station.

The planes. I'd rather not bring them up. But with Val so intent on my every word, she doesn't miss my phrasing. "What do you mean, 'we took the plane down to the Keys'?" she asked.

I wished I hadn't put it like that. I'm embarrassed by what it makes me sound like. But my childhood pictures include me and Aimee by an open airplane door, eyes squinting at the sun beating down on Freedom Field, just as Jim had pictures taken by his father's latest Chevy. How could I know when I was eight that it was a different life from everybody else? I was convinced I grew up in an average house in an average neighborhood and went to an average high school. We did normal things on the weekends, at least I thought so, but my first boyfriend at Cornell, who happened to be from Beverly Hills, pointed out that having a family plane and flying off to Maryland for the weekend was hardly average. He never even got to do that growing up, but he was in truth an army brat and had moved in with his uncle's family in the Hills to be settled in one place for high school.

I must admit he had a point. And now I was stuck having to explain all my family's eccentricities to a woman to whom each and every one of them mattered.

I tried to make light of our differentness. I told stories for Val, stories about the twin engine with wing latches that hadn't fully locked and the only thing lost was Dad's down vest, which parachuted down into green quilted cropland. And one time, one of the engines quit, and we had to make an emergency landing. I was there, but I don't remember much: I was too caught up in turning page after page of *Rage of Angels*. I was never nervous flying in those puddle jumpers. We always had Earl as our pilot, and I was safe in the back, eating doughnuts Earl brought for us or playing cards on a table that pulled up between the seats. Mom would try to keep our stacks of Solitaire from running together as the engines hummed, and I would try not to get airsick.

I even shared memories of times I couldn't remember, times I'd been told of so often, in such detail, they've become a part of me. Like when I was a toddler and we'd flown to the Bahamas, and Gramma Verne was sunburned so bad her eyes swelled shut. And when I was a baby and the heater died on the plane, and Mom covered us in newspapers to stay warm. The time Mom and Dad took a midnight cruise in the boat and the engine died, and when another boat passing by asked: "How many in your party?" my dad replied, "This ain't no party."

All these I told to Val. See, I was saying, I had a very good life. Be glad for what you did for me.

She soaked up every tidbit I gave her. Who doesn't love that, having someone hang on your every word? Though there is that point at which you have to acknowledge your foibles. Or at least admit you're holding back, not telling the whole about yourself.

That weekend, neither of us wanted to admit anything of the sort. We'd come close, then shy away, for whenever the emotions became too raw for either of us, we turned to pregnancy symptoms, a shared experience, a fall back conversation. Yet our soft underbellies were exposed, there for both of us to see, with Joe tipping Jim off as to what Val's search for me had done to their marriage. I'm sure Val saw my internal conflict, too. Though all she wanted that first visit was not to offend me, she's since told me. Me, I just wanted to get everything out that I might not otherwise get a chance to say.

"I'm glad you came to visit," I told Val. "If nothing else to clear up whether Jim and I might be related." A joke, but one that doesn't stray far from the truth. Especially considering a married couple in England recently found out they were brother and sister. And Jim and I, we looked so much alike that at his sister Susie's surprise fortieth birthday party, even Susie's father-in-law wondered which sister I was. Fortunately, even before Val, the calculations just didn't work. Jim's oldest sister would have been thirteen if she'd been the one pregnant with me, and she would have had to hide it from a mother who'd had seven other children at the time.

"We know that's not possible," Val said. She'd learned the hard way at nineteen.

"More coffee?" I asked, getting up. The morning, the last of our time together, was sliding by. A part of me grasped wildly for more questions to ask, more memories to share, anything to keep her there; another part couldn't wait to close the door behind them and take a deep breath, be alone with my own daughter.

"No, thanks," she said. "Time for me to get to work here." She pushed in her chair and then tiptoed up to Jen, who'd already pulled out her barn for the morning adventures of Carlos the horse. "Can I join you?" she asked, getting down on her knees.

Joe and I watched from above, in the enveloping cushioning of the green armchairs. We did not say a word, just watched as Val followed Jen's lead. Maybe I was tired of talking, tired of listening. Maybe I just wanted Val to get her fill, and we let her soak in Jen's words, bubbles of a voice lifting free from the depths of what Val had dared ask. Joe was the one who finally spoke the grown-up words. "We should probably get on the road," he said gently.

Val nodded and stood, smoothing her shorts. "Thank you," she said.

"I am glad you came," I answered. But we meant more than what was said. We hugged each other, and Jen and I walked them out to their car.

I stood on the stoop where they'd waited for me to welcome them in. This time, I was the one waiting, but words left unsaid untangled themselves and swirled by unused in the rush of good-byes.

They were in the car already. The doors closed, Joe shifting into gear. Joe turned around to back out, but Val kept her eyes on us. I slung Jenny on my hip and asked her to wave as the car eased down the drive. Val raised her hand to wave back. "Keep waving," I told Jen, as Val placed her fingertips upon the window. "Keep waving," I said, as the car slowly pulled away and disappeared over the knoll at the end of our street. I cupped my hand over Jenny's close cropped head and nestled her close into the crook of my neck. The cold of the concrete walk seeped through my socks. I realized I'd taken my daughter outside in late October without my shoes on.

"Let's go in," I said, more to myself than to Jen. God, I felt so drained I could barely bring myself to turn around and step up back into the house. I would call Jim at work and let him know how the final good-bye went. Val had never asked, not explicitly, when I would come visit her. Didn't even ask when or even if it would be okay for her to call me again.

Really, I can't say that I would have been as patient, as understanding.

A HARD-LEARNED LESSON, PROPRIETY. What is the protocol anyway for contacting biological relatives? After all these years, sometimes I still don't know what to do. No one did, at first especially. But we dared to try. And so the sister of my biological father called me again, asking if it would be all right if her parents met me. They would have a layover in Charlotte on their way to visit my biological great aunt. They wanted to know if I'd be able to stop by for a visit at the airport. I couldn't help thinking while on the phone with Nor, why in the world would she have to call to clear the idea with me first?

Why indeed, especially when I've laid out so many boundaries for Val. But I saw no inconsistencies until my editor pointed it out. "This surprises me," she said.

So I've been challenged to explain the difference, and I can't, really. Maybe it's because I'd been so long warned about The Mother being a threat to our family unity that I never thought to worry about The Father. Isn't the disaster you don't know to prepare for the one you should worry most about? Or is ignorance bliss? Depends on your perspective, I guess. And for me, it was a chance to meet the source of my imagination, without any prior restrictions. That David was dead maybe helped, too. No way my relationship with my dad could be threatened if The Father was dead, right?

So, maybe that's why I was so glad to meet David's parents. And that's why I could and did, without hesitation or trepidation or any other –tion, belt Jenny into her car seat to meet my biological grandparents out at Charlotte Douglas International Airport.

The only thing hanging over my head: Do I hug them hello?

I did, remembering how much it meant in college and after when my mother would greet a new boyfriend with a hug. (There weren't that many.)

Turned out David's mother was tiny, smaller than my mother-in-law, if that were possible. His dad was a towering older gentleman, with muttonchops for sideburns. For real. We walked to the gate for their connecting flight and sat down in the plastic chairs, and I told them my life story.

I brought pictures for them, including an ultrasound I'd just had, relieved I could finally share this secret with others now the first few months were under my belt. They were, however, more interested in Jen. We talked until we found where our lives had intersected. My high school band played at his alma mater. I'd been to Chautauqua, where he'd given lectures. But she'd lived in China, where her father had been a minister. She'd been court-ed by Robert McNamara, the Secretary of Defense during the Vietnam War. She'd biked across Europe for a family vacation.

It sounded perfectly lovely, the kind of memory I would have loved to have—never mind all the wonderful ones I did have. I groped for some-thing to say, not wanting a lull in our conversation. We did, after all, have so much to say.

Homer beat me to it. "Tempus fugit," he said.

"I'm sorry?"

He looked down at me, the happy crinkles around his bright-blue eyes quickly fading. "Tempus fugit," he said more clearly, as if I hadn't heard, as if it weren't a matter of me not understanding.

An Ivy League education, and still I wasn't prepared for this.

"It's Latin," he said.

Well, it certainly wasn't English.

He said it meant time flies, and I had a sense then, of other things flying—like my dignity, perhaps—right out the window.

I said, "It certainly does."

I felt very exposed, acutely aware of the people walking by, pulling their bags behind them, their eyes upon us. Another worry, too: Had we been talking too loud, sharing our secrets for all to hear?

Surely there was some polite question I could ask. But I was not able to have the presence of mind to thank this giant of a man, in stature and lore and mind, until he lay dying. And then, because I'd waited too long, I could only do it by email. I cried at his response, it was so much like my father's. So gracious, he thanked me, of all people, noting the strengths and talents I'd received from all my parents. He went on: "The thing we can all be most grateful for now is what you can do with it." Just like Dad would say. How perfect is this world, that the father who raised me would hold the same tenets as the father of the one who fathered me?

How human we are that we can't see it when first faced with it. At least I couldn't.

"You don't look like David," David's father told me as we sat in adjoining airport chairs—preformed, plastic, and identical. Yet he was so much taller, and I felt lost in mine.

"I don't look much like Val either," I said dryly. I wasn't sure whether he was denying his son's complicity or disappointed he didn't see any ghost of David in my expressions, in my voice, in my gestures. In what I knew. "I look a lot like my parents," I said.

It seemed to satisfy us all.

๛ 8 ๙

Thanksgiving, in So Many Words

I did not choose to tell this story. Not at first. I was born of a time when adoption was a private matter, long before webcasts or wardrobe malfunctions or morning talk radio contests where fathers guessed when their daughters lost their virginity. Still, Val would tell you I am a product of the sexual revolution.

That may be. More than that, I am of the Midwest, where even if you put your heart on your sleeve, you will cover it with your down jacket, for winters here, as in Sweden, are too long to add any more days wallowing in the dark.

I knew that not many beyond Michele and Christin would understood my struggle coming to terms with what my contact with Val would mean for the memory of my mother. I knew P.D. Eastman's book. I knew how others would see a visit from my birthmother.

It was hard enough sharing with Jim's family, and you'd think that would be easy, with the emphasis they put on family. Ten children, and Jim's mom still wished she'd had twins. Not to skip out on a labor, but because she'd have welcomed more. Bill and Teresa might have had twenty-two grandchildren when we visited that Thanksgiving, but their family hadn't yet faced what motherhood meant for an adoptee—especially one like me.

"How'd your visit with your mom go?" Jim's sister Sally wanted to know.

My mom? It still hurt when I heard the name, the pang of remembering she was dead. It'd been almost a year. It might have been worse, though, if in trying to be politically correct, Sally had called Val my Natural Mother. Or my Real Mother, for that matter. Ugh. What would that have made my Mom then? I swirled the water in my glass—a nervous habit. If I wasn't pregnant, I'd have some of that box wine my sisters-in-laws were drinking. The kind Mom always used to drink.

I said, "My birthmom, you mean?"

"Yeah, sure, your birthmom."

Maybe part of the reason I hadn't yet shared was I had no pat answer about what her visit meant. There were so many things I could say. A lifetime of questions I'd wondered about, packed into one weekend. And now I had to come up with a one-liner, something to sum it up.

"She's really a good person," I said. Okay, that was pretty weak. But true. "Amazing the things you learn are part of your genes, what's inherited."

For some reason, people are always interested in that high school biology lesson. The Punnett square filled with capital B's and small b's. What eye color did she have? Could I guess his?

The answer, though, lay outside that box. Hand gestures, speech patterns, haircuts.

Jim's other sisters, all of them, had gathered around, asking me questions under the bright lights of Bill and Teresa's kitchen. Yellow, like the kitchen in Rustic Hills, where I grew up and Aimee first told me the answer to a question I'd never considered asking. Now I was backed up against Teresa's counter, not because I was intimidated by all those sisters, but because I would need many years and thousands of words to come up with the answer to that.

I mean, I'm a writer, not a talker. And clearly no master of flash fiction, where whole stories are told in less than a few hundred words.

I was ready, then, for Bill to stand at the yellow flecked counter with his two-fingered whistle, to quiet all fifty of us in order to pray, "Bless us, O Lord." Dutifully, his brood queued up for a paper plate, letting new mamas through first for the pickiest and youngest eaters. Soft foods steaming in crock-pots, casserole dishes in Longaberger baskets with another nine-by-thirteen pan of potatoes warming in the oven and more heated canned yellow corn ready on the stove. Comfort food: exactly what I needed.

I loaded up a plate for Jenny and found her high chair. Teresa had put us at the main dining room table, a clear vinyl mat edged with ABCs lay under Jen's chair. I watched Jenny squish mashed potatoes between her fat fingers while Jim got in the turkey assembly line.

Teresa sweetly settled in next to me, as if preparing a turkey dinner with Midwest trimmings for forty was a snap. She made it all look too easy. That many guests and not only did she not ever run out of napkins or ice, but she still had the presence of mind to talk with me. My head would be in too much of a swirl to come up with any chit chat.

"So, Kate," Teresa said, cutting into her turkey with the edge of her fork, "I understand you had a nice visit with your mom."

Et tu, Teresa? The potato roll seemed to have lodged in my throat. It hurt as I swallowed. Then again, maybe Teresa had more on her mind than my picayune semantics. "My birthmom?" I said.

"Yes, of course," she said, and the words rolled so easily off her tongue.

I repeated what I'd told her daughters. A nice visit, with good long talks. I dubbed Val a plural: Good People. More than just the article (The Mother) she'd once been.

This at least I could grant her, without breaking my promise to my mother to be faithful. To not go back, to not consider going back.

My personal involvement had always been as marginalized as the mere article we'd given Val and David, The Mother and The Father. I'd not even register as a direct object in "Good thing she didn't have an abortion." Too troubling to put a name at the end of that sentence, even for this particular pro-choice writer (especially for this particular writer). And I was nameless, too, when my friends wondered whether my birthmother ever wanted to keep The Baby. Again, an article. As if The Baby was a third person, not me.

But Teresa made it personal. She asked, "Had Val always planned on looking for you?" A question, but as mothers we both understood it was a rhetorical one. Teresa's point, perhaps without realizing it: Val had always been looking for more than just a baby, more than The Baby and even more than for the baby with whatever name she'd called me.

Val, my birthmother, was looking for me, for the daughter she'd had.

Damn it all, thirteen years later I'm writing this down and I still can't bring myself to write those two simple words: *her daughter.*

"I'M GLAD VAL WAITED," I STARTED SAYING, after Teresa made her point about mothers looking for their children. Time could provide distance, if articles could no longer. Good that Val had waited until I had a baby of my own. So I could understand what it meant, to give away a miracle I'd had the privilege to be a part of.

But now I think it's more than that. I'm glad she waited until after Mom died. I was torn enough that year, to think I was where people were laughing and joking and death did not season our meal. Hard enough to split holidays with Jim's family, as Dad pointed out when I first told him about Val. And Dad's as sensitive about it now as he was then. I know because I just asked him last month if he thought Val's presence would be hard for Mom if she was still around. Hurt still edged his voice at the thought.

Being home for the holidays, though, is not so much a place as a time. And for my parents, my sister and me, that most precious time with only us four at home has passed.

I try and make it up to Dad. When we first lost Mom, I tried in my weekly calls. With words I'd tried to fill the void in his home that I could feel all the way over in mine. Often he would not answer. I would leave long messages, details of my week: Kindermusic on Wednesday mornings, Gymboree on Friday, walks to the park, play dates, children's hour at the library with

Miss Lisa. I hoped happy thoughts like these might fill his long journey, nine-ty miles, to and from work—a commute to fill the time, anything to not have to do anything in that big black hole of a house but sleep.

I'd agreed we needed to spend time with Jim's family for those holi-days, since we'd spent Thanksgiving and Christmas with my family the year before. But that first year after Mom died, it seemed to me Dad might need me more than ever. What a horrible idea it was to not be with him, when he was already missing his better half.

At least Ray had invited Dad to Thanksgiving. Ray and my dad had done business together for years, owned planes together, even. When Ray's marriage was dissolving, my parents fixed him up with Rachel, whom Mom had known since college at Michigan State. Ray and Rachel had been inseparable since, and the two couples would double date like college sweethearts. Had as much fun, too, going to ball games and gourmet dinners. Ray and Rachel always took in our small family as part of theirs for Thanksgivings. Good thing, too, with Mom gone and Aimee coming down from Michigan. No way Dad could beg off at the last minute, as he'd done so many times for dinners with friends since Mom died. This year Aimee and Dad would be swallowed up by Ray's family. Somehow two is so vastly smaller than a family of four.

But Thanksgiving was always Ray's to prepare, and it was a grand-daddy of production. He'd have a schedule of what dish went into the oven at what time. There'd be three different types of stuffing (oyster, cranberry, sage) and too many vegetables: Peas with pearl onions, corn soufflé, rutaba-gas, garlic mashed potatoes, maple-glazed sweet potatoes, honey-glazed car-rots, puréed winter squash. Salads like Ambrosia, and my mind so full of memories I can't remember anything else. Then again, maybe it was because of the wine—a different bottle for each course, and Ray could and would talk about any one of the bottles of wine on the table for longer than any som-melier.

For as long as I could remember, Ray put Dad in charge of the turkey. Dad would get up early to put the bird in the oven at our house, and finish browning it at Ray's. Mom was the only other one Ray would let in the kitchen; he could count on the chemist to make gravy smooth, not lumpy.

Rachel was put in charge of the conversation, since she came across as ditzy (read: nonthreatening) but could deftly maneuver discussion into and through the implications of the industrial revolution on Civil War strategies—and turn it into the most memorable topic of the evening (read: the kind that leaves your gut sore from laughing the next day). For carving, Dad was always given a chef's hat and apron. And a glass or three of red wine as well.

Maybe Dad mastered the art of cooking up a big bird as a kid. He certainly had plenty of game to practice with, for Dad had a trap line with a couple other high-school buddies. He'd walk beneath the snow-softened trees, tramping along in homemade snowshoes through borealis woods, checking traps he'd laid on an eight-mile run. He'd pull the stiffened animals from the iron jaws and reset his money-making machine. Even splitting the proceeds from the skinned pelts, they each made $3,000 a year, more than his father during those post-war years.

But Dad's trapping buddies were all gone now (the last of them honored in a five-by-seven spot in the *Wall Street Journal*), as was Ray's gravy maker. How lumpy and colorless the preparations could be this year without Mom. She'd held a special place in Ray's heart, too: In her last hours, he'd been there for her and Dad. We all sat vigil for her, taking turns by her bedside. We sat through one night and all the next day. And another. Nine-month-old Jenny was a patient baby, waiting with us, willing to have us hold her and read her books through those days. The doctors sent us home at night to sleep, sent us down to the cafeteria to have our meals. After one late lunch, Jim and I had to swing by our car to get a fresh diaper for Jen, and when we got back to Mom's floor, even before the elevator door opened, we heard a man wailing, keening through the halls. It was a voice we knew.

It was Ray.

As for my father—who from the first had refused to ask others for help, even if only to drive Mom to at least some of her treatments—his sorrows pooled silently. How deep I know those still waters run. Like a Swede's.

❧ 9 ☙

Denial and Other Holiday Treats

One holiday down without Mom, one to go. In between, the anniversary of her death loomed large. I needed all my coping mechanisms to hurl myself over that wall. It was how I got through law school: eating, sleeping, stressing. What better time to do all that than the holidays?

So I did it all with a vengeance. Baking cookies, shopping, sending out Christmas cards, decking the halls. I helped at Jen's preschool, dipping the kids' fingertips in different colored paints and pressing them against a teeny clay pot, connecting the fingerprints with a Sharpie marker to make them into tiny Christmas lights, and noting XMAS '95 on the rim. Then I made cookies for the preschool, and cookies for Santa, cookies to freeze and bring along to Florida. I signed up for the Newcomer's Group cookie exchange, too—twelve dozen cookies were needed for that. Twila, the woman who organized the exchange, had insisted it was the way her mother always did it back home, and I wasn't about to argue anyone out of their mother's traditions. And so I learned to make appropriate adjustments in predicting how many cookies each recipe made, depending on how many I'd need to sample.

Okay, let's be honest: I was eating my way towards Christmas.

The problem with making all these cookies (besides eating too many) is standing to bake them. When you're pregnant, it's Varicose Vein City in the making. I could feel a cord of vein burning up the back of my knees. And it was not my imagination—there, in the mirror, was the ugly truth: all up the back of both legs, corded blue fans of vessels—one set, and another, and another. I was so depressed that Jen and I spent the rest of the morning reading *Chick a Chick a Boom Boom* and a happy dose of Seuss on the couch, listening to Andy Williams sing Christmas songs, wishing I had legs like the skaters on his Christmas specials, the ones who wore pastel sweaters and faked their way through the bunny hop on live TV.

I pulled out Holly Leaf and Brown Sugar Pecan Cookies for after dinner.

"Where are all the Monster Cookies?" Jim asked.

"Gone."

"But you said you made four batches."

"I had to give them all away." Well, not all of them, but I wouldn't tell him that. The last two dozen of his mother's best recipe had been so tasty after my lunches that week. "We swapped at the Newcomer's Brunch. We have these now."

"But these are someone else's favorite cookies," he said. "Not mine."

I wasn't having much luck making cookies for Jim that year. I'd started out the season making my grandmother's Christmas cookies. The Swedish butter cookie with red sugar sprinkles was still my favorite, though I'd never forgiven Mom for what she'd done with a whole batch of them. I was maybe seven, just back from sledding, but the sense of treachery permeated the air as I stood in the entry, stomping the snow off my boots. "You made cookies without me," I cried from the door. And she had the audacity to refuse to make another batch. "You can help next year," she'd said, pulling the last tray from the oven. The red sprinkled Rudolph was hot and soft and perfectly formed, not missing any legs like the ones I'd made the year before with the cookie cutter. Oh, you can be sure I sampled the batch, but cookie treason leaves a bitter aftertaste.

Some things I just can never let go. I should, I know. Especially ever since Jim insisted I try his mother's iced Christmas cookie recipe.

There are certain inalienable truths in this world. This is one: Nothing beats Teresa's cookies. (If you must know, the trick is using butter-flavored shortening instead of just butter.) And yet there I was, trying to pass off Twila's Spritz cookies as an improvement over Teresa's.

Maybe I was just feeling sorry for Twila.

"You know, the woman who made the Spritz used to have a twin."

"Used to?" Jim asked, as if doubtful there'd been a legal dissolution of their relationship.

"He died," I explained. "He had AIDS."

Jim's face looked exactly like I hoped mine hadn't when Twila had told me, in the dark of her kitchen before everyone else had shown up.

"Not gay," Twila had quickly explained to me, but that wasn't what I'd worried about for her. To have someone so much a part of you, mainlining. I heard about the lies and the disappearances for days, betrayals on the heels of pleas for help. And then the slow wasting by a disease, like cancer will do. Twila and I stood in her darkened kitchen, the brilliant Carolina sun cordoned off and kept outside her windows, as she confessed why her brother had died just two years earlier on that day, an innocent victim.

"He'd been in a motorcycle accident—had a blood transfusion," I told Jim. "It was tainted."

I hadn't known her well, really, but she'd shared with me the pain that filled the void she'd been left with. I'd met her at Newcomer's, knew her as a mother of two small boys. I knew she lived in a lovely home on a fenced corner lot. She had damask wallpaper all the way up her cathedral ceiling, and at the top of the stairs there was a bonus room with a rainbow collection of tubs filled with toys for her sons, and downstairs in her lower level she had a sauna. I knew her as a woman possessing all this, but she knew herself as only half of what she'd been all her life.

Now I understood why she moved with an emptiness surrounding her, why her long face seemed thinned by sadness. She'd been born a California girl, tall and slender, blonde hair swept back from her face, with features that never quite seemed to fit.

Because they once belonged to a boy.

And I wondered, then, which was worse: to be defined only by what we have, or by who we miss.

WE SHOULD HAVE KNOWN MOM WAS DYING. She had cancer, so I guess we knew—but we didn't realize death really was coming for her. Maybe the question is, would it have helped, especially knowing who we are?

Shortly after Mom's diagnosis in 1992, First Union sent me to an executive development program. Life Therapy for one intensive weekend. Strangers thrown together to work through all of life's issues, to be better leaders. People were honest, painfully so, confessing emotional abandonment and abuse, the loss of children and the loss of hope. My turn, and I had nothing to confess.

"I really don't have anything," I said. "I mean, I lived a pretty ordinary childhood. Not that it didn't have its ups and downs, it's just—" I looked around the room, a circle of strangers patching the holes in their lives. Opposite me sat the facilitator, a powerful man in a wheelchair. What I'd need this group for hadn't happened yet. Would it be off point if I raised it? "A month ago we found out my mom has ovarian cancer, it's Stage Three, and she doesn't want to talk about it at all, even when we all were saying how much better people did when they focused on the positive."

Oh, she got really mad about that.

"And I'm afraid something will happen, and I don't even have a baby to share with her, and there's so much I don't even know about her yet, and I don't even know how much time we have—" and I couldn't go on, not without anyone being able to understand me through my tears.

The man next to me handed me a box of Kleenex. I tore one out, not wanting to need one. Desperately needing one.

"It'll be hard," the facilitator said. "Especially for you, as a sunny-side-up family. You won't want to talk about the pain. But it's there, and you need to say good-bye when it's time. You'll know when that is. You'll know."

That's the problem with denial. You know, and you don't want to admit it. I'd still like to think her stoicism and not my steadfast denial was the reason why, a year into the disease, I would start complaining to her about my morning sickness before realizing at least mine was something to be grateful for. Another year's worth of cancer treatments beyond that and we thought she'd been through the worst of it, with her CA 125 count back down to double digits. Her hair was coming back, and she wasn't so nauseous anymore. They were planning trips for that summer, after that last scheduled chemo treatment. A preventative measure, flooding her belly with poisons to make sure she'd be done with the cancer once and for all.

But it proved too much for her system. The doctors brought her back from the brink of death, but she'd lost her kidney function and her hearing, too. Who knew those organs were so interconnected? Dad had to explain several times to me: because of the nature of the injury, a hearing aid wouldn't help. We went for his birthday again, over the Fourth, and we did what we could around the house. We used a whiteboard to talk with Mom. I hated leaving, but we'd worn her out. I left my mom to spend the rest of her last summer in silence and in dialysis. She lay on the long couch in the great room, a kitten curled on her lap, turning pages of Ludlum and Clancy and Grisham, anything breezy.

What would you choose, I wonder, for the last books you'd ever read? I wonder now if she was too sick to read what she really wanted. Maybe mostly because those wouldn't be the books I'd choose for my last. What would she have chosen, if she would have been strong enough to concentrate on something else? She was too tired for her other favorite things. Like tending her roses, or just riding shotgun in Dad's boat.

Three times a week, Dad would drive Mom the hour to dialysis. They'd go first thing in the morning, and in the hours she'd have her blood cleaned since her kidneys couldn't do it, he made all his business calls and then he'd drive her home. Friends offered to drive, but he said he didn't need any help. "We're fine," he insisted. As if saying it would make it true.

Those first weeks Dad had to write everything down for her. This for a man I'd spent my adolescence wondering if he knew how to read or write, since he dictated his business letters and never read for pleasure. But for Mom, he wrote. He wrote notes to her, like in high school. In those days before email, we were lucky enough to have a fax at home, and I'd send a fax once a week, like my weekly call, trying to think of the questions I'd wonder about long after she was gone. Dumb questions, like whether she'd ever been to a Tupperware party. (Yes, at Eunice Shephard's. That's where she got the rolling pin and mat she used to roll out pie and pasty dough.)

Each week I'd ask, and Dad would insist he didn't want any help. "No, don't come up. We don't need you to come up. I'm fine," he said. "We got a cat," he said, as if the company of a kitten would solve everything for Mom. "We call him Shadow because he follows Mom everywhere."

I couldn't help but wonder if now was the time I'd been told about.

Aunt Mary knew not to listen to him. "I'm coming, Jimmy," she said, and she did. Mary had been a speech pathologist before she'd become an orthodontist's wife and a philanthropist. Mary put those skills to use again, teaching her sorority sister how to read lips. Mom was hungry for the spoken word, for understanding how to differentiate between "p's" and "b's," how to live without a white board or a notepad.

By Labor Day, Jim and I were surprised to learn the writing utensils were all back in drawers. Mom had mastered lip reading so well, we'd only have to remember to get her attention before we started talking. It was so good to see Mom, to see her smile. To hear her talk. And to have a conversation, something we hadn't been able to have all summer.

"I might come up again sometime before Thanksgiving," I said.

"What for?" Mom said.

"Just because."

We'd have time in October, I decided. Just us girls, just Jen and I. We spent quality time together: Mom on the couch, Jen in her lap with my silver baby rattle, Shadow the kitten tapping at the toy, then jumping across them.

Our conversations were easy once more—for the most part. Mom was that good reading lips now. I could be changing Jen's diaper, and Mom could still pick up what I was saying. Though Mom complained I made it hard for her. "You're not moving your lips at all," she said.

It's what I do. Sometimes, especially when emotionally charged or simply nervous, I freeze my mouth as I talk, smiling through my words.

I blame Billy. He was a ventriloquist's doll I got one birthday. He came with an instructional booklet, and I memorized it. I could make it look like he was doing all the talking. At least that's what my best friend told me when I made her listen to Billy talk on my knee. I'd pull strings behind his back to make his lips move while mine didn't.

I don't know why I still was doing it. Maybe I'd wanted to believe it was easy for her to read my lips, maybe I wanted to believe it wasn't hard for us to communicate. Maybe I wanted to believe it wouldn't be one of my last times with her.

"You still can't hear anything?" I asked her.

"Just the opera that keeps playing in my head," she said. "Pavarotti, I think."

"But you don't even like opera."

She just smiled. "The weird thing is, it doesn't sound like a memory. It sounds like I'm really hearing it, right now."

"Right now?"

I can picture her at the counter, with Shadow crouched on her shoulder and ready to jump at the flash. Mom's hair was just finally coming in again for the last time, a silvered crew cut. She was feeling good, I could tell from the way her eyes sparkled. But the opera thing was weird.

Maybe, just maybe, she did like opera, and I just never knew. For years she did sing for the Medina Community Choir. What I wouldn't give to hear her sing again, even though Jim insists she always sang flat, the very reason she never liked Sinatra.

When we visited at Thanksgiving, I told Jim she'd taken a turn. "She's weaker," I said when I thought we were alone. "And the singing in her head, it's worse."

"She seems okay to me," Jim said, but I knew something wasn't right.

I moved up my flight to come early for Christmas. "It's not like I have to ask days off work," I said to Dad. "I'll bring my work with me, if you don't mind." And we laughed because we knew I was talking about his grandbaby.

We didn't know I'd get to the hospital just in time.

When I arrived, Mom was sitting upright in the dialysis bed, arms outstretched, Christlike, to take Jen in. But Jenny, the little stinker, would not cooperate. She refused to curl up against my mother's chest. My daughter played Straight Baby, arms in front so you could not hold her close, legs straight out and toes pointed so you couldn't even stand her up. It was not the first time she'd done this to my mother.

I tried apologizing for Jen not being cuddly.

"You're not moving your lips again," my mother said. She bounced Jen on the bed, trying to get Straight Baby to at least flatten her feet so she could stand on her own. "I still can't tell what you're saying."

I tried not to smile, to enunciate better, but it was hard. I was glad to see her. "Tired of travel, I guess," I said again.

Mom nodded, but I don't know if she really heard me. She twisted Jen side to side to get a good look at her. Jen held her chin to her chest, her cheeks round and full, her eyes narrow and skeptical for a nine-month-old. "Crawling yet?" Mom asked.

"Not even thinking about it." She'd been so early, at only five weeks, reaching for the linked fish hanging from her car seat. But Jen preferred to snuggle against me than to go exploring on her own. If she needed to get anywhere, she just rolled over and over until she'd flip around at her destination, her wispy curls wild and her eyes grinning.

It bugged me she didn't take to Mom as I'd loved my grandmother. Jim had decided it was the way Mom tried to hold Jen, facing in instead of looking out at the world. Maybe, he delicately suggested, she wasn't used to babies like his mother was, since I'd been the last baby Mom had held before Jen.

Mom handed Jen back to me, a wry smile on her face as if she could read my thoughts. "You were just the same," she said. Not spitefully or even ruefully. Just a statement of fact. But she said it too loud. Mary hadn't been able to teach her how to monitor her sound level—that would have to wait until her next visit, she'd told Mom. She wanted to make sure Mom was well versed in understanding others first.

"She'll be ready for some good cuddles when you're all done," I offered, but that was the last time my mother ever held my daughter. When

I led Jen into a windowless waiting room, all I knew to pray for was that Jen would be patient in her stroller and that I had enough diapers with me.

But soon the nurse called me out of the waiting room. "Come quick," she said, rushing me down the hallway and around the corner from the dialysis unit. A woman gasped for air in a room nearby, and I wondered why no one was helping her. A tall man stepped out of that room and introduced himself to me. I recognized his name as one of Mom's doctors. Unruly hair tumbled across the top of his head, but he was calm, so calm asking if we'd discussed treatment options for what he called endstages. He was very clear: she needed a ventilator, or we needed to let her go. Two thoughts overwhelmed me. One, my mother was the one they weren't helping yet, and two, this word "endstages." Was that where we were?

Maybe only a minute or two had passed since I've been called out of the waiting room, but all this time my mother was gasping for air as if they'd been holding her under in the pool too long. *Let her up, let her up*, I thought. "I know Dad and Mom have talked about it," I told her doctor, "but I don't know that a decision's been made." God, she'd had cancer for almost three years, and we didn't have a plan in place? What happened to all the organization my mother lived by?

The doctor had no choice but to shove a tube down my dying mother's throat while I was left to spread the news. From a pay phone nestled against a bank of windows, I dared to call my father out of a meeting. "Dad," I said. "Mom crashed in dialysis."

"Jesus," was all he said.

The sun streamed through the windows, glowing all around me. I leaned heavily on the handle of the umbrella stroller, suddenly blinded by the reality of what was coming. "I couldn't tell them not to put her on a ventilator." I didn't tell Dad that the doctor had meted out words like "endstages" as if we'd known it all along. Hadn't we? She'd even said over Thanksgiving how someone had chewed her out for parking in a handicap spot at the grocery store—until she'd explained she was coming from the oncologist and couldn't catch her breath if she had to walk any further. Her voice filled with wonder as she related her story, as if amazed she'd reached this stage before sixty. Her mother had made it to sixty-three before cancer took her, her dad sixty-six. She was supposed to live at least that long. But cancer proved we knew nothing about actuarial charts.

And because I'd known nothing about DNRs, I'd ordered the doctor to resuscitate my dying mother.

"You were right to do that," Dad said to me, his voice tinny through the annelid phone cord. "Can you imagine? She'd be gone already."

Whether or not I could imagine it, her time was now.

Jenny and I formed a deliberate procession to a waiting room on the other side of the hospital. I couldn't visit Mom, since she was in ICU and I had the baby, so all I could do was find an empty seat a respectable distance from the family whose brother, a cop, had been shot through the nose. They had no time, no distance between it's coming and now. We'd had two and a half years.

I sat with Jen in that brown waiting room, reading to her one of the books I had with me, or making faces at her as she sat on my knees. The light was dim, as if anything brighter would have blinded us with hope. I did not have the heart nor the attention span to look through the out-of-date magazines on the laminate tables in the corners. When Jenny was bored with me, I packed her back in the stroller and did a lap around the room, past the empty avocado-green plastic chairs. I didn't want to walk the halls, I didn't want to miss the doctor. I skirted the cop's family. I'd no desire to make eye contact with this other family newly awaiting their inevitable, when I still wasn't ready to face mine.

It was eons before Dad came through the door. He'd already visited with Mom. "She's resting," he said, but we both knew it was a euphemism. He offered to take Jen round around the wing so I could spend some time with Mom. "The nurse can take you back," he said.

Betty zigzagged me through the halls and through doors. She held open a door to a room. "Just a few minutes," she said. "You won't want to wear her out."

Really? For someone needing final good-byes, the instruction seemed overly cautious. Even Mom's diabetic great aunt was allowed chocolate the last year of her life.

In a quiet gray room, Mom lay all stretched out on the bed. An oxygen mask covered her face.

"Hey," I said, laying my hand on her arm. "Mom."

She did not move. No flinch, no flutter of her eyes. I stood, waiting, rubbing her arm to elicit some reaction, any. This was not how it played out in Hollywood. I was trying to wrap my head around the idea that she'd been so eager to hold Jenny just a couple hours before, and now this.

"Hey, Mom," I tried again. "I love you."

Again, nothing. I smoothed back her shock of gray hair—straight and gray, like an old man's crew cut. So different from the dark curls she'd had before chemo, the ones she never knew what to do with when the weather turned humid. Curls like Jenny, though I knew that was impossible. I pulled her sheet up as best I could and patted her arm.

"You take care," I said, unable to come up with anything better to say. "You watch over Jenny for me over on the other side, okay?" And I backed out of the room slowly, wishing for one more chance to say good-bye, a chance where she could say it back.

Betty caught me as I passed, and the nurse's words barely registered as I beelined for the waiting room, in a hurry now for my baby to hold onto. I wish I'd acknowledged the nurse more for saying those words meant to comfort, meant to soothe.

I must have worn my pain on my face, for Dad, too, asked, "You okay?" All he was losing, and he was worrying about me.

So I nodded, not acknowledging my eyes filling full of regret for the years Mom would not spend with Jenny. "I should make some calls," I said. Dad slipped back by Mom's side, and I went on phone duty. Once I'd worked my way down the list, it would get easier, I told myself.

Even then I knew that was a lie.

I used words the nurse had told me. "It won't be long," I told Jim first.

"My flight's on Thursday," he said.

I hadn't been told explicitly, but I knew. "She'll be gone already by then."

There was a long silence, and then these words, reassuring even through their brokenness: "I'll see what's still open today."

My sister was not as easy to convince. It wasn't a good time at work (she was a sous chef at Ponderosa), and there was some sort of storm on the way down from Michigan. She came anyway, but called from Toledo. Her engine had died, having suffered years of neglect. Now of all times. But for Dad, it was a crisis for him to solve. One he could fix. A bus ticket later (that Dad called and paid for), Aimee showed up in Medina.

The funny thing was, if it wasn't for the car trouble, I wouldn't remember Aimee being there. It was all I could do to deal with my own grief.

In the interest of full disclosure, I should mention it wasn't the first time I'd been overly concerned about me and only me. Especially when it came to dealing with my sister. But blurring the difference between what happened and what we want to remember is something my family specialized in. That's why none of us counted that Christmas we had the day after Mom's funeral, when I gave Dad an eider quilt meant to replace the one Mom had torn apart in her chemo-frenzied sickness. He knew it'd been meant for both of them. I had not meant to give him a gift he would not take out of its package for two years. As for me, I would rather not remember returning Mom's presents. I made the clerk unwrap them all because I couldn't stand the thought of being the one to open them.

We would celebrate our first Christmas without Mom, then, a year and three days after she died. We'd celebrate in their condo down in Florida, where cancer had never invaded, and I would bake my way into believing the holiday would be good. It had to be. Ocean Reef was that way, it could make you forget any poverty of the heart (or wallet) as you lunched by the pool, watching chartered trawlers and 120-foot yachts glide through those mangrove channels. Jim started coming down when we got engaged, and Dad had asked before we'd unpacked how long it would before he would hear the pitter-patter of little feet.

Now Jen would finally be toddling around the place, and Mom would not be there to hear. We would try to blind ourselves to Mom's absence, as if we could with the sun's glinting rays off the Atlantic's broadside, which we'd solemnly observe from the condo's glassed-in sunporch.

We should have known better, though—known that changing locations would not change our hearts. Our sorrow could not be deterred, not even by the fever Jen developed on our drive down. We didn't realize until we unbuckled her from her seat. Jen was sweating, so hot to my touch. I gathered her in my arms and ran up the stairs to Dad's condo—as best a pregnant lady could—and burst through the door, Jim close behind.

"Well, hello there," Dad said from the couch, a drink already in hand.

"Jen's sick," I said, "Really sick." I was so frantic the baby inside me was spinning and kicking. I put a hand on my belly to calm it and went straight to the guest bath and swung open the medicine cabinet. If she'd been sick more than once before, maybe I'd have been more calm, or at least maybe I'd have known how to calm Dad while Jim called the doctor and I ran the cool bathwater, for all the while Dad hovered about, demanding whether I knew what happened to the brain at 105, the temperature Jen was running.

What he needed was Mom to assure him it would be okay, to remind him I'd run just as high temperatures when I had whooping cough at that age. No one else could tell him that the love we offer as parents is all we can give, that there's no need for any extra level of concern. He carried that added obligation anyway, he believed he agreed to it when he signed those papers saying he'd be our dad.

Here's how he told me he saw it: The Mother and The Father said we can't do it, we can't take care of our baby. We entrust her to you. With that kind of trust, he said, an adoptive parent had something more he needed to give, more than in the natural order of things.

For my dad the dealmaker, that was the kind of contract you could never break. No matter what was thrown at you.

ॐ 10 ॐ

Shadow of Our Former Selves

I n the morning, Shadow lay on his side in the sunroom. He held his head up, eyes closed and smiling. A Cheshire cat. Full grown now.

Jenny's eyes lit up as soon as she spied that tiger-striped beast. I set her down, and she toddled right to him. She crouched down and pointed to him. "Tat," she said, looking up at me happily. The back of Jen's head was matted from fever sweat, but her eyes were brighter now.

"Yes, Papa has a kitty, too," I said. I'd forgotten to tell her about the cat. She would not have remembered him from the year before. Shadow had grown considerably, bigger than any humane society cat I'd ever had. His height and girth testament to the strength an animal needed to get through what each passing day wrought for my dad.

"Careful," Dad said from the kitchen. "That cat is wild."

I got down on the floor in between Jenny and the cat, ready to mediate. Shadow laid his head down and rubbed it against the floor, grinning away, looking like he'd roll over if we would just give the command.

Just like Tigger, the cat I had growing up. I pet his tummy.

The cat hesitated, then rubbed his head again. Almost all the way over he went.

"He's still got his claws, Kate."

"He's playing," I said. Jen stood up and squatted again, this time right next to me.

"You putting his food in a bowl now, or just dumping the bag across the entryway?"

"Oh, I can't do that anymore. Not since the raccoons found it."

I put my hand over Jen's outstretched fingers, and with my other one I stroked the cat's back.

And that cat bit my hand. Next second, Shadow had jumped off to the side, back arched and tip of his tail flicking, and I'd scooped up Jen and held her close, feeling as Dad must have when he'd sparked the kitchen outlet by sticking a pencil in it, just to show us what not to do when I was young enough to know to listen to him.

"He get you?"

"No," I said, hiding the red marks on my hand.

"Careful with that cat," Dad said. "He misses being wild."

"You can take the cat out of the wild, but you can't take the wild out of the cat."

Jim shot me a look like, you didn't really say that, did you?

"You know he was wild, completely wild, while I had that apartment down in Dover," Dad said. The last couple of months, the ninety minute drive to and from work was too much; he'd rented a house on a hill next to work and let the cat back at home roam free.

"He was wild before then, too," Jim said. And Shadow was: back at the big house in Ohio, he'd climb over the top of the jaguar carved out of an African olive tree and waited, ready to pounce. If we sat on the couch, he'd climb onto our shoulders and then onto our heads. It wouldn't have been so bad if it wasn't for the kitten's claws.

"I locked him out one week and didn't know it," Dad said. "I was sure I'd lost him."

Was it my imagination, or was Dad getting all choked up like when he'd talk about Mom?

Shadow tucked his hindquarters down and, sitting upright, wrapped his tail regally around his legs. As if he were a gentleman who'd been snubbed.

"Amazing how a cat can settle in and find the condo out of all the others," I said. The condos here look so much alike that even my husband was confused which condo was Dad's at first. I wondered briefly how strong a cat's homing instinct was. Would there ever have been a danger he'd try and make it back up to Ohio? But he's a cat, not Lassie.

Dad said, "Oh, I haven't let him out down here at all. Not since I brought him down."

Talk about parallel, lonely lives. Both those boys so deeply grieving what they could no longer have.

YES, EVEN SHADOW. NO ONE REALIZED just how attached he, too, had become to Mom until after her funeral. Aunt Mary had shuffled us home, made a pitcher of martinis and poured the first for Dad at the beginning of the evening, the ending of a long, sad day. Thank goodness she took charge of the kitchen, since I didn't realize I could have.

"Your father didn't want any help this summer, you know," Aunt Mary had told me as I was cutting the potatoes. "But I came anyway. 'Too tall Mary is here, Jim,' I told him. 'And I'm here to help my friend.' Your mom is—was—a smart woman," she said, placing my mother once and for all into past tense. "She didn't know how to lip read at all when Dave and I first arrived." Aunt Mary heaped an extra syllable upon her vowels, as people who've lived in the South for years will do. She worked all the while she chatted. "I just showed her a few things, and we were talking and talking by the end, just like where we'd left off. He didn't know she still had it in her," she said.

Or didn't want to admit he needed help.

"She's a good mom," I said, unable to render her in the past just yet. At the airport, over Labor Day Mom had promised to come to look after Jenny, just like Gramma Verne used to do for me and my sister.

"She was looking forward to that, she was," Aunt Mary said, and her lips got thin as she poured the water out of the meat pan, the fat bodies lumping unceremoniously into the sink, and I turned on the beater and let the noise drain out the what-could-have-beens.

Aunt Mary laid her Southern charms out upon the great table my father had made, a plywood circle set upon an Ethan Allen base and covered by another one of Mom's elegant tablecloths. Everyone who was still in town after the service gathered round, since the table could seat seventeen. For grace, we always held hands, and Dad would offer up in a solemn voice a prayer giving thanks. But that night Dad left the offering of thanks to my Jim. Aunt Mary passed the comforts of what she'd made, and by the end of dinner, we'd pushed back our chairs, and we rested an arm upon the back of our spouse's chair, and we laughed until we cried once more.

And in the midst of this island of happiness, a kitten jumped up into Aunt Mary's lap, looking for the one who he'd shared naps with, the one who'd rest on the couch after tending as best she could after Dad. And we quieted as we sipped our coffee, watching that tiger-striped kitten kneading love into the crook of Aunt Mary's arm, working the question of where his lady could have gone.

Mom had told my sister and I that we'd be best friends when we grew up, but that's not how it worked out. We'd managed a truce over the years, ever since the time we'd drawn a line between her G.I. Joe and my Barbies. Every time I see her now, she seems smaller than I remember, but big sisters remain large in our memories.

I couldn't wait to tell her about Val when we picked her up from the airport that first Christmas without Mom. All the times she'd said she'd look for her Real Mom, a term used in part just to rankle Mom. To test her. All the furtive searching through piles of Hallmarks boxed up in the attic, talking about how she'd find her birthmother that way. Now I'd found mine. While none of those cards might have been from Val, all of that well wishing was.

The whole way down from the airport I'd been working on a way to broach the subject, but Aimee was the one brought it up once she'd settled into the condo. She was flipping channels, eyes on the screen. "Dad said you heard from your mom."

God, Aimee of all people should know what Val was to me. "My birthmom," I said. "Yes, she contacted me out of the blue not that long ago." It was back in March, I didn't want Aimee to know how far back it was. I should have been the one to tell her, and I wasn't.

Maybe I could make it up to her. I said, "You know, she told me how to start a search, if you want to."

"My friend Lisa told me, too," she said. "I've already registered, which is how you're supposed to do it." Was that a dig, that I didn't go through the right channels? And yet I knew even then that thirteen years later Aimee would be no further along. Somehow opportunity does not like to stop at Aimee's door.

"This group Val did it through, they give you counseling, help you understand the whole adoption triad. That's what they call it. It made a difference for Val."

"So that's her name, Val?" she asked, her eyes not on me, but the TV.

The way she said it, it was like another line drawn between us. I had a name, a person—while she had nothing.

"Yeah," I said quietly. "That's her name."

Aimee grunted and flipped the channel.

After dinner, Aimee cleaned up dishes faster than I ever could while I put Jenny down. (That was our deal, since I'd cooked.) As I was finishing up in the bedroom with Jen, I could hear the beginnings of Quite A Scene, as Mom used to put it.

I closed the bedroom door behind me to find Aimee trailing Dad around the condo. She cried as she walked, her head tipped back in freshly wrought pain, like her old baby photo. "I didn't know," she cried, claiming she didn't know Shadow was only an indoor cat here. She had left the kitchen door open while she was cleaning up dinner. "I didn't know," she said.

Dad fussed around the condo without turning toward her, as if there was no such thing as grief following him. "That's not true," he said.

Jim was in hiding in a swivel chair on the sun porch, trying to allow them some modicum of privacy in a fifteen-hundred-square-foot condo. He'd turned away and faced the darkness. The pool below glowed iridescent blue, outlining the low conch fence and palm trees clustered around it in shadow.

"He'll come back," Aimee said, as if saying so would make it true. She was following Dad so closely she was in Dad's face when he turned around.

"If anything, he'll go looking for home," Dad said.

I slipped past them, as much as a pregnant woman could, and stole a seat next to Jim along the southern wall of windows. Down below, beyond the glow of the pool lay the Atlantic, but no sliver of moon shone in that winter's sky. From where we sat, there could have been nothing, nothing at all beyond what was right before us.

As much as Jim and I would have preferred to be no part of that scene, in that small condo, we were.

Dad stepped around my sister. "I've told you not to worry," he said, waving his hand as if that would wash away her tears. "So you can stop your crying."

"But it's my fault."

"What's done is done. He's gone on his own for much longer up north," he said. "He'll be fine."

"But he was your cat," Aimee protested. As if it had been what Dad cherished most on earth. "It was all you had left of Mom. You've said so yourself."

"Besides us," I said. I couldn't help myself.

Dad made an odd noise, as if that point hadn't occurred to him. "He wasn't mine to begin with," he said. "Let it go, Aim. I have."

His voice was low and full of meaning, filled with the knowledge of what it was like to be removed from everything you'd ever known, to be trapped in a place that felt foreign. Like he knew what it was like to have a door finally opened, to escape in the night away from everything you've ever known because the pain of what you're in the midst of is just too overwhelming.

DAD DIDN'T LOOK FOR THE CAT THE NEXT DAY, either. Aimee sat on the couch, a blanket pulled up to cover her worries, her guilt. All that time growing up, and she always seemed so tough, so tomboy. I never saw how she took so many things to heart, I only saw how she pushed Mom and Dad to their limits, testing them. Older now, still pushing. It's what she knows. It's who she is.

As much as Aimee always flies off as if to check whether a safety net is really there, I'm the kind to never dare anything needing one.

To this day, I'm not sure I know which one is worse.

But you can imagine our epic fights when we were kids, then. I like to think I'm so much wiser now and know how to handle it when my own kids clash because of their perspectives from opposite sides of the spectrum—but I'm still not very good at it. We do what we can, though, and that's all we were doing with Jen, with each of us, that Christmas.

Jen's fever had broken, so Jim and I took her to the pool, to the ice cream shop, exploring. She chased a feral Reef cat hiding in the bushes as the sun brushed the ocean, pulling pink clouds out of the darkening sky.

The gloaming, the time of day my mother always loved the most.

That's when Jim spotted Shadow, wide-eyed and crouched behind an overgrown hedge of bougainvillea—not far from one of the feeding stations Ocean Reef provides for its feral cats, courtesy of an annual assessment of the members. My husband scooped up the tiger cat and managed to get to the stairs before it leapt from his arms—freedom! But it just glided up the flight and turned the corner. Tail pointing to the stucco hall ceiling, the cat danced at Dad's door, asking to be let in.

"Shadow," Aimee cried, leaping from the couch. "You came back." She picked him up and held him close—just what he'd escaped from.

On this side of the door, the cat had no choice but to be held so fiercely. And this, this, was what he'd agreed to return to. As if he knew it was all we had to give after everything we had lost.

How much easier it is to let go when you know the safety net stretches far and wide, when you know that even those who have fallen will be cared for. And as we finished up at the table that evening, Dad tipping back in his chair, Jim crossing an ankle over a knee, Aimee scraping the dishes clean into the sink, me fussing over Jen and the cat content upon the back of the couch, it seemed we'd come to realize, even though we'd felt lost for so long now, somehow we would still be kept safe.

❧ 11 ☙

Drawing Lines in Shifting Sand

afety net or no, I didn't want Val sending me a birthday card. Jim said I was making too big a deal over a piece of paper. But it was not just a piece of paper. It was a milestone, one Val would be sharing with me, but not Dad.

And Mom wasn't around to do that sort of thing for him anymore. Dad was forgetting to buy milk, pay the electric bill, feed the cat. He'd already asked for me to be the one to buy all the Christmas presents he'd give us. No way he'd remember to buy a birthday card, then. And if Dad wasn't getting me one, Val shouldn't either. Better for her to know that up front, before she started shopping the Hallmark aisle for me. Maybe she'd already started, as soon as she got home from that first visit with me. Jim thought I was being a bit presumptuous.

"Is it okay if my mom and dad send you a card?" he asked.

"It's different," I said. "They're family."

"Doesn't Val count?"

"She's not my mother."

FOR VAL, IT SHOULD HAVE BEEN A JOYOUS FIRST. For almost thirty years, only in silence and solitude could she mark the day her first child was born. As others celebrated Christmas and the New Year, Val would be preparing herself for an anniversary her parents and sisters would not want her to remember. An anniversary her husband didn't even know about when they were first married. She could not acknowledge to him, her family, or her friends, why she'd get lost in a black hole on that day of all others. But now she could. More than that, she knew who to reach out to, to celebrate instead of mourn the passing of a day. By all rights it should have been the first time for her to utter "Happy Birthday" to a child she'd longed to speak to, a child whose identity had once been lost to her but now was found.

But that was the year that child could not take hearing those words. So, yes, go ahead and think I was a snot for not wanting Val to send me a card that year. Because I was, wallowing in my self-pity that the one who'd made the cakes and sung the songs couldn't do it once more, so Val shouldn't either.

That's the shame, isn't it? Just when you need it the most, you push it away.

"Hi, this is Kate calling." I hesitated, then added, "Kate St. Vincent Vogl."

"Oh, I know who you are," Val said.

"I wasn't sure if you knew any other Kates."

Val laughed, gentle as when she talked about David. "Even if I did," she said, "I know your voice." Her voice swelled with happiness, just that I called. As if that alone was a pleasant surprise.

God, I was awful to ask what I did. I explained, or at least tried to. "I don't know what your plans are, or even if you'd considered it," I lied. "But if I could ask if you'd consider—" No, I didn't want to leave any room for her to think it might be okay. I definitely couldn't handle Val filling that empty space of my mom's that year. "It's just that, with Mom gone, and I know Dad isn't going to be getting a card or anything, it's just he won't, and I'm okay with that, but if I get something from you, it'd just be too hard. So, if you're thinking about sending me anything this year, just please, don't."

There was a long silence at the other end of the line. "No, I understand," she said, her voice soft. From concern or from hurt?

"I hate to put that out there," I said.

"No, it's okay."

"I'm sorry."

It was painful, I tell you, to wait to hear what she'd say next. I was ready to cut and run.

"Can I ask?"

"Go ahead," I said.

"I just want to be sure I'm within what you're comfortable with."

"I appreciate that," I fumbled over the words, so quick to get them out. We both had wounds we needed to tend.

"Would it be okay to send Jen a birthday card?"

Oh, my relief was palpable. "That's fine," I said. "That's fine." I don't know why that thought didn't gnaw on me at all, but it didn't, and I don't think it was just because her birthday was still three months away. Maybe because it was something Mom had never done—she was already gone before Jenny's first. Dad had no clue what to send then, so he mailed a painting he'd picked up for Mom on their trip to Italy. The same trip Mom found something blue for me to wear on my wedding day, and Jim and I had only been seeing each other two months.

"Yes, absolutely," I said to the woman who gave me life, "that's fine."

BEFORE BREAKFAST, AND BIRTHDAY CARDS from Jim and Jenny were already laid out at my place. Presents neatly wrapped in non-Christmas paper had been under the tree since New Year's. Jim takes after his folks, that's for sure.

The card from his parents had arrived the day before, no small feat with all the other holiday planning for who would be in town for the holidays (a small group, only twenty-three for Christmas) and taking into account days off, with New Years and all.

No card, of course, from Dad, but I didn't have to wait for the mail to arrive on my birthday to know that would be the case. He'd still want to wish me a happy birthday, that I knew. So I called.

"I'm glad I caught you," I said. "Listen, I'm going to be hard to get a hold of today, but I knew you'd be bummed if you didn't get to talk to me on my birthday."

A laugh, loud and deep, one I hadn't heard for too long. "That's pretty smooth," Dad said. "Thanks for the call." His voice grew somber. "I'm sorry, though, hon. I didn't even get a card for you yet."

"Don't worry about it," I said. "I know you're thinking of me."

"She used to do all that for me, you know."

"I know."

"A day doesn't go by, and I don't think about—" he began, but memories caught in his throat. "I've got to go," he said, and he hung up before the tears fell on either side of the line.

"I NEVER SAID IT," DAD TOLD ME LATER that night. "When you called before, I don't think I ever told you Happy Birthday."

My turn to laugh. "That's okay," I said. "It was implied."

"Good thing I paid for law school," he said. "So you can figure those things out."

A mixed blessing, I'm sure, for me to be home with his granddaughter. On the one hand, who better to raise Jenny? On the other, what kind of return on investment was he getting for what he paid into that Cornell degree, not to mention law school, too?

It bugs him, I know, that I have no interest in going back. Why don't you go back into law? he still asks. Why don't I just strangle myself? I think. All those lectures he gave me about being happy, and sometimes he worries so much he doesn't see that I am. I am following my passion, I want to tell him. I write. Law school gave me a singular insight, and for that I am oh so grateful. I do use it, just not in a traditional way. He gave me so much, he gave without question.

Well, there is the occasional follow up. Am I sure I don't want to go back and become a doctor, he even wants to know. Like Mom could have been.

"Oh, I'm sure," I tell him.

"Your mom was so smart," he says. For him it's no non sequitur, because she's still a constant point of reference in his universe.

For me, too. And that first year in particular, when I'd lost Mom and gained Val, I didn't want to lose that point of connection. Didn't help what I'd already forgotten, and it began at Mom's funeral. While the bishop intoned how she'd died so poetically on the darkest day of the year, I worked myself into a panic that I could no longer envision exactly how she looked.

No chance for one last peek, either. Not that Dad had her cremated. That seemed too drastic a measure for a two-minute conversation they'd had. But he knew for sure she wanted closed casket, after what she'd said on the way home from Papa's wake, when Grandma Jo laid her hand aside her husband's unmoving face.

Grandma had already knelt beside him and prayed so long Dad had to gently help her to her feet and lead her away. Her pumps crossed over each other as she stumbled, her hand lingering over Papa's face. It was when she touched him, cupping his cheek with her hand, that I realized what it was to be dead. I was in college and should have known already. But I saw it then, the way his expression did not yield to her gentle touch. No unconscious recognition, no flicker behind his lids, no slight upturn of the lips. Still she held on, more tears and her hand began pulling on his head—whether because she'd stumbled or because Dad was leading her away, I do not know. But I remember Grandpa Fred. All that drama, yet he remained immovable, unresponsive.

That's what it was to be dead, then: to be incapable of responding to those we love. To no longer be able to be touched.

At Mom's funeral luncheon, I grabbed one last chance to have that connection. Turned out her brother had her eyes, her face. A family trait, no less defining than his name—which just so happened to be Jim. Don't laugh, it's true: My uncle was called Jim, like my father and my husband. My grandfather, too. Either we're not very creative, or we were just trying to make sure some part of ourselves was passed on somehow.

Either way, I stared at my uncle relentlessly the whole time during that funeral luncheon, so much so I finally had to steal over to his chair, and

I crouched beside him to apologize. "Your eyes, Uncle Jimmy," I said. "They're just like Mom's. So sorry I've been staring, I just have been hanging on to the idea of being able to see her again in your face." I swallowed the end of my sentence. Maybe it was creepy to be told your expressions are that of the dead.

Being adopted, I'm not sure all that I've inherited, or from where. All I know is I wish I had something of my mom in me. It's all I have left.

So in my worry I won't be able to hold onto my memories of her, I now seem to only remember the times she was conspicuously absent. Like when Jim popped the question at the end of a family dinner party, and we didn't realize until after that Mom was no longer at the table. She was in the kitchen getting coffee and pie. "There's a ring?" she asked when she came out with the carafe. How could she have missed it?

She'd been there for everything. Even for my eighteenth birthday at the Japanese steakhouse tucked behind Summit Mall. She didn't like the food at all, but she loved me. There was a ring, then, too—a garnet from my parents. I wore it so much it bent into the shape of my finger. Just as the more I wear my memories, the more they bend to fit me.

VAL CALLED TO DOUBLE CHECK IT WAS OKAY to send Jenny a present for her second birthday. Not just a card, but a bona fide present—a toy. Maybe I should have deliberated more, especially with all the stink I raised about not wanting her to send me a stupid birthday card. Really, though, I didn't give it a lot of thought. Maybe it was how Val asked in her pretty-please way, maybe because it occurred to me how awful I would have to be to deny her. She was asking permission to be generous. How could I say no?

I was glad I didn't. The present was old-fashioned and clever: a wooden porcupine, one that ambled downhill when Jen placed it at the top of the ramp. It was not the impulse buy when shopping at Target for cleaning supplies. It was the kind that seemed like it'd been handed down, the kind to think about passing on to future generations. The kind I loved to give Jen.

So my decision seemed right. This, then, would be where Val and I would leave things. We'd have contact at birthdays, maybe a phone call at the holidays. I could send art projects as presents, which would have added meaning since David had been an artist by profession. Jen would write thank-yous. Val could even call occasionally, and I wouldn't mind.

I could live with all that.

I should have known how unrealistic I was being. Even if Jen inherited David's talent for sculpture, I couldn't send art projects year in, year out. More important, I should have realized Val wasn't the only one besides Mom who could claim a part of me.

ฆ 12 ฆ

The Play's the Thing

The Playwright called.

Val had tried to prepare me for her. "They all are so smart," Val had said about my birthfather's family, in her first phone call to me. As if intelligence was elusive.

It didn't occur to me then that it was the exact same thing Dad always said about Mom. In her graduate classes at Kent, the professor never could include her scores with the others, the Bell Curve would be thrown off that much. So I knew smart, I grew up with smart, I even was smart—in school, at least. But when Val told me about David's family, I felt the same intimidation Val always had. Maybe it was the spectre of self-doubt again, worrying that their intelligence might somehow be beyond me. Maybe I worried too much that all of mine had been twisted up tight as the Diaper Genie in Jen's Beatrix Potter nursery.

Maybe if I'd been told the Playwright was ornery, things might have been different. Ornery I can handle. I could handle that grumpy lawyer on the other side of the office who was four years from retirement and all he wanted was for people to pull their own weight. Do your job, do it right, soothe feathers. That I can do. Grumpy really isn't grumpy, once you get to know them. You just need to understand their motivation. They are usually quite sympathetic characters. (Scrooge more so than Archie Bunker, perhaps.)

Then again, maybe it wasn't anything so complicated. Could be I was just jealous, since Nor seemed to have already done everything I'd wanted to do when I was in college. But Dad—ever the engineer and most of all a realist—had insisted it just wasn't practical to pursue French as a major. As for my other desire, a Women's Studies degree: "What the hell would you do with that?" Couldn't make or fix widgets, what could it get you, then? I had enough of my dad in me that I didn't even dare take Creative Writing as an elective. I'd written bad poetry, a synopsis for a play, but I didn't trust myself to subject my passion to a grade. Nor, on the other hand, had been published. Often. I'd asked her the title of her books, the first time she called. *The Moon and the Virgin.* Women's studies, of all things. She was smart in what I wanted to be smart in, and I was so far behind where I wanted to be.

Regardless of the reason, when Nor called once more, I worried I'd be tested. I worried she'd cover topics already addressed, those I should have mastered. What would I do if she brought up how important metaphysics was to David again? No way I'd remember its meaning any better than the last time she'd called. And I'd looked the word up afterwards and everything.

Thankfully, she wasn't calling about that. No, more important: Another play she'd written was being produced at Duke. Would I have an afternoon free while she was here?

"Tickets? Oh, that's so kind of you to ask," she said. "I'm sorry, I believe it's sold out. It's a small theatre, you know." I could hear the English spelling of that noun in her strong voice, the kind of voice most useful in producing plays, especially ones I would not get the chance to see.

Not like I'd be interested in anything so urbane. Not like she'd have any connections, either, being the playwright and all. "That's okay," I said. "Probably too hard to find a sitter anyway, for Jen. Next time."

The distance I heard in her voice lengthened exponentially by my psyche. Dangerous waters I cross, using psyche to describe a conversation with a psychotherapist. Yet that's the only place that emotional distance I thought I heard existed. Because over the years, I've come to learn that smart is as easy to understand as ornery—or emotional distance, even the kind you think you hear but don't. Nor is most certainly smart, and more than that, caring—perhaps learned when she helped care for her baby sister Welling while her mother was ill. What she does now for all her family seems to be like what Jim's oldest sister does for his. And so Nor has been my link to David's side of the family, the one to carry on the connections, as I do—or hope to do—for mine. But I had yet to learn all that about her.

She's let me know other times her plays were produced, but we lived too far away from the venues for me to go. I caught one, finally, ten years later, in an overheated warehouse outside of Minneapolis. I brought Jen along, so she would know what we had within us. Together we watched as Nor's words sailed across the stage, borne on the voice of a princess pirate and the virgin queen she challenged. I'm not sure Jen knew what to make of the experimental play. She was only twelve and just graduating from seeing shows at the Children's Theater. I'm sure I didn't help, making comments about the video of the queen gnashing pearls in her teeth, how it shadowed the women pirates in the shallow pool below.

That's my struggle with literary expression. Intellectually, I find it intriguing. But I can guess what my father would say about it, the practical engineer that he is. And his words will pop out of my mouth, a Tourette's of sarcasm, even as I'm working on creations of my own.

So, probably better I didn't see the first play, when our relationship was green and as tightly wrapped as May Day hosta. Better to not trample upon what could be.

WORSE, PERHAPS, WAS TREADING ALL OVER what had been. I debated every Sunday phone call with Dad whether I should tell him about Nor. I could not, for fear of stepping on the ghost hanging low over our conversations. It'd been a year, long and sad. I'd gotten to a point where I didn't think of Mom every day, just when I spoke to my dad.

He'd lost half of himself when he lost her. They'd been childhood sweethearts. All those years, she'd never left his side except in desperate times, like when Gramma Verne was first diagnosed with cancer, or when I had Jen. He'd wanted her home when I was just back from the hospital with my newborn, and all Mom had to say was this, with tears in her voice: "Don't make me have to choose, Jim." He came to my doorstep instead.

But he had no choice when Mom died first. She left us while we were at lunch. We'd sat vigil at her bedside for two days, patient with each ragged breath. Wasn't this how her own mother had sounded, too, at the end? Slow and deliberate with each difficult draw, shallow now and soft. Mom died while we took a mere half-hour break to eat food warmed under heat lamps. We hadn't been gone long at all.

The nurse outside mom's door said her gasping breaths had spaced slowly apart, and then there were none.

"She died alone," I said. How could we let that happen?

The nurse stood up behind the station and put her hand on the tall counter between us. "Sometimes," she said, "they want to spare you that moment."

I stared at the offer of her hand, unable to take it in my pain. Instead I stepped towards the curtain, where Mom lay, as if I could make it up to her now.

"Don't go back there," Dad warned, holding my arm to stop me.

"But I have to," I said. "I have to see her, to make it real."

Oh, it was real. Her head was tipped back on her pillow, her mouth open. Not at all like she was asleep. Couldn't they have closed her mouth for her? But I didn't do it, either. One long leg was out of the sheet, the one with the oval birthmark just above her blue-veined ankle.

It was Mom, all right, though she didn't look like herself, not with the cruelties chemo had wracked. No curls left in her hair, just that spindly shock of white. Her eyebrows hadn't fully grown back, yet above her lips were a few wisps of hair. I'd come in to memorize her face one last time, once more before I'd forget with the passing of time. But this wasn't at all what I'd hoped to remember.

IN THE END, I WOULD NOT TELL DAD about Nor's first visit. A rationalization, to be sure. He'd given me carte blanche to get to know my birthparents. You do what you need to do, he said. I don't care. But whether he truly didn't care, or just didn't care to know more, I can't tell you.

What I can tell you was there was another a call I needed to make. "Hi, this is Kate," I said, unsure whether I needed to say more.

"Hi!" Val said, in full recognition.

I was just going to tell her about Nor coming to visit, but she had other questions first. For Val this time, there were only a few months to get caught up on instead of thirty years, and so she wanted more details: Where, exactly, did we put the wading pool? What did Jenny like to do in it? She wanted to know how I was feeling. She knew exactly how far along I was in this pregnancy, that I was past the scary part and at the point when having the baby would be okay. Because sleeping was already light and breathing hard.

I answered her questions and clumsily led her to what I had to say. "You know David's sister?" I asked. Guilt hung heavy over my words, as if I were setting up a meeting without the benefit of a court-supervised visit. "She's coming in a couple of weeks," I said. I explained it wasn't just to see me. Nor would be in the area anyway.

"They're such a smart family," Val said, and I understood again the intimidation she'd felt when David spoke so proudly of his family.

"I'll let you know what happens," I told her, hoping that would make it better.

"Send pictures," she said, though it struck me as awkward, taking pictures of a dead man's sister to send to his former _____. But I shouldn't think of them that way.

"You know we're moving," I said. When in doubt, throw in a non sequitur.

"After the baby?"

"No, before."

Jim had been transferred, given the premier account in the country. Fortunately, it was only two hours north, in Raleigh. Unfortunately, he needed to start right away. A whirlwind of decisions had led to actions that led to a flurry of results. And it all began with Jim's proposition, a bit more Taoist than he ever truly was:

"We'll just put the house on the market, and when it sells, it sells."

It sold the first showing.

"They want to close by month end," Jim had said, eyeing my seven-month belly.

"It's a heck of a lot easier to move with the baby in here," I told him, holding my tummy like Santa.

"You sure?"

I was, but our HMO wasn't. It was the early days of managed health care, when everything had to go through the general practitioner.

I made a two-hour trip to meet with a GP I didn't know. "Yep, you're pregnant," he said. At least he was practical enough to not make me undress to confirm the diagnosis. There was a trio of OB/GYNs he referred me to.

"You sure there's nothing I need to know about?" the OB asked, a Caribbean lilt in his voice. Apparently obstetricians don't trust women seeking a new doctor in their thirty-sixth week of pregnancy.

"My husband just got a promotion," I explained. "Great job. Terrible timing."

"Let's do an ultrasound," he said. "Make sure everything's fine."

The room was bright when the cold jelly touched my big belly. The skin tightened—Braxton Hicks contractions—and the baby moved. "Look at that," he said. "There." He traced the outline of the head, the limbs, and for once I could see it all without a doctor's help. Only took two kids and three ultrasounds.

"You want to know?" he asked.

Of course I wanted to know whether the baby was a boy or a girl. We could pick out a name, pick out nursery colors. We could know whether we should save Jen's baby clothes or buy new baby-blue ones. Jim and I had talked about how it would be nice knowing for the second one, if we had the chance.

But it was just me at the doctor's that day. And if I found out, I would know before Jim. There'd be no other to share the joy in that single moment of discovery. "No," I said. I couldn't.

"How could you not find out?" Val asked when we spoke. "The doctor could have told you right then?"

"Right then," I said, sure that my husband would not have taken that burden by himself, either, if that had been somehow possible.

Maybe I made too big a deal out of nothing. Maybe, though, a part of me realized how lonely it would be to find out about a baby all by myself. Like thirty years before, when a young woman lay alone in a hospital bed, holding tight to the knowledge that the baby she'd just had was a girl because that alone was what the nurses let her hold onto. Val had not been able to savor that moment of joy, of discovery, of new life. She had no one to reassure her, no one by her side but a nurse with judging eyes and a doctor whose silences walked heavy upon her heart. As if emptying a womb was dirty. Excretory. Something a parent should forget.

ဢ 13 ရ

More Is Found

These are the things I remember from my first meeting with Nor and her daughter Deirdre: I wore a borrowed maternity dress, navy with white sailing boats. Proof I was nervous—I only wear dresses for holy days and sacraments. Perhaps I understood how important it would be to Nor and her family that I be some sort of stand in for their dearly departed David. How difficult that would be, considering I never knew him. It would be a test I couldn't study for, like an eye exam. (Those were the worst, if only because those were the only kind of test I never passed.) All I knew of my birthfather was buried in half my genes, and who knew if they'd ended up as recessive? I had the distinct feeling Nor would be looking for something of her brother in me, and Lord only knew if I had what it would take to pass.

So I did what I could to prepare. I was a cleaning banshee before the visit, worse than when we'd prepped the house for the showing. I'd been running so hard that even after I'd changed, my dress clung to my back when the bell rang.

And when I opened the door, there were three. A tall, thin older woman with wheat-blonde hair like Aimee's—go figure—and two college-aged woman. One a curly redhead, the other a Mediterranean beauty. Nor had let her daughter bring a friend along to see the play and to meet the biological cousin. Didn't matter who was who, what bothered me was this:

Is there no one out there who looks like me?

Nor's father's words began ringing in my ears: Not from this side of the family. So much for recognizing long lost relatives while walking down the street. I took my guests through the house, and we talked as if we were distant cousins who'd felt obligated to drop by because we'd need to report back to our parents. I served an egg bake with croissants and feta and spinach, the recipe I'd found in a sorority cookbook my Aunt Mary had sent me. I played the role of hostess, one I learned at my mother's side, sitting on a pillow under the tasseled green tablecloths she used for bridge club.

What to ask, what to ask. When Val came to visit, I had so many questions for her. But David took so many answers to the grave with him. Besides, some questions in these situations are, shall I say, rather delicate in nature.

I had to ask. "So, I was wondering, who in your family knew about me?" How much had David shared? He could have hid the whole thing.

"Only a couple knew, bits and pieces," Nor said. "Steve had managed to piece it together. Mom, though, tried to even keep it from herself, so she certainly didn't want to share that first letter with any of us."

That first letter from Val, written years before, when she was at the home for unwed mothers. Several pages worth, but the baby wasn't mentioned until the end.

"The baby" being me, article and all.

David had taken everything when he moved out of his parent's house. Nothing personal left—no pictures, no awards, no memorabilia. "If the sheets hadn't been Mom's, he would have stripped the bed and taken those, too, I think," Nor said.

But he left the letter and only the letter, opened and flat in the top dresser drawer.

"Talk about a Freudian slip," said Nor, the Jungian psychotherapist. "Mom wouldn't have opened the drawer except how he'd left the room. It was like he wanted her to find it, but he couldn't bring himself to tell them any other way." She looked at me then, as if she could measure my mettle. "You know they called you Carrell Anne."

After his mother.

It's strange how adoption works. It's as if I am two people. I am me, of course, but I am also The Baby—the one given up, the one wondered about for years. The one born in dishonor and yet named in honor of a mother who was not supposed to know. I feel no connection to that being, but that's how Val had known me since I was born and how Nor imagined me now. It's what Teresa had pointed out to me that first Thanksgiving.

I was left at a loss as to what more to say. I felt spent. The meal was over. I pushed my big baby belly up out of the chair and brought them out to the back porch, where Jenny's azalea—the one my coworkers gave when she was born—was finishing the last of its bright pink blooms that breezy April afternoon. I walked Jen to the blue plastic slide we kept on the deck and had the others settle around the table.

Only so much time we had, and the questions I still needed to ask were ones I should've asked over the phone, to allow for distance. Better she was there with me, though. Better to see your fairy tales come to life.

This was why I hadn't wanted to tell Dad. Without his warnings about what I would make of my time with Nor, I was free to make whatever I wanted of it. A birthmother, you need to have your guard up. A birth aunt, though? Those we allow. We had Aunt Mary, after all. Tall and blonde and Swede, and it took me years to put together that she wasn't a blood relation—just a college roommate who'd joined the same sorority.

It didn't take anywhere near that long to figure that a connection with me was a way to reach out to David. That's what I wanted to explore. Understanding why he was gone, why karma or fate or God meant for me to have alive only one parent, whether birth or adoptive.

"It was an accident, then?" I asked. We all knew I was asking about David.

Trees crowded our back deck, and yet the Carolina sun still managed to reflect off Nor's round glasses. "He was on his motorcycle, turning left. The guy didn't see him," she said. "Not at all."

106

"I'm sorry." I wondered then if dying in accidents could be hereditary, like cancer. "Did he have any children?" I asked.

Nor looked at me peculiarly.

I hadn't considered Nor might have counted me among the survivors. It was, instead, my own little test. Nor's dad had forwarded me a family tree that indicated that David and his first wife had a little girl. "Adopted" typed next to her name. I was appalled. Mom and Dad would have done no such thing on our family tree.

"A girl," Nor said. "She was a foster child he and Jan had taken in and adopted together. Raised her as their own."

Just as Jim had assured me. I really should listen to him more often.

"I'm sorry," I said. Another apology, this time for questioning whether this family treated an adoptee any differently. Nor's words told me no, and somehow it made sense to me that a foster child would want some acknowledgement for her other home. Though maybe I think so only because my homes have always been filled with love. "It must have been difficult for her," I said. Losing a parent too young, something we could commiserate over, if I ever would contact the only child who'd known David as a father.

We watched Jenny climb up and down the slide. I wasn't sure I should ask anymore; if I did, could I be accused of going back? Instead, I asked Deirdre and her friend about school, about where they planned to go for college. Polite conversation in the midst of such personal questions.

A girl cousin. I could have had a little girl cousin. She wouldn't have beaten me up like my boy cousins did whenever we visited. Never made sense that meant they liked me. We would have taken her along on trips, like when Mom took Aimee and me and our cousin Ricky to Williamsburg, and Ricky found out he didn't have to make his bed on vacation because that's what maids were for.

No, it would have been different trips. Different mom, even.

"So who does Jenny look more like?" Nor wanted to know.

"Hard to say," I answered. "With Jim and me looking so much alike. Did I tell you how glad I was when Val called? A part of me worried Jim and I were somehow related."

Jenny raised her hands as she landed at the bottom of the slide. "Ta-dahhh," she said.

I hesitated then, afraid I'd say something wrong. "Probably a Vogl baby, though," I said. "She does have this dimple on her chin, we're not sure where that comes from."

Nor smiled, a silent smile, and I took it as unwillingness to admit the mystery gene came from her family—that's how convinced I was that I might not be considered of them. "You ready for your move?" she asked.

Changing the subject, something I would have done to avoid an-swering, to avoid disowning that mystery gene. I was so busy second guess-ing, I didn't see her care and concern. "The company takes care of the hard part," I said. "They'll come and box it all up and take it away."

"Still, it'll be hard, getting established in a new town with a new baby coming."

"We lucked out with the new place. There's a club around the cor-ner, the ladies' book club meets once a month. That's all I ask," I said. "That and a walk every day."

I shouldn't have brought up books with a poet. I didn't know any she recommended, even though my group was founded with Cornell grads and attorneys. My turn to change the subject.

"Did I tell you what my friend Christin had to say about this whole thing?" I said, waving my hand over the three, as if this gathering could be defined. If only there was a way to separate myself from the awkwardness of where I kept leading the conversation, if only I could make light of it all. All I could think of was how my friend, my best defender, gave my birthparents names so awful I could only laugh. "So we call him Sperm Guy now," I said, my face red at the words. How could I be telling them that?

"Oh, you won't believe this," Deirdre said. "My biological dad, I call him BioDad. Same thing."

Thank God, absolutely. Only I wasn't about to ask any details. That wasn't my business. Deirdre was with her Egg Woman. In time, I was sure the story would follow.

Years later, Deirdre would tell me she finally felt like she met someone in the family just like her. I had to have the olive-skinned brunette explain.

"None of this clutter, this messy professor stuff like my mom has," she said, her full lips breaking into a wide, apologetic smile as she glanced at Nor.

I didn't have the heart to tell her it may have only been because our house had been cleaned, organized from top to bottom, in preparation for our move.

Nor, I knew, might be reaching out to connect still with David. Never occurred to me Deirdre might be looking for something, too. As for me, something seemed to fall in place the more I found out about Nor. The love of the writing, the love of symbolism, in addition to what I already shared with Val— that undercurrent of caring for family and others and in discovering what that meant wherever life led. I shouldn't worry so much about not understanding what Nor would say. I knew it already. "I was the signature performance for an Iron Workers convention once," Nor told me. "I wore red opera gloves, had a single spotlight on me. Everything else black—my dress, the stage, the back-drop. I read from my *Zillah's Lament*, and of course my epic, *The End of the Iron Age*. It was quite something," she said, her voice glittering.

I couldn't imagine what my dad would have to say if she'd shown up at the kind of conventions he attended. World of Concrete in Vegas, Bucyrus Erie heavy equipment distributors down in Ocean Reef. Probably better I hadn't told him about her. I wanted to keep her all to myself, without anyone else judging her, without anyone else painting upon my picture of who this woman was, and who she was to me.

In reaching out to me, Nor may have been looking for something of David. I was looking for ghosts of my own.

THE PROBLEM WITH BEING A HOSTESS—for me anyway—was that it was hard to relax. Welcome the guests, make them feel at home, finish last details like tossing the salad and pouring the wine while putting and keeping your friends at ease. Along the way, the conversational gems dropped, and I never found them until everyone had gone. All the questions I could have asked David's sister but didn't. At least Nor left pictures I could pore over later, after everyone had gone.

The first on the stack of photos was a shot of her parents, on a bench and smiling big, happy grins. Their backs to each other, they are holding umbrellas full of color and happiness high above. In another shot with Nor and her daughter, the Alps stretch grandly behind them, and they all look very much at home there together. Or at least in a place they traveled often.

There were other pictures, too, from long ago, when her family was whole. A black and white Christmas card of the kids gathered at the piano. Suave in his pompadour, David didn't seem fazed at all by the toddler next to him, fist raised, ready to bang out a high note. Nor stood behind him on flute, Deb on violin, and Steven on cello. Ingrid, the exchange student, played the recorder behind them, game for the pose. I was glad to be able to see him at the keys, for Nor had said her favorite memory growing up was falling asleep to her older brother playing Rachmaninoff downstairs.

Another shot of David, at an up angle, his smile easy. "Still with hair," Nor noted on the back. He had hair in the last photo, too, but not on top of his head. The eight-by-ten Nor had copied showed David in a red flannel shirt, seated in a captain's chair by a fireplace. With facial hair—something Christin and I had resolved we'd never tolerate in a man. But you can't say something like that to a man who would be your father.

David when he was about thirty.

When imagining what my biological parents would look like, I'd always thought they'd be the same age as my parents. They weren't. Val and David weren't of the fifties, but of the sixties, of free love and Woodstock, protests and activism. They'd been dubbed the black sheep of the family, whereas I'd always been accused of being the favored child. (Don't get me wrong: conformity in the preppy 1980s was quite the blessing.)

The children in the photos Nor sent were well scrubbed, young enough that the psychedelic sixties fashions hadn't set in yet. Even without that distraction, I could not see my features in David's or any of the children's faces, for that matter. Nor told of an idyllic life: family bike rides, a cabin in Vermont, visits to Chautauqua, community theater, and church choir. Everything I had growing up, and still this sounded better. No, I had not grown up like that. I was not of them, not anymore.

Damn recessive genes.

NO MATTER I HAD STRONG WOMEN LIKE VAL and Nor becoming a part of my life. There's still a part of a grown woman that misses her mom. Whoever she is, she's part of who we are. So we hold on to every little bit we keep inside, even if we're given more. Maybe it's out of selfishness, maybe it's to hold on however fiercely to our identity. Or to salvage what we've always thought it was.

All the struggles I had hanging onto memories of my mother, and she was there all the time. In my peanut butter jar, of all places. It's a comfort food, and I'd no idea how much comfort it could give.

This I learned from my cousin. Robby was flying through Minneapolis on his way back to his home in Coto de Caza, and he stopped for lunch and a short visit. His voice and his easy laugh took me back to summer road trips north to the Upper Peninsula of Michigan, with all of us—Ricky and Robby and Aimee and me—sitting around Grandma Jo's formica table, drinking milk freshly poured out of a plastic bag set inside a Tupperware pitcher. How different was it when Dad and Aunt Joan sat as children in Grandma's kitchen? How much the same?

Now it was my kitchen, just Robby and me. And we were laughing again at how I'd been scared to death of him, a gangly boy with hands as big as my head, how I hid underneath my reading cot even though I heard Mom and Uncle Rugg and Aunt Joan desperately calling my name for hours, checking the bottom of the pool and frantically checking the lake. I'd been so sure they'd go to the park without me, take that large-handed boy with them, and leave me to the wooden puzzles I had of school buses and police cars and a clown with balloons. I was three and believed I could be forgotten.

You'd think by now I'd understand it doesn't work that way, that I should have known I couldn't forget my mother, either. Not even after all these years. I'd given up on remembering her face. I had never realized how much she was a part of me.

I needed my cousin to tell me how. Robby sat at the kitchen table, his long legs stretching almost to the counter. As he's aged, he was looking more like my dad (his brother even more so), but I hadn't told him this. Maybe because he still had his deceased father's eyes. Maybe because it might matter more to me than to him. Mom and Dad could have adopted a little boy, but they'd let that chance go. She'd been pregnant, and it would've been too much to take on another.

They didn't know they would lose that baby. So close, closer than ever before, and still not full term. Another life I could have lived, as middle child. But none of these parallel lives were mine, and that baby boy was now someone else's son.

I stood to make a snack for my girls. In the pantry I found the peanut butter jar.

"Get a load of that tub," Robby said. "Man, I didn't think anyone could like peanut butter as much as your mom."

"She did?"

"Swear to God, that's all Peri would eat. Peanut butter on toast."

My favorite lunch. How could I not know that? I remember she liked eggs. Eggs with ketchup. But peanut butter? You would think I would know my own mother better than my cousin did. So many things I missed about her, things I never learned. And I never would, until others who loved her too unbundled their memories and shook them out, letting them drift over time and in our conversations, so I could watch in wonder, enjoying such a light and simple thought as picturing what Mom would pull out of the cupboard for lunch. I bent my head as I cut through the homemade bread and smiled, a quiet smile I could keep to myself. Maybe a smile like Nor had once given me, but there in the kitchen with my cousin, I was thinking only of my mother.

"Yep, you and her are so much alike," Robby said. "It's uncanny."

The peanut butter spread thick and smooth over the bread I'd made. Maybe I don't need to be able to imagine all the little details about her. At least not within a still picture, and certainly not as she was at the end in that hospital bed. I had her with me in what I did and in all I loved. After all, I could remember her in motion, I could remember her in life.

I remember her race walking back to the RV on the hillside, chasing after our miniature schnauzer. "Don't anybody mess with my dogs or my kids," she'd said.

I remember her handing me a sleek banker's lamp out of the trunk of Dad's green Eldorado, just after my swearing-in ceremony for the Illinois Bar. "It's from Grandma Jo," she said, but she was the one who'd known I'd need light during the dark hours I'd spend poring over documents.

I remember the way her widely arched eyebrows raised even farther when my father said something outrageous. "Ji-im," Mom would say, her voice drawn out, an edge to cut his raucous humor, but the apples budded on her cheeks, her smile wide. I can hear the echo of her words now, as I say the same to my own husband, Jim.

And when I say nighttime prayers with my girls, I remember Mom reading me Raggedy Ann and Andy next to me on my bed, while snowflakes gentled past the spotlight outside my window. Words she intoned low and even, bestowing upon those rag dolls adventure and joy and life.

And so I will remember that hospital room on that winter's solstice all those years ago, when I reached for my mother's arm—it was not yet too cold—and I wished, how I wished, that I, too, could wield such magical power. That I could pass it on for the ages.

∞ 14 ∞

To Give and to Give Over

One of my favorite childhood memories is visiting Disney World. Not because of the Mouse, but because it meant we could stay at Aunt Mary's. Waking up in that eyelet bedroom to her singing "Rise and Shine," I wanted nothing more fiercely than to be able to live there forever. And maybe I could. After all, Mom and Dad had brought down the paperwork for Aunt Mary and Uncle David to be my guardians "in case anything would happen."

I was young enough to wish it would.

I wanted to be able to stay in this house with the willow steadfastly overlooking the lake. And inside, spread across their living room wall, a mural of a garden gazebo, lush wisteria winding up the lattices. I'd sit on the counter eating pound cake while Aunt Mary and Mom talked late into the night, at least for a five-year-old. During the day, Erik and Karin and Aimee and I would roll up our pants so we could watch minnows school around our legs and we did cherry bombs on the swings, riding so high the whole set heaved with each pass. And after nap time, which Aunt Mary said we had to take for little Karin but we all were glad for the rest, she'd bring us up cheese slices to eat in bed, and I tried it only because of the way the plastic peeled back from that perfect square.

For Aunt Mary, her duties as guardian didn't end when Aimee and I turned eighteen. So when Mom died, even though I was nearly thirty, she made it very clear she would be there for me. "You let me know when you're ready for Baby Number Two, Kate," she said. "I'll be down."

I don't know if she knew what she was in for. Since we ended up moving when I was eight and a half months pregnant, I had to take her up on her offer. Jen and I picked her up at the Raleigh/Durham airport and brought her to our brand new home. Boxes had begun filling the rooms. Our two living room chairs were already in their new spots, and the white couch sat opposite, naked, waiting for pillows out of one of those boxes. Upstairs in Jen's room, two men kneeled upon her floor, putting her bed together.

Jen stopped to watch, holding her blanket close to her face and sucking on her tongue.

Aunt Mary went straight to work in the kitchen, unloading one of the dish boxes. "Do the kitchen first," she said. "And it'll start feeling more like home. That way I can start on my other job here, too."

The next two days, Aunt Mary scolded me to go look after Jenny as she and Jim unloaded boxes and made sure every last kitchen utensil and play toy was in place. When the last of the boxes was unpacked and broken down and stacked in the garage, she went back to work in the kitchen, pulling out recipe card after recipe card in my file, and she made batch after batch of casseroles and desserts. She wrapped them in plastic and put post-it notes on the top before she put them in the freezer.

1 hour @ 325°
let stand 10 min before serving
(Cheeseburger Strata)

I didn't tell her Mom kept the chicken whole for her Chicken Divan instead of shredding it. At least I tried not to. As I filled the cupboards with the rest of our dishes, I worried over the chicken pieces in the bowl. It's going to taste different, I thought. I can only handle so much cheese being moved at once. Still, I needed to stop being such an ungrateful wretch. That I should have something worse to worry about.

"My Karin loves this one," Aunt Mary said as she separated a raspberry chocolate bar into three sections and covered each with Saran Wrap. "She made it for a Tri Delt luncheon, and it was the first one gone."

"Aunt Mary," I said. "I can't tell you how much we appreciate everything you're doing for us here."

"I'm just doing what Peri would have done for you," she said.

"It's more," Jim said as our heads hit the pillow that night. "Your mom would never have done all this."

He was probably right.

The half moon shone through the tall windows of our room. I plumped my pillow and covered my eyes with the crook of my elbow. There's no way to sleep on your stomach, much less bury your face in your pillow, when you're nine months pregnant.

"She's just trying to make up for it," I said. "For Mom not being able to be here."

"It's not her fault."

"No," I said. "But at least she can do this. Give us what Mom can't anymore."

Something we all wanted. Something we all would work as hard for—especially for this baby, who wouldn't ever be able to know her.

FOUR DAYS LATER AND WE WERE COMPLETELY unpacked, dinner for two weeks in the freezer—with desserts. And Aunt Mary was already home. "When baby comes," she said, "that'll be a time for just the three of you to share. I'm just getting you ready."

And just in time, too. Two days later, my contractions started coming five minutes apart. Jim called his secretary to come stay with Jenny, since Lee was the only mom we knew in town to ask.

We walked the halls of the hospital, still debating over boys' names as we had two years earlier with Jenny. We lingered by the windows to the nurseries. In the neonatal ICU, a woman sat in a hospital gown next to a plastic bin. Her hand stretched through a hole into a glove to rest over a baby with a torso no bigger than her palm. Tubes taped to the little red body led to machines, silver and menacing in their effort to keep the being alive.

"I'm so glad we're past that," I said.

But we weren't where we thought we were, either. My contractions had slowed. Worse, they stopped hurting.

No way was I still in labor.

The nurse tucked me in bed and secured a monitor to my belly. "Go to sleep," she said to me and to Jim. "We'll see what happens."

I woke to the sun streaming through the window. Jim uncreaked himself out of a chair.

"No baby," I said.

"Don't worry about it," the nurse said as she unstrapped me from the machine. "A lot of people get false labor. Take a long walk today. We'll see you again later."

I pushed Jen in the double stroller all along the parkway that day. Two blocks from our house we were on the back side of a golf course and a pool. Our pool—we'd joined the day before—but even my maternity suit didn't fit anymore.

I sang all the verses of "Hush Little Baby" as we walked the length of the lake, past the French stucco mansion with a flagstone facade, past the golf villas and the gardens. As we turned to head home, the contractions began again, and I had to stop to let them pass.

I called Jim when I got home. "I need Lee back on call tonight," I said.

And so, for the second night in a row, Jim's secretary and her husband came after dinner, and Jim and I were back walking the halls on the ninth floor. This time, without having the stroller to push, I sped up through the contractions.

"Didn't your doctor say it was when you had to stop that it was real?"

"Oh, honey, these are real," I said, as I turned the corner ahead of him.

The doctor on call that night was the one I never had an office visit with. So much for rotating through the doctors. He shook my hand and then got down to business. "Now push," he said.

"How?"

I'd looked forward to knowing what I was doing this second time around, but here I was, not quite right in the head with whatever they'd given me. I couldn't even do what had come so naturally the first time around.

Jim held my hand. "Baby will share your sister's birthday," he said. It wasn't quite eleven o'clock.

"Push," the nurse said.

For the life of me, I couldn't remember what to do. Women had been birthing babies for God knew how long, and here's me with no idea how to finish the job. It was all I could do not to laugh. "Can you remind me how again?" I asked, sheepishly.

Maybe I wasn't meant to know how to birth a baby. First time, I hadn't known what to expect. Couldn't very well ask Mom questions, how could I ask anyone else? This time, when they shut out the last of my pain, they shut down my body's way of knowing what to do. Weird, how that works.

Midnight came and went. I'd gone through four rounds of pushing. I laid back on the gurney. "I really don't get it this time," I said, ready to give up. "Isn't that funny?" I'm pretty sure I giggled, too. "I'm all goofy," I said. "That stuff I got before the anestheseewhatsit got here, it made me all goofy." I smiled. What a funny word, goofy. Or maybe I was thinking about the late night news ad we'd just seen: What Insomniacs Watch Most.

Goofy.

Nurse Cratchit came back. "I'm serious this time," she said, which made me not. "You've got to push."

"Okay," I said, up on my elbows and trying to keep a straight face. "Can you remind me?"

"FIRST BABY OF THE NIGHT," THE NURSE said, placing my baby girl on my stomach.

"You missed your sister's birthday," Jim said to me, his hand cupping the top of Julia Teresa's tiny head.

I encircled them both with my hands. I tipped my head back against the bed. For as goofy as I was, I was still spent. "I got Aunt Mary's," I said.

THOMAS JEFFERSON WAS A GREAT BELIEVER in luck. He once said the harder he worked, the more he had of it. I can't say that work had anything to do with my having Julia on Aunt Mary's birthday. It was just sheer dumb luck. But there's a great deal of truth to what he said. I don't think he meant to define work as drudgery, I think he meant it as effort. The effort of making connections others don't think to, or simply haven't before.

When Jen was born, I hadn't known Val, so I hadn't known to call her. It wasn't even on my radar screen. Thirteen years later and I'm so used to Val being a part of our lives now, I've almost forgotten how I'd debate whether and when to make that effort to call her, whether I should bring such luck—namely, the joy of a connection. But I can still bring myself back, back to the hospital room after I had Julia. I remember thinking in those early morning hours that she would want to know, that I wouldn't want to be the kind of person who would deny her that kind of singular joy in life. A joy I could share without losing any of my own. Like Dad had said, when I first told him about Val. What luck, isn't it? That it works out that way.

When I was in high school, I was sure my father didn't understand anything I was going through. As I've grown older, I am learning I am the one who doesn't know. Every day brings us something to learn. It's up to us how we use it.

So far I've been learning how God brings families together, in so many different ways, at so many different times. I said that to Val recently and realized it sounded like I'd been working at the church too long. "Whatever you call it," I said. "Karma or fate or God or Buddha. But there's always room at the table for family, for more family." Sometimes, though, it's

119

hard to see you can make the room, especially when you've never set an extra place there before.

So maybe—probably—I called her out of obligation the day Julia was born. For whatever reason, Val later told me how incredible the connection was that she felt, something she hadn't had the chance to experience when Jen was brought into the world. My only regret now is that, as I write these words, I've forgotten the actual call and the joy we shared in it. Perhaps I've forgotten because of the worries that followed, the kind I'd so glibly thought we were past during my last night of labor as Jim and I pitied the young mothers bending over oxygen tents in the NICU end of the maternity ward.

LATER THAT MORNING, in the reasonable hours when the sun was up, a nurse brought Julia into my room and laid her on my chest. "Here," she said.

I smiled in thanks, wondering if I would be a bad mother if I sent my little one back to the nursery. There was no way I could stay awake, holding her. I was ready to crash. Four hours sleep both nights, too many sleeping hours spent trying to have a baby.

"I've got to show you something," the nurse said.

But I know this time, I wanted to say. When I had Jen, the nurse had to show me everything, even how to change a diaper. Somehow I'd never thought to ask Mom all that. Jim was the one who filled me in on the rest, with everything he'd learned from his mother. He'd been the one to tell me that babies needed both morning and afternoon naps. Who knew?

This nurse, though, was about to show me what I still needed to learn about being a parent. She pulled the receiving blanket off Julia's chest. "See how she's getting blue?" she asked. "When she does that, you need to rub her chest. Remind her to breathe."

With that, the nurse turned and left the room.

Wait a minute, I wanted to call after her. Am I really qualified to be left alone with a newborn infant who forgets to breathe? While I'm on the verge of falling asleep? Maybe I wasn't so tired anymore. Stay pink, sweetie, stay pink. What if I couldn't tell she wasn't pink? Then what? I started rubbing Julia's baby chest just in case.

Another woman walked in. "Hello, I'm Dr. Roberts," she said. "I'm the pediatrician on call. We had to run some tests on Julia this morning, based on her performance last night," she said.

Excuse me, didn't she have a nine on her Apgar? It was all so confusing, so wrong. But I have healthy babies, I wanted to say. Everything comes easy to us.

"She failed."

Dear God, she's not even a day old, and she's already failing tests?

It wasn't strep. I'd had the Group B Strep shots my new doctors had insisted upon. (And I thought they were being overcautious.) Still, there was a white spot on Julia's lung—sometimes these things just happen—so they would need to treat it as pneumonia.

The nurse was back, lifting my baby out of my arms, and then they were gone.

I called Jim. "There's something going on with Julia," I said. They had to put her in an oxygen tent, I told him. They had to give her medication. "There's a chance it might affect her hearing."

"What does that mean?"

"There's a chance." For the first time in these crazy couple of months, I felt overwhelmed. A move I could handle. A new baby I could handle. But this, this I wasn't sure I could handle. The room seemed darker than it needed to be. The window was higher, too high to see out. And this time, there were no white blossomed pear trees lining the drive outside as there'd been when I had Jenny.

. As soon as I was able, I walked down to the neonatal care unit. I'd been so smug, thinking we were past this. A nurse showed me how to cover my clothes and shoes with germ-free protective liners, how to wash my hands and hold them so I wouldn't get new germs while opening the door to the unit.

Julia lay on an incline inside a clear plastic box, a white bundle with a tan scrunched face. A small sign at the foot of her bed read, Congratulations! in pink. For her name it just read Vogl. *Her name is Julia*, I wanted to tell someone, but the nurses all seemed busy with babies too tiny to be alive.

121

I pulled up a chair next to her bed and sat. My arms ached to hold her. I don't know how long I was there.

"She's a good eater," a woman said behind me. She wore pastel zoo print scrubs. "She took a half bottle of formula."

"But I gave someone my colostrum to give her," I said.

"Oh, that little bit," the nurse said. "She wanted more."

"MARGIE TOLD ME SHE'D NEED MORE than one IV," Jim said. "That they would put it in her head." Margie is his oldest sister, the one who looks after everyone, but more important, she is a nurse and the family consultant on all things medical.

"Well, she doesn't," I said. "And they didn't."

"She said her head would be need to be shaved for it."

"It isn't that bad. Really. You should let everyone know."

Julia had responded well to the medicine. They'd been able to pull her out of the oxygen tent after just twenty-four hours. Jim and I took turns visiting her, while the other would stay with Jenny. Jenny seemed huge now, a giant compared to her little sister. I snuggled with her in my hospital bed.

"How do you like our new house?"

"There's a bunny here," she answered. Jim showed me pictures later: a rabbit that nibbled on the hostas outside the hospital.

"Tell me about the bunny," I said, my eyes closed, just holding her.

"Hop hop hop," she said, little sing-song voice.

Everything was wrong for her, I knew. I'd been the one to give her a bath every night, until Julia. My little one was too used to meals and snacks and bed all at those appointed times, my sweet little German. But the one she'd always counted on, her mommy, couldn't stay home with her now. Jim had tried last night to give her a bath, but she'd thrown a fit, water splashing all out of the tub, all over him.

"It's okay, Jen, it's okay," he'd said as he pulled her out and held her tight, even as still she thrashed, wet and slick. "I know," he said, "I know, Mommy's not here."

And he covered her in a bath towel my mother had saved for me.

When I was big with Jen and we'd gone back to visit my folks, Mom had pulled my old towel, some washcloths and a stack of wraparound baby tees from a square cardboard box. Inside, too, were matching kilts from preschool days for Aimee and me, and the embroidered dress I wore for fourth-grade pictures. "I'll give you the rest when the baby comes, if it's a girl," Mom said. But there were other distractions, then, other things we wished we could pull out of a box.

Jim did what he could for Jen, without me, when Juls was born. By the time Jen's tantrum had dissolved to tears and she'd crumpled under the weight of it all, he wrapped her in that terry so soft and worn, and he carried her to bed.

I'D BEEN AT THE HOSPITAL THREE DAYS. I was too healthy to stay any longer, and Julia wasn't healthy enough to go. She'd been moved to an open crib in the neonatal unit, but she still had an IV that looped outside of her blanket. At least I could hold her.

Val had told me all she ever wanted was for her baby to be held. She may have only been nineteen when she had me, but she knew what a baby needed more than anything.

"Here," the nurse said when I was discharged. "You'll need this." It was a machine, the size of a shoebox, with two funnels attached to it by tubing. Briefly she pointed the funnels to my chest before she set them down gingerly. "Your baby will be here a week," she explained. "You'll need something efficient to express your milk."

Holy cow, that thing was high powered. The suction alone scared me.

"It's not so very dignified, is it?" I asked. Birthing babies is, more than anything, a humbling experience. Doesn't matter what you get on the LSAT, your baby's coming out just like that birth-slicked foal (except yours better come out head first). Knowing our Charlais cows and the Clydesdale mares also stomped in pain with nursing wasn't exactly any consolation for me. You forget the pain, other mothers told me. But I never knew to ask about the humility learned, didn't see until then that our babies' birth process is no more sophisticated than any barn animal's. And now I'm convinced it's all practice for what more is coming. Because we mothers don't just give of ourselves. We give over. And we learn just how much will be demanded of us through that initiation—the birth. For Val and for my mother, missing the other part made their giving over that much more difficult for them.

That physical trauma of birth happens whether or not you're lucky enough to take your baby home. If you've had a baby, you remember how your body aches afterwards. For weeks, in some areas.

And I can't imagine being a teenager, unwed, going through it all. The fifteen-year-old daughter of some friends of my parents had a baby, and I remember going to their house for dinner the week after she relinquished her child. (I suppose it should be no surprise we hadn't gotten together with them in the months before that.) I was not yet ten, and I remember not understanding why Mom was surprised the girl could already walk up and down stairs. Now I'm surprised the girl still had it in her to smile, knowing she'd never see her baby again. Five years later, I wasn't old enough to wear a grown-up bridesmaid dress for her wedding, yet I was the same age she was when she became pregnant. In our car on the way to the reception, I said, "Too bad there's a baby out there who's lost to its parents forever," but my mother remained silent on that score. I said, "Do you think she would have married him if it weren't for the baby?" Enough, finally, for Mom to turn around and give me The Look.

I was glad it was not me who'd faced the chasm that girl endured, between what she had and what could have been. For only one week I'd brinked a schism, a fifteen-minute drive each way between my newborn and my firstborn. But I will say, coming back home from those hospital visits to nurse Julia, nothing beat my welcome at the door, the cry of "Mommy!" I didn't need the patter of little feet, the arms thrown around my neck, though I loved that, too. It was what I saw in those eyes, the light of recognition of what I mean to her world, and it was in that moment that I belonged completely, irrevocably, to her, more than she would ever belong to me.

It was hard enough to leave that hospital without a baby strapped in tight in the backseat. How awful it was to walk away from that nursery and know my baby would cry and I would not be there to hold her with the love she was meant to have.

Val knew exactly what that felt like. And to think, her worry would last a generation—thirty years. She'd been told it was the right thing to do, the only solution.

Last year, Val told me she didn't believe that anymore.

I must admit, as awful as it was walking away from my own baby for just a few hours at a time, Val's newfound conviction still scares me a bit. And yet there's nothing either of us can do about it, except move forward.

Together.

ɷ 15 ଔ

Covering Up, Carrying On

J ulia had been home from the hospital for a few days, and I was talking with Dad during my regular weekly phone call. "I'm coming down for a visit," he said. "Are you ready?"

As ready as we could be, having just moved and birthed a baby.

"It'll be weird," I told Jim, "without Mom."

"It's not like you haven't seen him without her since she died," Jim said.

But I had every day without her here, this place where she never had been. When Dad came, it would only be what? maybe the twentieth day I'd spend with him without her.

"We could show your dad the video I took when Jenny was born. Your mom was on that."

"She was?"

"There's a whole bunch of your mom on it."

So I sat on the floor, Julia in my lap and Jen leaning against me while Jim got out the camera and the battery and the wires and hooked them all up to the TV set. With Jim, it did not take long. If it'd been my dad, it would have been a half-day's search, looking for the wire hook-ups.

I was as excited as Jenny watching her favorite video. *It's starting, it's starting*, I thought. I could relive that week Mom had been with us. Those moments I'd find out just how fiercely she'd hang onto whatever time she would have as a grandmother. It started when we called to tell her I was in labor with Jen.

She and Dad were up visiting Rattlesnake Island in the middle of Lake Erie, and there they were stuck. "Damn fog," said the lady who never swore.

She kept calling back, to give us updates on whether Ray's plane had been cleared for take-off yet. "Can you believe we're still stuck on this damn island?" she said.

"You can meet us at home," I said.

"No!" she said. She hadn't yelled at me like that since I was three. "I'll meet you at the hospital." She'd missed taking her daughters home from a hospital. She would not miss taking home a granddaughter.

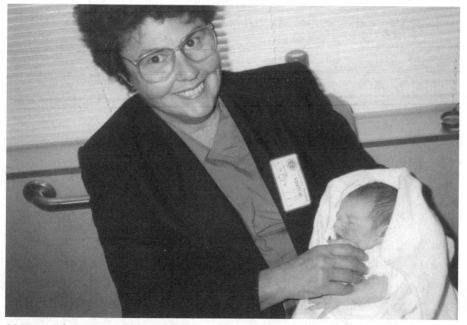

Mom with Jen at the hospital.

127

Especially with there being such a chance that she'd miss so much more—her granddaughter's wedding, high school graduation, other milestones I could name but won't because I don't want to imagine she'd thought of the times her mother had with us that she wouldn't have with Jen.

So if Mom couldn't demand more time, she would demand more from it, from the moment Jen would take her first breath. She would be with us when we left the hospital, she would be with us that whole first week, through that first doctor visit when I wasn't sure whether to sign in my name or the name of that little bundle who'd been part of me until just a few days before. My mom would make a difference, in that little bit of time that she could make one. And we were about to view the fruits of that effort in this video.

Jim flicked on the power—and then out of the darkness came my mother's voice. She was clanking dishes in the kitchen, but the camera was on me, balancing a sleeping baby on my stomach. Jen was curled into a comma, like a thought not quite complete.

Mom kept saying something in the background, but Jim's voice drowned her out, describing the date and time of Jenny's delivery, as if we wouldn't remember it.

"She came on a Monday," I said. "Like she was my new job." I was flailing my hands for emphasis, I was so giddy and short on sleep.

In the background, Mom's voice moved closer to the camera.

"She's almost here," I said.

"Who, mommy?" Jenny said.

"Almost," I said. Almost on screen, almost on screen—and there! that's her foot—and then the frame of the camera twisted upside down, and the screen went blank.

"Who, mommy?" Jen asked again as Jim fast-forwarded through the next frames, searching desperately through the next nine months that my mother would be alive. I'm sure he wanted nothing more than to return to that day, to capture the moment we'd hoped to be able to play over and over.

As good an editor as my memories can be, sometimes nothing beats one last replay. But all that Mom gave us was never meant to be recorded on film—only written upon our hearts.

IN THE FIRST WEEKS JULIA WAS HOME, I learned why the nurses had such a hard time getting her to sleep. This one always wanted to be up, to see what was happening. She still doesn't like to miss out on anything. And so, though it was almost dinnertime the night Dad was due to arrive, my newborn had only napped for twenty minutes that day.

All you moms out there will know that makes for a fussy baby—and a fussy mom as well. Because the secret for new moms is to nap when the baby does. This I learned from my mother-in-law Teresa, since I didn't have Mom to tell me. Teresa is the kind of mom who has this whole fountain of information but she has the patience to wait for you to ask for it first.

I still haven't been patient enough as a mom to put that one into practice. But we can only do what we can, so there I was, with Julia fussing and squirming in my lap as I sat outside in a folding chair. I felt bad for my neighbors, though I'd already tried all of Teresa's tried-and-true suggestions: putting her down in her crib and in her car seat and in the swing, and I'd even tried putting her back in the crib with the vacuum cleaner on in her room, any sort of white noise to get her to sleep. All this and still I had Jen with me, trying to keep an eye on a two-year-old who desperately needed Mommy's attention. So I gave up, and let Julia fuss on my lap while Jenny stepped in and out of the wading pool.

Never in my life had I been more interested in seeing water being poured out of a big blue container and into a little yellow one. And ever since I have been horribly sympathetic to anyone with a crying baby.

After maybe seventeen demonstrations, Papa's white Towncar pulled down our driveway.

"Jen," I said, "say hi to Papa."

"Papa?" Jen asked.

Dad got out of the car, his arms wide open. "Jenny!"

Kids are amazing. Jenny hadn't seen the man for six months, which for her was a quarter of her life. She ran to him anyway, like he was her favoritest person in the whole wide world. He scooped her up and hugged her tight.

"I love you, Papa," she said into his shoulder.

I held Julia out to him. "What's with the mustache?" I asked.

"Got tired of shaving there," he said. "How's this little one?"

"Fussy."

His mouth drew tight under his bushy salt-and-pepper mustache, and he set Jenny down carefully. "Anything wrong?"

"No, she's fine," I said quickly. I did not mean to worry him again, not after that pneumonia scare. "She just wants to keep up with big sister. She just gets fussy at the end of the day, that's all."

"You were like that," Dad said.

"I was?" The things my parents have kept from me.

"You had it so bad—thanks Jim," he said as my husband pulled a bag out of the backseat, "that your mom took you to the doctor and made him give you something, her headaches got so bad."

And I always thought I was an easy child.

"Hey, Vogl, I got something in the trunk I'll need help with," Dad said.

Jim gave me a look as he brushed past. "What you got for me this time, Vinnie?"

"Not for you," Dad said. "For your girls."

Inside the trunk of that Lincoln Towncar, perched at an angle, was a Barbie Jeep. A mini motorized car, just for Jen.

"Awesome," my husband and car aficionado said. "I can't believe it fit in there."

Each Jim took an end and hefted it out of the trunk.

"Look, Jenny," I said. "Look what Papa brought you." Holding Julia tight against my chest, I led Jenny to the driver's seat and had her sit.

"I got this one because it had a seatbelt," Dad said, sounding proud of himself.

It was pink and had a shoulder strap and was secured with Velcro. With all its slack, it hung limply off to her side, below her hip.

Jenny grabbed the wheel and grinned.

"It's perfect," I said.

Dad bent over Jen and flipped a switch. "Now you can make it go," he said, but he needed to press down the pedal with his hand before Jenny understood.

She took off up the hill of our driveway, straight for the street. Jim ran after her and turned her back down toward the house.

"She'll need some direction," Dad said.

"Don't we all," I said.

Jim ran alongside the Jeep, helping Jenny steer, while Dad and I tried not to laugh and giggle too much.

"You know you didn't need to bring anything," I said.

"I know."

Jim tried to sit in the Jeep, but it was like flying coach—his legs just didn't fit.

"Did you have a hard time deciding what to get?" I asked.

"Oh, I had a whole cartful before I came across this," Dad said. "I picked this up, just left the cart."

"Did you really?"

He nodded, grinning, his eyes on his granddaughter circling the yard.

Jim sprinted around to the front of the Jeep, arms out and hands spread. Anything to stop her from running over the flowers. "Okay," he said breathlessly to our daughter, "you need to be done."

"More!"

"Tomorrow," Jim said firmly, leaning down awkwardly as he steered our third car into the garage.

I picked up what I could carry with a baby in the other arm, and we climbed the steps up into the house. I set Julia down and began readying for dinner.

"I'm not going to have much to eat tonight," Dad said.

"Not hungry?"

"No." He laughed apologetically, if not sheepishly. "I've got something going through my system."

"You're not sick?" A newborn mother's panic. Who knew what new germs he was introducing to my fragile newborn to begin with, and now he tells me this!

"I ate something bad."

"Some bad pie at a truck stop?"

"I think it was the pasties I had back home." Somehow we managed to get him to admit that the meat had gone gray and he'd stuck it in the freezer anyway. And then he ate it a year later.

"You need Aunt Mary to come take care of you like she did for us," Jim said.

"She really outdid herself," I said. "We had Mom's Chicken Divan the first night home from the hospital," I said. And wouldn't you know, it tasted even better the way Aunt Mary had fixed it.

For a moment, I wondered if I'd said the right thing. Would Dad be thinking of the first week after Jenny was born, when Mom came to fix dinners and tend house while I figured out what it meant to be a mom. Julia's first week had been so different from that, with her in the hospital and the rest of us in our new home. Different enough so there was no longer any comparison for me, though I wasn't sure Dad could see it that way.

But Dad was laughing. "Oh, that Mary," he said. His eyes were red, and I wasn't so sure it was from a long day's drive. "You know she used to write me letters, tell me about how she was looking after your mom for me."

That was when Dad was in Korea, in those years so strange to me, when Mom had started Michigan State and my parents' lives were not yet officially tied together. Those letters from Aunt Mary must have meant so much to him in those lonely months spent in a South Korean cave. Mom must have sent him letters, then, too, but I don't ever remember either of them mentioning those. Some things are private, even among family. But he told me stories about the letters his schoolmarm mother sent back, her red-lined corrections of grammatical mistakes he'd made in the notes he sent home.

"He's not safe by himself." Jim said, after Dad had excused himself for the night and the girls were down.

"He's always been like that," I said, but it was the first time I'd had enough distance from my own hurt that I could see the pain gathered in my father's eyes. It's easier to see in others once some of it is cleared from your own.

"Your dad's worse now, though," Jim said.

I let it go as I stood at the sink, washing smashed bananas and buttered noodles off the high chair tray. He was still in the darkness, but I was on my way out. Someday he would be, too. He had to be.

"And what's with the Guido mustache?" Jim asked.

I laughed. "It is awful, isn't it?" It was big and bushy, not quite as terrible as the handlebar mustache his grandfather had, but it was close. "He grew a mustache after his father died, too," I said.

"So he's hiding behind it, then?"

Maybe. Maybe he just needed to keep everything tucked inside until he could face it again. Until then, he'd be able to look in the mirror and see a separate person. Someone that was easier to see than the one missing his other half.

And the time would come, it would, when he could see himself whole once more. Of that I was certain. We were, after all, a sunny-side-up family.

Baptism by Fire

Picking a godmother is harder than picking a maid of honor, I swear. Even with all the hype that went into weddings, a maid of honor had to step up to the plate only that day. Godmothers had duties that lasted an eternity. Considering I'd made my mom sick over my choice for maid of honor, I was hoping to do a better job choosing this round, even if Mom wasn't with us anymore.

Let me explain, since I really did make her throw up. I could say I was young and didn't know better, but I did. I knew family trumps all else in sacraments, but I also knew I could count on Christin for whatever I needed on My Day. And so the Bridezilla in me won, and I rationalized the decision by remembering how Aimee had abandoned me in the haystacks when we'd played hide-n-seek almost twenty years before. Sibling rivalries can last forever if you set your mind to it. So when my folks came to my tiny Chicago apartment to help plan my wedding and Dad laid it on the line that I needed Aimee in the honorary role, I balked.

"No way," I said. "I'm not going to ask her."

Mom got up and left the room. There was no place to go but the bathroom. Dad and I sat at opposite ends of the room, classic standoff.

"It's my day," I insisted to Dad. But that's where we left it because through the walls of that renovated girls' school we heard Mom retching into the toilet at the thought I would choose my best friend, not my sister, as maid of honor.

I was stubborn and would not fully relent, insisting they would share the title. I like to think I would have granted Aimee full title, if I'd known my mother would be dead in three years.

Now, once again with Julia's baptism I had to choose who would stand by our side for a sacrament. This time, though, others in the family had a larger claim to the title. With all Aunt Mary had done for us, you'd think it would be the least we could do for her. She was certainly qualified: "Praise Jesus" was as common a phrase out of her mouth as "Diet Coke, please" was for me. Not to mention how involved she was in the prayer chain in her church. I won't even tell you how she drove nursing home residents to her church's weekend masses, or how she searched Orlando's streets in the midst of an oncoming hurricane's torrential rains to look for her homeless friend, to take her in during the worst of the storm. As religious as Aunt Mary is, though, she's not Catholic, which unfortunately falls short of the Church's godmotherhood requirements.

So Jim and I did the next best thing and talked to Sally, his next oldest sibling, the one he was closest to. We asked if she'd look after Julia's spiritual well being.

"If you trust me," she said and laughed, like that would be a joke. But she'd had twelve years of Catholic education, which made her eminently more qualified than anyone else I knew.

I don't know I understood the full import of what it meant to be a godparent, even with one daughter already baptized. To me, a godparent was someone who showed up at the baptism and the responsibility ended there. Because, however much my godparents have prayed for me without my knowledge, I still have no idea who they are.

Neither do my parents.

It's not that my sister and I never asked. I remember clearly Aimee swiveling in her kitchen stool to face Mom and ask, "Mom, do you know who my godparents are?"

135

I'd been reading the paper at the table, and I stopped to listen. I'd never thought to pose the question.

Mom didn't look up from chopping the vegetables. "I don't remember," she said.

"Would it be the Wrens?" Aimee asked. Mr. Wren worked with Dad, and our families got together on weekends. We kids chased each other around the house while the grown-ups lounged on the screened-in porch, drinking beer and eating cheese and crackers. "Booze and cheese," we teased them from the bushes below.

"Maybe."

Aimee called Mrs. Wren her second mother. My sister has always needed that extra support and wasn't afraid to look to others to provide it. Something I never did. Put me down, I'd said as a toddler. Didn't mean I didn't want hugs—just on my own terms.

Independence had its down side, though. Whereas Aimee had that knack to connect with people, I didn't. Told myself I didn't want it. Granted, I would rather curl up in the armchair with a good book instead. But as good as all those Nancy Drews were, I was jealous of what Aimee found with people—especially with Gramma Verne. When she came to visit, Aimee always got to have sleepovers down in Gramma's room. I tried it once, but was jolted awake in the middle of the night by a lion's roar. I couldn't move, I was so terrified. When I finally garnered the courage to reach over and warn Gramma about the lion, I saw it: I saw Gramma snoring. Kept me awake the rest of the night.

I didn't mind so much I never got a turn after that.

"Is Mrs. Wren my godmother, too?" I asked, dying to know mine if Aimee was finding out hers. I didn't feel the connection Aimee had, but as a kid I was pretty sure their daughters walked on water. Their youngest, Pammy, did something even better: she was a pearl diver at Sea World and once arranged for me to be kissed by Shamu.

"Maybe," Mom said. "Probably."

I'm not sure why Mom led us to believe it was something a parent couldn't be sure about. That if it would be anybody, it would be the Wrens.

Maybe she wanted to give us something she knew she couldn't. I do know it bothered her, not being able to name our godparents.

The Catholic Church has a way of outing these things. When Jim and I were getting married and had to meet with our priest and hand over our papers, Mom insisted on coming along. Mother hen, I thought. The priest ushered us all in his office, giving Mom a look, too. I felt so justified in my annoyance at her joining us.

"I'm here to give you the baptismal certificate," Mom said.

"Oh, yes," the priest said, reaching across the desk for the paper.

"Do you really need an updated copy?" Mom held my certificate from long ago, the crease down the middle worn into a tear over the years.

The priest took Jim's current copy, crisp and clean and precise. "It's mandatory," the priest said. "Absolutely. You see, all sacraments, from Baptism to First Communion to Weddings, are all recorded at the church of the Baptism. This way all sacraments are conveniently recorded in one place, and we know for sure no parties have any previous marriage."

"But she's had her first communion and confirmation here," Mom said.

"Was she baptized here?" the priest asked patiently.

"No—"

The priest shook his head. "It needs to be where she was baptized."

"But all I have is this," she said, her voice shaking. My mother was a precise woman, a scientist. She played by the rules. That she couldn't provide the right document probably kept her up the night before. "At the time they said it was all we would ever need."

The priest began again, leaning into his words, holding onto his patience. "Where she was—"

"But she was adopted." There, Mom said it. After all those years and all that love, someone could tell her it still made a difference. That I wasn't really hers. At least not at the beginning.

"Oh, then," he said, sitting back in his chair. "That's fine, that's fine." As if there could be a salve for the rawness we thought had healed over so long ago.

Ironic that now I work in a church, collecting baptismal certificates from brides to be. Recently, I confessed to the other secretary I work with that I still don't know my own godparents.

"So isn't there a way for you to check now?" she asked.

There is, but a part of me doesn't want to find out. I prefer to think there's a little nun at St. Ann's, somebody like Sr. Marcene who teaches first grade at our school. I pass her door on my way in to work. She sits forward in her rocking chair, smiling down at the children sitting criss-cross apple-sauce on the floor. I've heard her tell them, just as she told my youngest six years before, "Yes, I think I will be one hundred seven this birthday." I'd like to think someone with her sense of humor and dedication was a godmother to all the souls born to unwed mothers, and that kindly woman knelt down every night and prayed for Grace and Love for each and every one of us.

I hope she's still out there for me, whoever she is, because surely I need it.

I AM ON MY THIRD DRAFT OF THIS CHAPTER and I still cannot bring myself to return to the time of Julia's baptism, when Jim's family came to celebrate and there was no one from my side of the family there.

Part of it is a personal issue, when I have people over. I was doing it today, even: Dad and my stepmom, Jackie, are visiting for Thanksgiving and Dad is talking and all I can think is, I have to go and take care of that mess in the kitchen and then I have to get Julia out of bed if we are going to have any chance of getting to the Nutcracker display up at Macy's today before the crowds get unmanageable, and I had to make myself stay seated, to remain in the moment and listen to the dinner conversation. So if I can barely be in the moment having two guests for a weekend, imagine how scattered I was with ten at Julia's baptism.

In Jim's family, for a sacrament, that's a party. So, of course, Jim's parents, Bill and Teresa, came—one of the last times they would drive themselves. And it wouldn't have been a sacrament without the chosen godparents, Jim's sister Sally and her husband, Nathan. Recently married and as yet kid-free, the two offered a convenient godparent package. Other sisters came, too—like Annie, the aunt who comes for every sacrament, and Kathy and her family, too. (I think just because they love babies that much.) For much of that weekend, then, Jenny got to play the Who Do I Get the Most Attention From game, which is really fun with cousins. The game was even more fun for Julia, a newborn who napped only twenty minutes a day to keep up with all the action. Especially where doting aunts were involved.

"So, your dad couldn't come?" Sally wanted to know while I was doing my little survey of what I could tend to in the room.

"No," I said, realizing I didn't really know why he wasn't there.

Funny when you consider Dad had been the most vocal about getting Juls baptized. And I doubted he'd been to Mass in the two years since Mom's funeral. I'd tried to explain to him that babies didn't go to Limbo anymore, not since Vatican II, but old fears die hard. And that one had been in place 1,600 years, when St. Augustine was looking for a reason for believers to commit their kids at an early age, to bring more into community. For all his concern, Dad still didn't come for the sacrament, even though he'd come up just after she was born. Not because he didn't lay the same weight on this sacrament as Jim's family—but because he just couldn't bear the thought of being at a family event without Mom.

"And your mom?" Sally asked me at that event.

"What?"

"She couldn't come either?" Sally had a smile on her face and in her voice as she always did, you can't help wanting to be part of that party. She wasn't being facetious, or ironic. She was genuinely asking.

"Oh," I said, "Val." Maybe—just maybe—this was something she might have wanted to come for and not just get a call about, whether she cared about Catholicism as much as Jim's folks did or even if she wasn't practicing at all. "You know, I didn't even think to ask her. I really should have," I said, thinking aloud. I was a young enough mother to think resolve will make it into practice; I was blissfully ignorant of the years it takes to change.

Sally raised her eyebrows and brought her glass to her lips. She did not drink—that time—but just smiled a silly, embarrassed smile for me. "I guess," she said.

"I SHOULD SEND A TELEGRAM," DAD HAD TOLD ME, when he confessed he wouldn't come to Julia's baptism.

"You don't need to," I said. "I know what you mean."

He and Mom weren't at Jenny's baptism either, but it wasn't because they didn't want to be. It was right after Mom's last chemo treatment, the one given just to be sure since her CA125 count was still double digits. We almost lost her "on the table," Dad had said, just like all those years ago when Mom lost The Baby—the one who would have been my younger sibling.

When the time came for Jenny's baptism, Mom was still in the hospital recovering. And so when we traveled to Iowa to celebrate that sacrament, I had to explain Mom's absence. Again and again, I had to say: No, Mom wasn't okay now, not anymore. With that last dose of chemotherapy she'd lost her kidneys and her hearing. Suddenly I was an expert, describing how the ear canal and kidney function are related, formed at the same time in utero, which was why both were affected. Dad remained at Mom's side, but he'd been given explicit instructions to send the telegram, just like her father had done when she was born.

That paper is still tucked inside Mom's childhood album, the thin rectangle glued against black pages. No silver writing under the entry on this page, the thirty-five-dollar hospital bill and the official document with an eagle soaring across the top said it all.

WELCOME TO THE WORLD STOP KEEP YOUR MOTHER COMPANY UNTIL I CAN BE THERE TO HOLD YOU STOP.

My grandfather served with the Michigan attorney general and was working in Washington when Mom was born. When she first showed me the album, Mom had to explain there were no cross-country flights in 1935, no room for telling a boss during that Depression era you'd prefer to delay the trip.

Now, for Mom, history had a strange way of repeating itself, and she wanted to follow it to the letter. If she couldn't be there for Jenny's baptism, she wanted that telegram sent. She scribbled words on a scrap piece of paper, echoing what her father had sent almost sixty years before, ending each sentence with "stop."

I imagine Mom laying back in the hospital bed, spent from the effort. "You'll send it?" said the one responsible for all the details in their thirty-seven years together. "Please, so they get it before the baptism."

Dad tucked the paper in his pocket. "Consider it done," he said, sitting down by her side.

We called from Iowa to let them know how the ceremony went, a quiet affair in the back of the church, with Father Bob's voice low and resonant and Jenny holding tight the whole time to the string on the end of her silk bonnet.

"You got the telegram?" Mom wanted to know.

"I did," I lied. "It meant so much."

Our next visit home, Dad slipped a folded paper in my hand. "For you," he said. "Later."

I waited until back in my room before opening it. It'd been folded tight, creased in his pocket as he drove back and forth to the hospital those dark summer months. I held the paper in my hand, studied her handwriting, the precise slant of her words even in her sickness, the even loops she made writing "love" and "Gramma Peri," a misspelling I made as a child for her mother that Mom never corrected. I folded it back up and tucked it into my purse.

Thank God Dad never sent it. It means so much more having the paper she once held, to be close to the movement she made with her hands, wishing so much love to a baby girl she had wanted to hold as much as her father had once wished for her.

DIFFERENT, I SHOULD KNOW BY NOW, does not mean better or worse. Just different. And Julia's baptism was different from Jen's. For this one, the first at St. Michael's, we stood in the back of the church by the baptismal font, a copper basin centered in granite. Jim picked Jen up, and she curled against his shoulder, a splash of color in her bright pink dress, her nummie blanket in her hand, against her cheek. Looking all the world like I did, at her age.

Sally had turned serious, intent on her duties—ingrained from her childhood under Teresa's watchful eye. So Sally knew when to hand the priest a flask of water from the River Jordan, from when my parents had visited the Holy Land on business. I remember Mom handing me two flasks when they returned. "You're in charge of the one for Aimee's kids, too," she said. "You keep it safe."

I made a note to double-check the keepsake box when I got home, to make sure it was still tucked inside, in the silk bag Christin had made for my wedding. It'd been something new then. For Aimee it would be something borrowed. Or something old?

I could be in this moment, I told myself. I should be in this moment.

The priest uncorked the glass flask and poured the water in the basin.

I lurched forward, as if to stop him. He was supposed to pour it on my baby's head, he was. But the precious few drops he poured were now mixed with the rest, the not-as-holy water.

"In case we have lots of babies," Jim explained to me later. "This way, there'd be enough for them all."

My friend Christin didn't want to take any chances. Next time she went to the Holy Land, she brought back a flask for each of my girls, one for each of Aimee's hypothetical children as well. "Next priest can dump the whole damn thing on your next baby," Christin said.

But I was left at the side of that basin, searching for a trace of that most holy water Mom had brought and the priest had unceremoniously poured and then set aside. I held my baby close, her white satin gown as cool as comfort against my arms as the priest intoned the ritual words. Julia's head tipped back and forth, like she was watching something. Or someone.

She was studying the flame of her baptismal candle, entranced by the flickering light meant to lead her out of darkness.

I watched with her, the flame dancing on the wick, and I remembered evenings spent watching the fire with my mother's mother, Gramma Verne.

A crescendo from the choir, and I am caught in the moment. I am there, and not there, for there are a thousand other moments I am thinking of, moments in the past I wish I could hold onto in this present. I hold so tight to my baby I lean forward with her when the priest gestures for me to hold her low, so he can scoop waters from the font, waters joined and separate, and let them trickle over her.

She stares in wonder at this holy man and this everyday miracle he performs. Her mouth forms a perfect circle, all the wonders in this world, and this is what my little girl sees, and she cannot say it but I see it in her face—my father saw it when he first laid eyes on her and said, "Oh, little honey, there is so much in this world for you to see, so much for you to live."

And I can barely see that flickering flame. It is all I can do to not let go of that sight. I am glad for the darkened hall, for my eyes are so full of wet, and I am holding so tight to my baby I cannot let go, I cannot and will not wipe away the love gathered in my tears.

Jim's mom, Teresa, found me afterwards. "How are you doing, little mama?" she asked. "That was a beautiful ceremony." She looked up at me, eyes proud.

"The songs," I said. I could still barely get any words out.

"The songs were beautiful."

Which is, sad to say, unusual for a Catholic service. Seems all the musical talent in the Church had agreed with Martin Luther's ninety-five theses. Our priest had joked at the opening of the service, "Wow, we sound like a bunch of Lutherans today."

Like the choir Mom sang in when she was little. I hadn't been able to pick her out of the line up of fifth-grade girls in her choir picture, but at Julia's baptism, I could hear the music as well as the words of a woman who'd spent her last days in silence.

"You couldn't have picked better songs," my mother-in-law said.

"But I didn't pick any." Not said in protest, but in wonder.

I admit, I did not know much church music then. We'd gone to church more in those few months than I had in years. Each reading I heard, I heard for the first time. But the songs sung at Julia's baptism I'd heard before. For each of them, the opening, the psalm, the communion song and the closing, each were the same ones sung at Mom's funeral. And I'd had no hand in planning either service.

"I have to tell you," I said, gathering strength. "The music—it spoke to me."

Some part of an everyday miracle: Still here with me, still here with us. Not anything I can see, but flowing through it all.

Like some kind of most holy water.

❧ 17 ❧

The All-New Brady Bunch

At Mom's funeral, one of her friends gave us a poem and this advice: "It'll take two years before your dad will start coming out from under." She meant, of course, that's when he'd begin dating again. I nodded, feigning agreement, but I was resolutely appalled. At least Dad was never one to follow expectations. Surely, he'd never date.

Though he still kept the remote control gate up in the middle of the drive and still would not take any phone calls, it was in fact just over two years after Mom died that we walked in the door over Labor Day and found Mom's mahogany desk had been moved to where the bird watching chair had been, under the conservatory windows in the great room. A woman had a ledger spread before her, her back to the view of the pool and the waterfall that cut through the wood below. She stood to greet us, glasses hiding her eyes. She had tousled dark curls. Her figure backlit by the sunlight, for a brief startling moment I wondered if my mother was welcoming me in her arms once again.

"This is Linda," Dad said. He'd warned me she'd be there for our visit, though he hadn't put it that way. He'd met her while working out in Vegas, where all his new business was.

Never mind all the hugs my mother gave my boyfriends, I did not know whether to shake this woman's hand or give her a hug hello.

I offered one hand and hugged with the other and was caught off guard by the bitter smell of cigarettes lingering in the air. After all Dad's complaints about their good friend Donna smoking whenever we skied with them.

"Jenny, can you say hello to Miss Linda?" I asked. Southern charm, calling grown-ups by their first name. I loved it until I realized its roots derived from slavery.

"You moved the desk," I said to Dad as I gave him a hug hello. At least he smelled the same, of grease and Old Spice. The relocation of the desk was bothering me more than the idea he might have already kissed this woman not my mother.

"I'm getting a pool table," he said. But in the cherry-paneled office just off the great room, there was nothing but a gaping hole. The desk's footprint still weighted heavily upon the forest green carpet.

We got settled into the bedroom I'd never lived in, only visited when home from law school and work. Back downstairs, Dad was well underway making dinner, dishtowel already thrown over his shoulder. Linda by him, glass of zin in her hand. She scooted away, but not before rubbing his shoulder affectionately. Intimately. Had they more than kissed? I guess I knew this time would come. I'd just hoped it wouldn't be happening already.

Linda backed into one of the stools at the counter, set her glass on the counter and fiddled with her empty hands. Jim made us drinks, his a gin and tonic, mine a chardonnay, and I fell in beside my father. I fumbled my way through helping, knocking over measuring cups and almost my wine. Trying to be more controlled, I poured the broth slowly out of the measuring cup, but the liquid hugged the glass and wet the counter, and I could hear my mother's voice. "Surface tension," the chemist once told me. "Water's is the strongest. You've got to be strong enough to break it. The faster you dump it, the better."

My husband tried to comfort me later that night, telling me he'd heard that the sooner widowers date, the more the relationship meant. "He's just looking for what he once had," my Jim said.

Small comfort when you see your dad reaching for another woman's hand.

Dinner was better. Dad opened some wine and told some stories. Laughter peppered the table.

"Excuse me," I said. "I should put the girls down now." I left Jim to be sociable with the happy couple, and I lifted Julia up into one arm and took Jenny by the hand. The foyer stairs swept in a wide circle to the second floor, encircling a brass chandelier. Taking the steps one at a time, one little girl at my side and one clutched in my arm, I couldn't help but notice the dust layered upon the brass. Mom was probably the last to clean it at my wedding five years before. In the room, I tried to change Julia quickly, then helped Jen into her Cinderella jammies. I held both in my lap and read *Hop on Pop*, the pages yellowed since I'd read it as a child. It was quiet up in that room I never called my own, quiet in solitude and respite. "I should go back down now," I said, but I pulled Julia against me and stroked the back of Jen's head and wished for all the world I could stay with the both of them. Or at least when I went back down that it would be a different woman at the table easing Dad back into life.

I'd just sat down again and was laying my napkin back in my lap when Dad broke the news. "I'm helping Linda get set up in a new home," he said.

"I'm so glad for you," I said. It was all I could do not to repeat what Dad told me when I moved into my newlywed apartment the week before my wedding: You're not married yet.

"It overlooks the strip," Dad said. "You'd love the view."

"I'm sure I would."

Dad waited until it was just the two of us before he talked about her son, how the teen had become a lost soul after her divorce. "I'm going to help him out," he said. "He needs someone to point him in the right direction, and I can do that."

"Sounds like he'd like that," I said. "And I bet it would mean a lot to Linda." Polite conversation, the kind Mom taught me to have. Manners to fall back on when you'd no idea what to say, how to feel.

"It was a pleasure to meet you," I told her when we left. I made a point of asking about her when I called over the next several months.

It didn't surprise me when Dad later told me, "Linda and I have decided to go our separate ways. Did you know she smoked?" He said, "I'm still going to be a mentor to her son, though."

Out my window, the trees silhouetted against the setting sun in the gloaming, Mom's favorite time of day. "I'm sure that would mean a lot to him," I said, but we both knew it would probably mean more to Dad, to give life after a relationship had died.

LESS THAN A YEAR LATER AND DAD had this question for me: "Will you be home for Thanksgiving?" he asked. "I have someone I want you to meet."

"Okay," I said absently, focused on cleaning countertops. He hadn't mentioned dating in so long I'd been able to tuck it in the back of my mind. "Sounds good."

"She's easy to talk to," he said. "We've got more in common. Background kind of stuff, you know? Doesn't play much golf, but she does do tennis and bridge. And she went to Ohio State, but I can forgive her for that." We were covering the Big Ten—he and Mom had gone to Michigan State, I'd gone to University of Michigan for law school, and Jim went to Iowa.

Turned out she'd grown up in a little farming town outside of Columbus. "She's just more my kind of people," Dad said.

"I look forward to meeting her," I said, cradling the phone on my shoulder as I clouded the mirror with glass cleaner. An idea was forming in my head. For two years, Val had been asking when I'd be in Cleveland next. And if Dad thought this was a good time to be introducing new people into the family, then . . .

I said, "Maybe that might be a good time for you to meet Val, then, too."

I caught his hesitation.

"Not for the actual meal," I said. He had laid down the rule about not sharing holidays. "But maybe they could come on that Friday, and I could introduce you."

"Maybe."

My Jim wasn't as positive. "Won't it be enough, you meeting this new girlfriend of your dad's?" Ever the voice of reason.

"It's just his rebound person," I said. "Whatever. I can handle it." I couldn't wait to tell Val.

"Are you going to be in town for Thanksgiving?" I asked her. "Because if you'll be around, I'd love for you to come over on that Friday and I can introduce you to my dad. You can see the big house."

I could hear gears spinning, thinking she'd be able to imagine me in the house I grew up in. "They moved in when I graduated from college," I said. "That's when the bishop blessed it." How do you like that? Had no idea who my godparents were, hardly a churchgoer, and we've got an in with the bishop to bless the floors we walk on. Crazy world, isn't it? "I started law school that summer, and then I worked over the summers. So it's only been a place to visit for me. A very nice place to visit."

But my folks had sold the old house my junior year, which had begged the question of where they'd lived in the meantime. The answer: "Above the barn."

Oh, there goes a whole another conversation. How many people do you know have an apartment above the barn? It was lovely, too: Three bedrooms, two baths, a kitchen and dining room, great room, and game room. Mom decorated it in 1970s red and gold, with brown accents and Dad's hunting trophies—ducks he shot while in Canada and a caribou he shot on a trip up in the Arctic Circle. I don't know what was done with the polar bear he nabbed with his buddy Zipter. They'd been helicoptered in and caught it the first day. "No cell phones," Dad had told me. "So I was out there a frigging week, freezing my ass off before that plane came back." Yes, there are definite advantages to having cell phone service now.

What's funny is that I write of these trips he took and the farm we had and it all is a wonder to me now. It was a different life, a different time. A different family. At least, a different understanding of one.

AN HOUR BEFORE WE WERE LEAVING for Dad's for Thanksgiving, Jenny threw up. Of course I rushed her in to see the doctor, hyper-worrier that I am. Maybe I was just being diligent, or maybe I was looking for an out—so I wouldn't have to meet whoever Dad wanted me to or live through the uncomfortable moment of introducing Dad to my birthmother. But the doctor pointed out it was just a little bug, she'd be sick either way, and we should be with family over the holiday. I don't think Jim would have minded staying home, though. I can guess because he swore under his breath all along the ice-slicked ribbon of highway through the mountains of West Virginia.

It was late late by the time we pulled into the driveway in Spencer, past one in the morning, but the sleet had stopped the last half hour of our eight-hour drive. And what a relief to see the big house with the French doors splayed, the light from inside spilling over the half circle of brick entrance steps. Jim and I flanked the car doors, each lifting a sleeping girl from her car seat.

Dad greeted us at the door. "You made it," he said loudly, then, "You made it," more quietly for the girls.

"There was that patch in the hills where we weren't sure we were going to," Jim said, teeth still clenched as he carried Jen over the threshold.

"Bad, huh?"

"And your daughter has a habit of sleeping through the worse of it," my Jim said.

We tucked the children upstairs and hurried back down. Two older women sat on the couches in the great room, but they stood as Jim and I entered the room. Dad put his arm around me. "Jackie, I'd like you to meet my daughter," he said, his voice low and sober.

The younger woman about Mom's age smiled, and her whole face shone, as if she'd just discovered a dear friend in a place she'd never been. "Oh, Katie, I am so pleased to meet you," she said. As much as Linda looked like my mother's little sister, Jackie looked nothing at all like her. Jackie had a button nose and wore her strawberry-blonde hair straight and long. Her smile was toothy and warm as fresh-baked bread.

"Me too," I said. "I've heard so much about you."

150

She feigned pulling back in horror.

"Oh, it's all good," I said, laughing. "All good."

Jackie then introduced her Aunt Justine. I took the older woman's hand gently in both of mine, and I shook it.

"And this," Jackie said, acknowledging the cocker spaniel at their heels, "This is Buddy." The dog wagged its tail and squatted, dribbling pee in a circle upon the carpet.

Next morning was Thanksgiving and we had much to do before the rest of our guests came. Nothing like preparing dinner for fourteen to get to know someone. Jackie cooed over her elderly aunt and chatted with me easily, fussing about the kitchen. Dad basted the turkey in between house cleaning and tweaking. Jim was sucked in with that round of duties, while I was in and out of the kitchen, pulling out old toys of mine to set before the children as I helped with the sweet potatoes, mashed potatoes, and bread.

Dad recruited me into the dining room to help pull the chairs from around the large round table. The last time Dad had filled this table was the night of Mom's funeral, when Shadow had found comfort in Aunt Mary's arms. Unceremoniously, Dad pulled the salmon tablecloth off the top, revealing the workman's plywood circle beneath.

"I thought you wanted me to set the table," I said.

"First we're taking this apart." Dad pulled the bare wood towards him and off the center of the rectangular table below.

"What are you doing?" There was silverware to polish, potatoes to peel, and yet Dad would have me stand before an undressed dining table, doing nothing but waiting for carnage to unfold.

Dad came back in with a circular saw. "Vogl, can you hold this steady for me?"

With that, Dad flipped on the switch and rendered in two the table over which we'd broken bread as a family and with friends.

"Won't you hack the table underneath?"

"For Chrissakes, I've been working with tools since I could reach my daddy's workbench," Dad said. "I know how to handle this."

But he wasn't handling the tabletop, he was mutilating it. Edges raw and splintered, piece by lonely piece processed out upon my husband's shoulder.

Jackie stood in the doorway. "What's going on?" she asked. She didn't know what was to come: Dad cutting through what he and Mom had built together, patching it over. As for me, I could not see that day, that date as one in a succession of new beginnings for my father, but rather just another in the succession of endings.

Perhaps my sister was the only one to get it right. She and her boyfriend did not show for Thanksgiving until we were sitting down at the table, and it was not until well into the first course that I realized her quietness was not so much from her lack of willingness to partake as it was her lack of ability to focus. She'd numbed herself to her pain. I'd thought I'd been through the worst of mine, but coming home, I felt pain all anew. This was not the first Thanksgiving without Mom, but it was the first one I'd had at the house without her. Quite frankly, I wasn't sure I was any better now than I'd been almost three years before. No wonder Aimee left as the sun rose the next morning, excusing herself with work. No one wanted to take the shift she'd been given, the day after Thanksgiving. The excuse was convenient and offered relief from the pain, palpable and throbbing wherever and however we moved through our mother's house.

I was on my hands and knees when I met Val's children. The doorbell rang and Buddy peed, dribbling telltale dots in her tail-wagging circle. And so, when Val and her husband and their children walked through the door, there I kneeled, Cinderella style.

Not at all as I'd imagined when swinging on the swing set, conjuring tales of my long lost siblings.

Chris was tall, much taller than I expected, his face gaunt as if recovering from a leftover growth spurt. As for Allisyn, she was pretty but wore too much make-up, probably not unlike me at her age. Something I did not expect, either, and yet I should have—they were young, so much younger than me.

And blond.

Definitely their father's children. I had to keep reminding myself he was not my blood relation, though they'd been married twenty-five years already. Joe was her rebound man, the one she met just after she had me.

"Let me wash my hands first and then I can say a proper hello," I said. Dad and Jackie already had. His greeting more than cordial, relaxed. Dad had pushed his glasses up onto his forehead, a habit of his. A towel thrown over his shoulder. He'd been cleaning up. He was Dad as I knew him, not a polished version to present to company. (Anyway, that's something I do, not him.)

When the conversation lagged, as it will in a meeting so heavily laden with emotions, Dad suggested I take them on a tour. A house that size, people wanted to see it. By today's standards, it's probably just another McMansion on a big lot, but in the mid 1990s, it was two or three times as large as most folks lived in.

And as I was taking them around, I saw the house through their eyes, saw its luxuriousness and even its excesses. It was my parent's dream house, the one they'd planned for so many years, the one they'd only enjoyed four years before Mom's cancer showed up at their door. I began the tour by taking Val and her family through the main floor, where my parents did the bulk of their living. The Queen Anne guest room, with not one but two Drexel Heritage dressers, a bed needing a stool to climb up into, a fireplace with the two wing-back chairs recovered and recycled from our old house, so stately in their old setting, so modest here, though they flanked the rose brick fireplace. Dad had put new *tchotch-kes* on the mantel, but it still looked wounded and bare of the Italian painting he'd sent down for Jen's first birthday.

"Dad built it big like this so his mother could live here," I said, realizing the room was big, too big even with a cot so Jackie and Justine and Buddy could keep each other company in one room. "It's handicap accessible," I explained, pushing on the wide cherry door leading into the shower only bath. He'd built it for his mother to come stay, but she never did. He never went to visit her, either, those last two years of her life. Both too stubborn to give in and go to the other.

But I didn't mention any of that. I was lucky to come up with words, any words, for this basic tour.

Val said she'd be bringing her kids, but it hadn't occurred to me this would be my chance to get to know them, too. I'd been so busy worrying how the meeting between Dad and Val would go.

Of course he was gracious, considering everything she'd once given him. I struggled to be the same to Val's children, but I found myself at a loss as to what to say with them here, now, in front of me. It was all I could take in that these two existed. That they were somehow related to me. I couldn't imagine it.

And yet here they were. Chris was taller than I, something I hadn't expected. I should have; he was a grown man of twenty-five. Allisyn was shorter, like Val's sisters. Her eyes crinkled in a perpetual smile. Nervous, or happy? She reminded me of me when I was in college, wanting to make a good impression, to please, but I dared not say it for fear of sounding like a doddering old aunt instead of what I was.

What was I? Half-blood sister, but I felt more like a distant relative. Weird to discover these intimate connections when you're too old to start calling someone you just met "family." Other than in-laws, I mean.

So now imagine showing a birthmother and her kids your parents' bedroom. Can you connect with them and still be proud of the beauty of the room? Or should you be embarrassed at its extravagance? Don't forget to point out the sauna/steam room/tanning bed along with a TV in the bathroom. They'll admire the bedroom couch and chairs grouped around a coffee table and overlooking the deer run for which the home was named. Call it your dad's room, since he's the only one sleeping there anymore. And that way you can avoid the use of the word "mother." It will be something to avoid for years.

When Val had come to visit our house in North Carolina, I'd told her that Mom would always be Mom to me. Now I wondered if she'd shared that with her kids. Dare I refer to Mom as Mom as I led these people through the house she dreamed into being? Or would that seem like I was saying Val was somehow not worthy of the title? Better to avoid that whole quagmire if I could.

So I tried to give a tour of my parents' home without ever referring to my mother. Good luck if you do the same because sometimes you just have to swallow and use her name. To call her any less wouldn't be fair to the dead.

Val's family lingered in the bedroom, mostly because that's where all the family photos were. Val was studying a memento tucked away above the bed, upon one of the cherry shelves. Could have easily been just the decorator who put it there. For a finishing touch, he'd gone through the house with a box filled of treasures, strategically placing the tiles Mom purchased on trips or awards Aimee and I had won. What caught Val's attention was a simple plaque I'd bought for Mother's Day when I was in high school and knew I needed to get Mom something, just didn't know what. It cost less than five dollars, but you'd think it was priceless, the way Val was holding it, cupped in her hand.

Allisyn peered over Val's shoulder, to see what was so important. A ceramic rose clinging to cream-painted wood. A Mother Is Love, is all it said. I couldn't hold Val's eyes. Would I have put more effort into the gift, had I known it's later significance? Or was this something guided from above, something for us all to see and understand? I only wished I'd felt the higher power that Mother's Day so long ago. Felt the significance of the time—and for all that was to come.

"Let's go upstairs," I said. Anything to break the longing look in Allisyn's eyes as she watched Val linger over the stupid plaque. *It doesn't deserve this much of your time,* I wanted to say. *I'm sure Allisyn put much more thought into what she got you.*

I led them up the winding staircase, which led directly into my room. A four-poster bed, just like in the guestroom for Grandma Jo. But by my rose brick fireplace was just one wingback chair. Everything in pink chinoiserie. Julia's pink Pack-n-Play matched.

"A reading nook," Allisyn said, rushing to the dormer window. "My favorite." Mine, too. I only wish I'd had one as a child, but I'd had my reading cot instead.

In the other dormer, a built in desk. A picture of me from Cotillion. At first Val thought it was from my wedding. Allisyn studied the girl in the photo, twenty pounds heavier than the me who stood before her. I was heavier in college, too, I wanted to tell her. But that's not something you say to someone you just met, even if they are family.

I leaned back against the wall, a mural of a Chinese garden, perhaps not unlike what my biological paternal grandmother had grown up near. Everything I had to show Val's family today, everything was beautiful but just a shell of what we'd had. I don't mean tangibly. Our home had been lovely growing up, too, with a pool out back and a baby grand in the living room. More important to me, even more than the dolls living on my bedroom shelves or the fish in the aquarium in the kitchen (at least until Mom backed into it while vacuuming) was the love we'd filled it with. Christmas bonfires at the end of our driveway, picnics out back in the summer, reading marathons curled up on a toile loveseat, *HeeHaw* and *Carol Burnett* down in the family room, where we all watched together, even Gramma Verne.

This house, though. The big house. It was empty of all that, echoing Mom's solitude in the silence of her last days. No Pavarotti, either.

I led them through my sister's room, with ballet slippers upon the wall for the girl who hated taking tap but loved Nureyev. The back of her closet opened up to a secret hallway. There Mom kept pictures of grandparents, senior portraits of me and my sister, a portrait neighbors had done of the house I grew up in. Jim hated how we kept our family pictures hidden, not adorning the living spaces. But it's what I've always known. We kept our family private.

I tried to ask Chris and Allisyn questions, at least as best I could. I had more experience as a tour guide than I had as a big sister. I'd no idea how to relate to a brother. Thankfully, we were old enough now that he didn't have to hit me to let me know he thought I was okay. That broad, full-lipped smile he'd flash whenever I'd do the backward tour guide walk let me know instead. Beyond walking them through the house, I had no idea what to say, what to ask. All the questions I knew had to do with school, and Val had said Allisyn wasn't interested in going back to Kent in the fall. Questions about them growing up? We settled in on talking about pets, dogs we loved and lost. Allisyn's eyes crinkled with joy at sharing the memories. When she smiled, I realized she had her mother's chin. And mine.

The back hall connected to the apartment above the garage, with a kitchenette and living room, bedroom, and bath. It even had a balcony over-looking the waterfall, the best view in the house. Again, I felt I had to explain the extravagance of the place. "It's in case they ever need someone to stay here, to care for the place," I said. Dad hadn't arranged for anyone yet, even though my parents knew it would be too much to handle on their own from the start. At least Dad had patched the holes in the ceiling the hornets had eaten through. I tried not to stare up where the holes had been, tried not to draw attention to the scar in the house.

Back down into the house, we were back where we started—in the office, which no longer housed the desk (that was in the great room) or the piano (Dad had shipped that off to me). Instead, a pool table filled the cher-ry-paneled room, as Dad had said it would. It was Jenny's favorite part of the big house, pulling billiard balls out of the leather pouches and rolling them across the green of the table. Val lingered, entranced by watching the little girl.

On a bookcase filled with college texts and classics, as well as Ludlum and Clancy and Grisham, stood a curved frame Mom won in a golf outing. Allisyn seemed drawn to the twin photos, one of me with short hair, and another of Aimee, a senior portrait when she had a perm she never would wear again. "So this," she said, picking up the awkward curve of glass and studying it intently in her hands. "This is—"

And I began nodding, yes, yes, she recognized us even though we looked so different.

"This is your other sister?" Allisyn asked.

"Yes, of course," I said, realizing my mistake as I'd led them through a maze of rooms not their own, through a tangle of relationships I'd known from only one side of the branches of a family tree. They'd known a ghost, too, ever since they could remember. Surely they'd felt it even though Val had never named my presence, not until just a few years before. "Yes," I acknowledged. "That's my other sister."

Gently, my half-sister set the photos back down beside a misshapen bird I'd sculpted out of wood in seventh-grade shop class. And then, stepping back as if to appreciate a new perspective, she cocked her head, and she smiled.

≈ 18 ≈

A Wedding Made in Heaven

New Year's Eve, and Jim and I were bringing in 1998 at home. We kicked off the evening with me in the bathroom, giving the girls their evening bath. My hands were covered with soapy bubbles, trying to scrub Jenny's birthmark off her back once again before I realized what I was doing.

Jim opened the door and bumped my foot, and I lost my grip, sliding into the tub, my hands looking for purchase in the depths of the bathwater. "Phone," he said. "It's your dad."

Dad was down at the Reef with Jackie, and I knew what that meant. Starry night, music at Buccaneer, dancing until they forgot it was early morning and had to return up north, back to reality and the cold of winter. He'd be high on life, a happy call. He didn't mean to, but he'd be taunting me he had a party that night and I didn't.

I can be really, really good at feeling sorry for myself sometimes.

"I'm up to my elbows." I tried not to sound annoyed. "I'll call him back."

Jim held the phone out to me. "I tried to tell him," he said. "He insisted."

Sighing dramatically, I took the phone and tucked it on my shoulder. "Hi, Dad," I said. "Happy New Year."

"Hello, Kate," he said. He called me Kate only when he was in a good mood, ready to lecture, or if he's been drinking. From his tone, I was guessing it was all three tonight. "I've got some good news I had to share with you."

"I can always use some good news," I said, trying to get on with this bath.

"Can't we all," he said, laughing.

He was up again, up like I hadn't heard him in forever. He'd been like that for a while now, maybe all fall. The widow had said two years it would take him after Mom died, and it had taken three.

"Hey," Dad said. "Something special happened tonight. Jackie and I got engaged."

"You didn't," I said, standing up, frantically pantomiming to Jim to take over the girls. "You're engaged?"

Jim's eyes widened as he dropped to his knees onto the plain white tile.

"Did it happen tonight?" It seemed so backward, to have Dad calling me with this news. He didn't even ask me beforehand. I wanted to blurt, "Too soon, too soon," like my mother did when Jim and I started talking about getting married three months after we met.

And then Mom had pointed out my Jim hadn't even talked to my dad yet.

I'd laughed at her. "What, to ask for my hand?"

Mom had been serious; life was to be taken one step at a time. And so the planning began for making our engagement official. We planned out the weekend Jim and I would make the six-hour trek home. On Saturday we all would play a round of golf, and Jim and Dad would have a cart to themselves to discuss my future, and that evening we would have a party. With champagne.

Mom hadn't planned on the rain. Morning of the much-anticipated golf tourney, and windows sheeted with a hard, drumming rain. Washed away all the groundwork Jim had me do, including a call to lay out explicitly the reason for the visit. "We know!" my family echoed back on the speaker. Now, Jim's the planner, not me, so that morning when an alternate plan of attack needed to be made, all I could do was ask what to do.

But no one else knew either. Not Mom at the stove as eggs sizzled ready. Nor Jim, whose face was white as a freshly torn sheet of blank paper.

We had breakfast as if we'd nothing planned. I felt like a kid waiting for the grown ups to say what to do. Aimee kicked me under the table, just to smirk at me.

The rain started letting up, but no way would the club allow play on the sodden grounds. My usual Taoist approach seemed so inadequate. Jim had said there needed to be a plan, and now there was none. I'd no idea how life would play out that morning, and for the first time, that worried me.

Dad pushed back from the table. "I think I might get some work done," he said.

God. All hope of any plan forming seemed lost, so lost. We girls slowly started picking up the table. Jim dutifully helped.

I heard the sliding glass door open. Dad was outside, picking up.

And then Jim was at the door, going outside, too.

We took a long time washing the dishes that day. It's hard to be quick when your eyes are riveted to two men outside, one slowly, methodically vacuuming a pool, the other cleaning off a patio. It took us awhile; it took them forever. But when Dad started pulling the long steel rod from the pool and Jim reeled up the hose, Aimee slid open the door.

"Coming in?" she asked. The wait was killing us.

"Vogl here had some important things to say out there," Dad said, stepping up into the house. Tears began forming in his eyes. "He says he wants to marry my daughter."

Jim beamed at me.

"And you want to marry him?"

"Very much."

"There you have it," Dad said, taking off his glasses to wipe them instead of his eyes. He chuckled softly. "I feel like I just paid off a mortgage."

To think my father felt so emotionally invested in me. Criminy. But I know what he meant, that he meant well.

For me, there was no debt relief when Dad told me of his intentions with Jackie, but I knew how he felt, knew he deserved that wealth of happiness I didn't think could still be possible for him.

"It's magical," Dad told me, his voice brimming with the moment he and Jackie just shared. Possibilities lay ahead again for him. Once again, there was hope.

Jackie gave him more than love, she gave him life.

When my father-in-law turned sixty-five, he held a retirement party. When my dad turned sixty-five, he had an engagement party. Jim and I drove the girls to the edge of Lake Erie, to a nondescript three-room office building that hugged the side of a road. A chain link fence divided the small parking lot with the tarmac, and beyond that the landing strips criss-crossed the acreage between the one-room terminal and the Great Lake. We pulled our duffel bags and diaper bags out of the trunk. Dad had reminded us to pack light, that there wasn't much room for luggage in the back of Ray's Cessna 182, and it was better to have soft-sided bags that could be shoved into nooks and crannies.

The heat was stifling, but Jen wouldn't let go of her nummie blanket (her long-legged George the Gibbon was tangled up somewhere inside) and Julia cradled her black bear in one arm and Dumbo in the other. I would have sat on my college duffel as we waited, and pulled the girls on my lap, but it was too hot even to think of resting my legs against anything, much less a scratchy old duffel.

We stood in the sun for what seemed like an eternity, but it was only a ten-minute jump from Rattlesnake Island to the airport at Port Clinton. Long enough to remember that perhaps I should be nervous flying again with Dad's friend. Ray was, after all, the one who'd almost flown my parents straight into the Perry Monument. Granted, it was foggy that morning. But when a 352-foot limestone tower looms out of the milky gray and you live to talk about the layers of pigeon shit on the copper top, you know you beat death by mere inches. "It's not foggy today, not foggy at all," I told myself as we waited for the buzz of the blue-striped plane.

The 182 materialized out of the Erie blue sky and rounded the rim of the landing pattern for its descent. And then the plane was hanging in the air for that brief wondrous moment when the engine was cut and the craft was floating on nothing but a cushion of air before it glided to the runway surface. The Cessna taxied up to the tarmac, and the door popped open before the plane rolled to a stop and the propellers wound down.

I carried a car seat up to the door. A blast of oven heat poured over me as I popped my head in. "What's up with the door latch?" I asked.

"Just so damn hot," Ray said, conducting his pilot check in shutting down the instruments. Sweat had darkened his gray hair. "No air-conditioning, see?"

Was that worse, or better, than Dad not being there to co-pilot the plane?

"Oh, there's no way you're going to fit that in here," Ray said, noticing the car seat I was trying to shove into the back. "If we go down, hon, we're going down."

What great comfort. I grumbled all the way back to the car, and life was no better once I crammed in the back with the girls. Jim didn't have it much better up front, either, in mom's old co-pilot seat, but I had the fuzz from Julia's black bear pressed against the heat of my skin. "Can we move this to the back?" I said, taking hold of the bear. But Julia only held tighter. Two years old in her pink-striped overalls, she had no idea what I'd put her into. Nor did Jen, who held her Sesame Street nummie up against her face. The heat might have been oppressive, but it could not cancel the comfort those loveys provided for each of my girls.

A short blast down the runway, and the plane grabbed the air, climbing high and fast, courtesy of the stoll kit Ray had installed. The airport at the island we were going to was so short, the modification to the wing from the flaps to the tip gave an uncanny extra lift on takeoff—a must after seeing those last two feet of Perry's Monument so up close and personal. The engines were loud, especially with the tiny pilot's window open for air. It made me nervous with it open, but I can't imagine how oppressive the heat would have been with it shut.

The shoreline quickly receded behind us, and Lake Erie lay dark below. Islands, I knew, would soon appear. I knew the flight path well, though I'd only been to Rattlesnake a few times since my family first started coming when I was in law school.

"But that's owned by the Mafia," my roommate had said.

"Oh, that's just a rumor," I said. "Keeps the riff raff off the island." I'd never heard such a thing before. I never knew about Rattlesnake before my parents went, how could Ann have heard stories about the Mafia there? Granted, both Ray and Dad were in construction, and Ray's name was well known in the Cleveland area. (His eponymous company signs were among the lit billboards lining the hallways of Cleveland Hopkins Airport.) And Dad had begun consulting for a waste management company. But being in those lines of business didn't automatically mean either was part of the mob.

The islands of Erie began to draw close beneath us: the first of the three Bass Islands and there, there's a smaller one, that's Sugar Island, the one I always thought was Rattlesnake at first. South Bass was beneath us, and there on the north shore was Put-in-Bay, with its towering monument. To the west now a smaller island with rock outcroppings—rattles—dotting its tail. Ray banked into landing pattern, flying north along the length of Rattlesnake Island, then a slow turn on final, and we bumped onto the grass field and seemed to come to an abrupt stop. Again, the stoll kit, giving as close to a helicopter landing a plane can get.

"How's that for first class?" I asked the girls. "Be sure to thank Mr. Ray."

"No problem," he said. He helped us pull our bags out of the back of the plane and dropped them in the empty golf cart parked by a small cabin. He told us to take the Niagara suites—a two-story building with hotel-like rooms, with dark cedar on the upper level and the lower level trimmed in limestone. Its sliding glass doors overlooked the lake to the south.

"You get settled, meet us at my place," Ray said, climbing into his Model T, which he kept to tool around the island.

164

"Sounds good," I said. I swung onto the cart, Jen between Jim and me, and took Julia in my lap. The cart lurched forward, and we were off, across the grass landing field that doubled as a golf course, up onto the gravel path and past the lamppost. The last time Jim and I were on the island was five years before, over Memorial Day, and the three of us had crowded into the back of Ray's old car. Mom wore a bandana all weekend; her hair was completely gone at that point. And as we played bocce ball, she talked candidly about her first symptoms, how within just a couple of weeks she'd bloated so much she couldn't wear any of her clothes anymore, how she'd been so sure it was something in her large intestine.

"I even took that awful barium test," she said. "That's when it showed up." It being the cancer, of course. Those awful days when they told her she needed surgery within two weeks or she'd die, and they couldn't get her scheduled for four. That weekend was one of the only times she talked about the cancer, what it meant to her. She was, after all, a Swede and not prone to discussing feelings. Not at all. Once we tried to get her to talk, enthusiastically chatting about the power of positive thinking in the treatment of tumors, and that's when she cried, "Stop! Just stop already. I'm taking this just one day at a time, I can't think about what I am supposed to be thinking or not thinking. Just let me be." We'd all fallen silent, but not before she added another, more plaintive "Please."

RAY LIVED IN THE NORTH LODGE ON THE ISLAND. It was my favorite, better even than the South Lodge with its towering stone fireplace on the screened-in porch and the islands of Lake Erie painted on its floor. Ray's Lodge had a full kitchen and bath and maybe three bedrooms, but what I loved was the great room; hanging over a Hearst-size fireplace was an oil painting of Perry's naval victory in the War of 1812, stormy and dark and full of poetic angst.

From the back porch came bubbles of laughter, and I could hear my father on a roll with that devilish giggle. "Can you hear Papa?" I said, pushing Jen towards the door. We would need to figure out what term of endearment to call Jackie. "Miss Jackie" didn't seem to impart the role she'd be playing in the girls' lives, but at the same time, it seemed strange to give her the same title as Jim's mom.

"Girls!" Dad said, standing up and throwing his arms wide. "Come to Papa!" And as they did, he scooped them up in his arms, and he held them tight. "You remember Jackie," he said to Jen and Juls. Jen nodded, but held her nummie tight to her face. Julia tipped her head against Papa's shoulder.

"Of course they do," I said for them. "Hello, Jackie," I said, giving her a big, long hug. "It's so good to see you."

"You, too, honey."

I gave another hug to Ray, for good measure, and one to Rachel, the love of his life, as he would call her at Dad and Jackie's reception. "Oh, Katie, look at you," Rachel said, in her high, cracked voice. She was shorter than I but held her head up in a way that seemed as if she was looking down at me, appraising. Her eyes had grown milky since the last time I'd seen her, at Mom's funeral, and it made her look old. "Peri would be glad, you know," she said quietly, gesturing over to the happy couple.

"Of course," I said. Maybe she was rationalizing, maybe she felt responsible, since Dad and Jackie had met the previous summer at Rachel's sixtieth birthday party. I said, "She's put twenty years back on his life, so we all love that."

"She has, hasn't she?"

It was hard not to see it, the way he looked at her with love in his eyes. How she shone under his gaze. How could a daughter not love that?

"Katie!"

From the patio, a blonde with a wide smile and a deep tan waved me outside. Jim motioned for me to go, he had the girls.

I stepped across the grass to the concrete square. Rachel's daughter had been sitting alone on the lawn chairs facing the sunset over the lake. She stood, waiting for me, her blue eyes sparkling like the light upon the water.

"Rachel," I said. "I'm so glad you're here." Yes, her name is Rachel, too. They are as creative with girls' names as my family was with boys'. "There's something I wanted to tell you," I said, after we'd talked of our daily routines and our most notable exceptions thereto.

166

"Yes, I heard you had something to tell me," she said. "About your mother."

I had to pause at that. She knew my mother. She even knew my mom was her mother's big sister in their sorority. And she was adopted, too, so it's not like she doesn't know the lingo, to use some version of birth-mother. Aimee I could rationalize, using the word—she might have only wanted to get in a dig. But Rachel? "You mean Val," I said.

"Is that her name?"

I swore it seemed the light in her eyes was dimming with the sun going down in the water.

I launched into my story, about how Val had called and I thought she was notifying next of kin. I told about Val's visit, and about meeting my birthfather's family as well. Strange, but it seemed this fellow adoptee's interest seemed to fade as I went deeper into my story. And so I pulled back, didn't tell the details that made it interesting, at least more so.

"I tell you all this," I said, "because Val can hook you up with the group she used to find me. You can look, too," I hesitated. "If you want."

Rachel leaned back, away from me. "It's not really a need I have," she said. "But you know I'm so glad for you, you know that."

"I never wanted to look, either," I said. "But then I got the call."

"No, you see," she said, flipping her hair over her shoulder. "That wouldn't make a difference for me."

I measured her, evenly. I did not, could not, know her story. There are many reasons, you know, why a woman would give her child to strangers. Mine was banal, trite. A girl got in trouble, and her parents told her it was the right thing to do. There were other means of arriving at the same end. More interesting stories, perhaps, for a book, but not the kind you want a part of your life. A child can be born of violence, of a stranger grabbing you in the dark vestibule, holding a knife to your throat, making you take him into your apartment where he would rape you and rape you and rape you. Or it could be the date you thought was kind, making sure you had something to drink, and another and another, and you awoke hours later with blood between your legs and an awful realization that what you'd saved was lost forever. Then again, maybe it was a stepbrother, who made you believe it was all your fault. No, you would not want the child born of any of that to visit your doorstep. Nor, conversely, would you want to find out that was your whole reason for existence. And then, to meet the woman who was your future, to see her three divorces later? No, some things are best left unknown.

"It's different for everyone, of course." Or maybe it wasn't. Maybe she'd made the same promise to her mother that I'd made to mine.

"It's not that I'm not happy for you," she said, reaching for my knee. "I am."

"I know."

She leaned back again in the chaise, let the waning sun warm her face. "Does Aimee know?"

"She does."

"Is she looking?"

"I've given her the contact information, but I don't know that she's doing anything about it." Rachel and I watched the martins swooping in and out of the bird hotel Ray had just installed. In and out, whichever babies were there they'd feed. I said, "Dad and I are a little worried for her."

"What do you mean?" Rachel asked. "She won't like what she'll find?"

"It's not always a happy story," I said.

"No," said Rachel, settling back into her chaise. "Sometimes, it just isn't."

"HAVE YOU MET J.I.?"

Everyone had wanted to know. J.I. had quite the advance team. I knew much about him before we ever met back at Dad's house for the wedding. J.I. was surely a formidable combination: a Notre Dame grad and a lawyer. Nothing like having God and the law on your side. He did not practice, but ran the new lawyers division of the Pittsburgh Bar Association. He arranged to have all new members admitted to the Supreme Court—how could he not be loved? At least by the lawyers. Apparently, he loved too much: he'd had some ten children. Jackie had trouble recounting, wasn't sure whether to include children from previous marriages for a couple of his wives. That should have been warning enough, but I was too naïve.

"Where's the goddamn—" were the first words I heard from him as he took the length of the entrance hall and past the bar in three great strides.

Jackie's other brother turned him around to face me. "J.I., this is Jim's daughter Katie," and he nudged his big brother's arm to encourage him to extend his hand.

"J.I., it's a pleasure," I said, but I wasn't so sure of it anymore. I could tell people now that I'd met J.I., and they would say, "Hoo, hoo," as if we were both in on the joke now, but I am not sure I ever got it or thought it that funny.

Boo and Emmy, on the other hand, I met at the bridal luncheon. Jackie's girls. Boo, all right brain, was art editor of a magazine, and Em left brain—all numbers and finance. Their brother was left brain, too, but being a boy he was not at the luncheon. Aimee was supposed to be there, was supposed to have been at the house in the morning helping out, but she had disappeared along the way somehow and Jackie's family, having a bit of Southern gentility in their bloodline, and knowing what it was like to have a sibling who could go astray, were kind enough not to ask any questions, at least not of me.

We carpooled to the luncheon, to downtown Medina. In the 1970s, Medina went through a major downtown renovation, and all the shopkeepers discovered that beneath the sheetrock facades lay master brickwork from a Victorian era. One even uncovered a stained glass window, an Art Deco masterpiece, four feet high and spanning the width of his building. There were treasures inside, too, with a high, tin ceiling, rough hardwood floors and exposed brick walls. It was supposed to make it more beautiful, but somehow, maybe because I was fussy over what was happening, I had the impression that everything had been peeled back, and maybe it would have been better to leave in place some of the trappings the years had accumulated.

"SO IS IT BRADY BUNCH OR CINDERELLA?" Jim asked when I got home from the luncheon.

I busied myself with folding Jenny's nummie, a particularly useless task. "Neither, I suppose." I said. "It's not like they're not nice because they are. It's just that—"

"It's not like we're growing up with them and will have to learn how to share the bathroom."

"No, no we're not. Not like anybody's going to make me scrub floors instead of going to the ball, either," I said. "It's fine. It'll be fine," I said, but I spoke more to convince myself than to tell Jim any different. The connection I felt with Emmy and Boo was akin to what I'd had with Val's kids. Whatever our stepmoms or birthmothers had intended for us to share, undoubtedly it was more than what we kids could offer. As a child born and raised to please, I worried it would never be enough.

"Aimee back yet?"

"No," Jim said.

No word, either.

We did not dare discuss my sister's absence as we chopped vegetables and prepared sauces, set tables and brought up all the chairs from downstairs. There were others in the house now: Jackie's brothers and her sister and their families, and their chatter filled the air. We worked silently, helping Dad prepare the rehearsal dinner, and the worried conversation we would have over my sister we could play only in our heads as the afternoon simmered away into the musk of evening. I was filling the water glasses, and Dad was dumping noodles out of a Dutch oven full of hot water, when I finally had the nerve to ask if we were going to wait for Aimee before we started.

"If she's here, she's here," he said. "I can't wait for her, I've got all these people here." He waved his hand in the air, the one holding the spatula, as if I hadn't noticed there was a reception going on.

Later, much later, Dad would open up about his relationship with my sister. She was doing it again, he told me, asking for money to fix her car but not telling him the whole story. I was old enough, I thought, to tell him he shouldn't help her this time, though I knew as I told him he still would. Dad insisted what he was doing wasn't enabling. It was patience.

"When I took this kid on," he said. "They told us about The Mom. She'd been using, so we knew there could be trouble. I knew it then, and it's up to me to hold up my end of the bargain now." Someone he knew had adopted a baby who turned out blind. "They gave it back," he said incredulously. "That's bullshit." He'd seen sixty years of deal making, and for him, that was worse than reneging on a deal, it was reneging on your kid. So Dad helping Aimee out, even when she fudged the truth, meant simply he was loving her as he'd promised he always would.

"Here," Dad said. "Come help me lay out the dishes." He picked up a serving dish and walked it outside. We laid the dishes around the rim of the covered hot tub, which actually made for a wonderful buffet table. Pot roast and chicken, ribs and a pork loin, all in a row. The nieces and nephews began lining up before Dad, Jim and I were able to shuttle the rest of the dinner outside. Their mood light as the summer breeze. Jackie found some music, some Broadway melodies that joined happy memories of her yesterdays with this day before her wedding. Women in dresses hued of ripe summer days, men in Bermudas. A Chinette in one hand, a chardonnay or a gin and tonic in a plastic cup in the other. One by one the guests, Jackie's family, found a patio chair, a chaise lounge. I hurried back into the kitchen to re-stock, and there was Dad at the stove again, telling Aimee dinner was out on the patio as her new boyfriend skulked behind her.

"Where—" I tried to ask, but Dad shot me a look. Didn't matter where she'd been, she was here now. And as to what she'd been doing all day, whether skipping stones across the creek we'd waded through as kids, or holed up in some hotel room with some drug dealer, or something somewhere blandly in the middle, we were here all together now, as much as we could be. And as hard as it was to keep our perspective, for all of our blessings we should be thankful.

It was my father's wedding day and it was hot. August hot, made worse by no air conditioning, made unbearable by the fact that I forgot to douse myself with cold water at the end of my shower. I was just barely out of the bathroom and already sweat was forming rivulets down my back and my front.

Lovely, it was absolutely lovely to stay at Michele's house that weekend. She'd been my best friend since middle school, she matched me up with my first boyfriend, we were pregnant together for our firstborn children. And it was Michele who watched Jen during Mom's funeral. She was the only thing left from growing up that hadn't changed, I'd wanted to think. She even lived on the same street as way back when. She had a meditation room and a closet full of toys that fell on you when you opened it—two things you'd never see in my mother's house. No, her house wasn't my home, and the deeper into the weekend I fell, the more I came to realize my home would never be the same. Not that the big house ever really was, but Jackie would be there now, along with all her things and all her family.

The heat of the day pressed upon me, and the weight of the heat or maybe my thoughts made it too hard to breathe. I took my cosmetics bag and my hose, and I brought them down to Michele's screened-in porch, and I threw it all in a wooden chair.

"What are you doing?" Jim asked. He was dressed for the wedding, a dress shirt and a tie that would match the dress I didn't have zipped up yet.

I turned my back to him and held up my hair. "Mark's not here, and everyone else is just girls. I'm dying." I stood, waiting, my dress unzipped and still I felt the world too close upon me. "Can you help me out here?"

"Everything's going to be okay, you know."

"It'll be fine," I said. For the love of God, please don't patronize me.

After he secured the hook at the top of my zipper, I showed Jim my hands. "Look at me," I said. "I'm a wreck." My hands had a tremor worse than Janet Reno's.

"Relax."

"If only my brain could tell my body that," I said. I pulled on the front of my dress to cool myself off. "I'm not the one who's supposed to have a dad getting remarried, you know. I don't know a couple who was more in love."

"And that's precisely why your dad is getting married today. You know what your mom would say about it. She'd say you can't make your dad live in the past. He's got Jackie now. Let them be happy together. Even you were saying how smitten he was."

I was on the verge of ruining my eye makeup, but I held back my tears. "He's like a teenager on the phone with her, he is."

"Twenty years, you said, she's added to his life."

"You did."

"Whatever. Be happy for him."

"I am," I said. "I am."

But to be perfectly honest, I was sad for him, too. For as perfectly lovely and Columbia smart as Jackie was, she was not the one he'd planned to love until Death stood at his door.

J.I. WAS GRUFF AND PROBABLY DRUNK ALREADY by the time we arrived at Dad's. Jackie was radiant, a dress of summer flowers and a graceful, broad brimmed Kentucky Derby hat. Perfect. Her only sister, tall and resplendent, as if she could have been a mother of a bride.

"Where should we be?" I asked Dad, but I was looking at Aimee, making sure she stayed within my sight that day. I couldn't stand another day wondering where she was, if she was safe.

"The garden," he said. His suit was black, and his face just as somber.

"You ready for this?" I asked. He looked gray to me, as if he were already standing on the dock at the River Styx. I stood above him in my heels, a vantage point I hadn't yet realized I had. I had to bite my tongue not to ask whether he was shrinking.

"She's a neat lady," Dad said, but he sounded as if he were the one needing convincing.

"She sure seems so." I spoke with the whole of my heart.

"She picked this day because it was her mother's birthday," Dad reminded me. A sweet tribute she'd mentioned to me the night before. Jackie had only lost her mother the year before.

I couldn't help but note with a pang of jealousy her mother had spent thirty-four more years on this earth than my mother had. That was more than the whole of my lifetime.

Like at the rehearsal dinner, I took Dad's wedding one moment at a time. I did not know until we gathered at the stepping stones in the front garden that a judge would preside over the ceremony. I don't know why I thought there would be a priest, with Jackie divorced, and no annulment vitiating the sacramental nature of her marriage (not the fact that it ever happened). But there we stood in the garden the driveway encircled. Park benches faced each other in the center of the garden and created a natural aisle with the judge at the head. The guests gathered in the grass behind the benches. The garden was lush and green and verdant, more than I'd ever known, and I'd wished I'd spent more time there before.

And then there was Ray, walking around the path and then up the aisle with Jackie's sister, who looked so alive there was no way of knowing she held death within her and cancer would take her before the year was out. And J.I. then, looking the role of the dapper older lawyer, his baby sister on his arm, and Jackie glowing and happy, as a bride should be.

The judge wore black for the solemnity of the occasion, but it struck me as the wrong color for a summer afternoon wedding. Maybe only because I was still picturing a priest in his white robes and vestments.

Dad took Jackie's hand, to have and to hold, from this day forward. "'Til death do us part," he said, and the sixty-five-year-old's voice cracked.

I felt the softness on my shoulder, a large wet tear from the heavens. Though the sun still shone upon us, one by one the droplets fell, heavy and full as a day lost to longing.

"'Til death do us part," Jackie said, happily. She turned to the families, her arms spread wide as Jo March. Jackie would have offered her first kiss to Marmee, too, if she'd been there. "Tears of happiness, all happiness," she cried. "You can tell, with the sun. Mom's crying for joy, can you feel it?" she asked, but I did not share in it, not yet, I was still lost in remembrances of darling Peri, who was lost and gone forever, oh, our darling, lost to time.

∞ 19 ∞

For the Cause of the Union

There'll be teepees," Dad said. "We're going to have them lined up on the driveway, and when we light up that bonfire at night," he said, his hand casting the picture before him, "it's going to be cool, man."

My dad, the visionary. He was newly married, smitten in love, and filled with great ambitions for bringing the family together. He'd have a reunion, or in this case, a union. Somehow he'd manage to find all those teepees, he would, and he did. I'd left him and Jackie to their own devices planning the event honoring their alliance, since Jim and I had wrapped ourselves up in a move to Minnesota.

Time came for us to leave our new home and go visit my old one. A thirteen-hour drive, and the longest part was edging up the gravel drive, all the way through the cornfield, through the woods and the gate. There, before us, on the concrete loop circling the garden where Dad had been married two years before, twenty-six native homes stood proud upon the drive.

But that was not all: There were blonds in my father's house. Whole families of them, and I was supposed to count them as part of mine, now. But we Vogls had the coloring of Snow White, and these were Cinderellas. Different fairy tales. I felt worlds apart.

"Dad?" I said. A question, as if wondering whether he was still himself. I gave him a one-armed hug, since I held Julia with the other. She was curled up against my shoulder, still sleepy from the trip.

"Hello, darlin'," he lilted, and led us towards a three-by-three box in the middle of the great room. He reached in and grabbed a handful of khaki tees. "Make sure you get the right size," he said.

Red letters spelled out "Smith-St. Vincent Family Reunion" above the outline of a teepee and the year 2000.

Teepees set up for the Smith/St. Vincent Family reunion.

"You're right," I said. "This is cool, man."

Jackie appeared from out of a throng of blonds. "Hello, dear," she said. "Have you seen the basement?"

"It's finished?"

We'd been up just a few weeks before, when the walls were just getting buttoned up. Workers crawled over each other, dry-wallers and electricians and plumbers. Dad had walked us through his vision for all the rooms, but it was hard for me to see beyond the bare stud walls.

"It's a riot," Jackie said, and would have even if Dad was still in earshot. He'd disappeared to get a drink for one of Jackie's brothers.

"We'll check it out after the girls have their snack," I said, poking a straw through a juice box. "Your nieces here?" I asked. I'd met a few a couple of years before, at the wedding. There was one from Columbus, the blonde who sent the girls stuffed puppies. And there was the nurse from Birmingham who had triplets. Managed them all on her own, without fertility drugs of any kind, she told me within minutes after we met. These are the things you learn to say to people you meet, because you know they are thinking them anyway. I've learned that, since I've met Val.

"Is your mother coming to visit?" Jackie asked.

Sometimes I don't bother correcting people anymore, especially when they know who means what to me. "Val and Joe can come tomorrow night." I said. "How are you doing, hon? Is it hard having everyone here, without your sister?"

Four months after Jackie was married, her sister Patty, the tall and resplendent one who'd stood up for her, had died of bone cancer. I'd tell you it was the same day my mom died, the fourth anniversary of her death, but you probably wouldn't believe me.

"Oh, Katie. You're right. It is hard. I don't go a day without thinking of her," Jackie said. "She was my sister. We talked every day. You know how it is."

Only, I don't. I don't talk to anyone every day. Except Jim and my girls, and I live with them. Maybe I've grown to be a recluse. Maybe I'm withdrawn. I just don't have a need to talk to someone everyday, not since high school. But I did know what she meant, how difficult it was to get tripped every time you went past the hole of someone not there. "It's raw again, isn't it?" I asked. "When the family gets together."

She hugged me. "It is, it is."

Patty's husband breezed through the door. He spread his arms wide. "So," he said, "has anyone seen the love of my life?"

Jackie took my arm and leaned in close. "I don't think I've told you," she said. "Dave's remarried."

I recounted the years since Patty died, but still only came up with one and a half. "Since when?"

"Since about four months ago," she said.

Dave wrapped his arms around a petite blonde.

Seriously, it seemed there were more blondes in Dad's house now than at a summer band concert in Minnesota. We'd seen one first hand, with our recent move.

"Don't ever leave me," Dave said, a little too loudly.

I exchanged looks with Jackie. I ask quietly, "How's the family doing?"

"It hurts a little, I'm sure," she said. She looked me over. "Well, you know."

Dave let go of his bride, perhaps a little reluctantly. He rubbed her arm, looked at her adoringly.

Jackie's expression captured what I felt the first time I saw Dad put his arm around a woman not my mother. How different was that from what Dad must have felt when I brought Val in to meet him?

"Just shows how much his marriage meant to him," I said, using the same words Jim had once given to comfort me. "You know how much he loved your sister."

"Thank you, Katie, you're right," Jackie said. But under her breath, she said, "Still."

"MICHELE," I SAID. "COME IN." My hippie friend and her family, in all their tie-dye regalia, stood at Dad's French doors, swimming towels in hand. The more the merrier, Dad had said. Go ahead, have them come over for reunion weekend.

"You have to see the basement," I said.

Being peaceful people, they agreed. Swim towels trailed down and around the stairs, past the poster-sized pictures Dad took from his first African photo safari. I took a left at the bottom of the stairs, toward where Dad now kept the pool table—by the tack for the eight-horse hitch, polished and shining, from when we owned twenty-six Clydesdales. Not your typical household decoration, I know. Some of Jackie's nephews, ones I hadn't yet met, were playing pool as if they belonged against the backdrop of my childhood. "Oh, hello," I said, as if it were perfectly natural they were there.

Beyond the racks for the cues, the back wall was covered in slate shingles, like the outside of a home. The door even had an eave above it and to the right, a mailbox, flag up. The Grandma Moses room. Inside, a pencil post bed, a writing desk, a country border across the middle of the room. The first of the four themed rooms. On the other side of the stairs, on the way to the others, was a red phone booth, like the kind Superman used. The kids, being kids, ran inside and closed the door. Jen sat on the bench, and Julia tried the phone. The light wasn't working in it yet.

I couldn't help but wonder how much of this Mom would have let him get away with. Maybe it just would have been executed differently.

There was more, like the log cabin room with a false window looking out upon a deceptively real picture of a lush waterfall. The kids ran into the closets on either side, so they could step in front of the scene. They pressed their faces against the window panes and made faces at us.

"Doesn't it look like Camp Mohican?" Michele asked.

"Except for all the dead animals on the wall," Mark said, drily.

"Nobody likes the antlers," I said. They were smaller, the Lower Peninsula kind, posted on fake log walls, all around the three sets of bunks in the room.

"You could put a whole scout troop in here." Mom and Dad had hosted my troop once, but we'd camped out in the back pasture, and I refused to go to the bathroom in that hole in the ground all weekend long. Was this so the girls could camp here in comfort?

At least the Scout master would have it easy—she could stay in Africa next door. The Sahara room had a double bed with mosquito netting draped above, a zebra print chair, and another false window, this time overlooking a baobab tree.

"Folks," Jim said in his tour guide voice, "I'd like to address your attention to the wonderful view we have here, complete with our very own Tree of Life."

Yes, we'd all seen our share of *The Lion King*.

Next door was the Spanish room, with saffron-hued adobe walls and a Santa Fe pine armoire.

"You know," Michele said, "he could totally make this into a bed and breakfast."

"I think he wants to make it easy to come visit," Jim said.

As if Dad needed something to lure me back with Mom not there. I don't know what Mom would have had to say about Dad finishing the basement, or any of the projects he's undertaken since—including pulling a load bearing header out during one of his construction phases. "I'm an engineer," he said. "I know what I'm doing."

Jim's theory is that the construction would still have gone underway, but he probably would have been on a different timeline. And involved more finish carpenters, especially with the projects he's undertaken down at the Florida condo as he's neared retirement. I have to agree, but I worry that I've lost touch with what Mom would have done, what she would have wanted.

Pool time, and Michele and I climbed in with the kids while Jim and Mark sat and had a beer. Which meant Jim played gopher for Dad as he prepped the grill for hamburgers.

"Vogl, go get me the cheese out of the fridge," Dad said, wire brush in hand, scrubbing the grill clean.

Jim came back, a block of cheese unwrapped in his opened palm. "Vinnie, looks like you've only got gorgonzola here," he said.

"Slap it on."

"But the kids—"

"They'll be fine," Dad said. "Slap it on, Vogl."

Well, you can guess how many parents had to scrape every last bit of cheese off their kids' burgers that night.

There were, all told, over sixty people at that reunion. And Dad was doing all the cooking, all the meals. "Jackie wanted to get a caterer," he said. "But this way, we bond together, getting everything done."

Only we'd never had family on that scale before. Dad and Mom each only had one sibling. When we got together, it was one side of the family or the other, never both. Even if we had Dad's sister and her three kids and Mom's brother and his three boys, we would only have seventeen people all together. Which was how many we would have for the big dinners mom used to put on, and growing up we always had friends over more than family.

Mom and Dad had several close friends. I remember the dinner parties, where I'd help put in the extra leaves on the dining room table. Aimee and I laid the table with china and crystal. We'd set the forks in proper order and turn the wine glasses so the proper cut showed, and I'd roll up the napkins like they did at our favorite restaurant, the Oaks. That was before Dad made the plywood circle top for the big house, the one he'd sawed in two, and so sometimes we'd have to snuggle a card table against the side of the dining table and lay matching tablecloths on each, so no one would have to sit at a naughty table (a.k.a. the kids' table) in another room.

Papa grilling at the reunion.

In the summer, Mom served strawberry or cucumber soup or sometimes gazpacho, and in the winter she pulled Oysters Rockefeller out of the oven just as the Haddads or the Wibles knocked on the door. Dinners were elaborate affairs, the *Bon Appetits* and the *Gourmet* magazines would be spread out upon the table as Mom planned out the menu. She'd start preparing days ahead, write lists for the week, and the day of, timing down to the minute when to put the rack of lamb in the oven, when to set out the mint jelly.

But we never had a party for sixty. At least, not that wasn't catered. There are ways to manage having so many people over for a long weekend. Jim's family seems to have worked out a plan: For the past few years, thirty Vogls got together for a long summer weekend to celebrate VoglFest up at a lake cabin. What made it work, besides looking forward to the Paper Plate Awards, was that everybody got along and everybody was responsible for something. Everybody brought their own beverages, which cut down on the problem of people forgetting where they left their drink and deciding just to open a new one. Such a waste, and no one but the host was left to pick up the half-used cans. When we knew Lisa liked Diet Pepsi and Ron liked Mountain Dew, we could ask them if they're finished, but if we didn't know the people and didn't know what they were drinking, we didn't know who belonged to that apparently just opened can of RC cola abandoned on the coffee table in the great room. Conversely, too, if the can wasn't marked, people couldn't be sure it was theirs, and so opened a new one. A vicious circle.

And then there was the problem of getting all the food made and on the table. It was hard enough to do for just my family, never mind operating a small restaurant. Dad had chafing dishes, so theoretically he could make it all work, it was just that doing it all was a big job. The niece with the triplets had picked up some macaroni and cheese for lunch for all the kids, five boxes worth, and they still ran out. The niece from D.C. and one of her cousins took care of shucking all the corn, and it took an hour.

At VoglFest, where we had half the number Dad had at the Reunion, we designated two families per dinner, and then they were responsible for clean up. Dad figured others would step up to the plate, and some did, it's just that no one realized how big a job it was until in the middle of it.

Aunt Joan and Uncle Rugg came for a day, just for the afternoon and dinner. "My little brother told me I should enjoy myself and stop helping, so I'm not helping anymore," said my aunt, who'd always been what my mom called a "worker"—someone who you could count on to get things done. Besides the help Aunt Joan had already given at the reunion, she'd

182

prepared dinner every night she stayed with us when Mom died. And now she wrapped her arms around herself, as if that could keep them from reaching out to put away the RC Cola left upon the game table.

When Val and Joe showed up that evening, I was so relieved to see her. A familiar face, even if it meant another guest to serve. I offered a drink, but Val refused.

"We're here to help," she said. "We're going to help."

"No, you're not."

"Kate, do you know how many people are here?"

"I don't think I have an exact number, but I think it's over sixty."

"And you and your dad are putting this whole thing on?" She didn't let me answer. "You guys aren't from a big family. You don't know what you got yourselves into. We do this all the time."

Dad had planned this approach would bond people together, but mostly it was bonding for him and me and Jim. And now, Val. And Joe.

What a relief. I could finally relax my shoulders. I'd wound them up to my ears by that time of day, with the clean-up from lunch and the prep for dinner. I hadn't sat down all day. My poor little girls had wanted to play in a teepee all day, and I'd never had time to walk them out to the front, much less let them have time to pretend to be Indians. I'd yet to look over one of those things, to see how to adjust the opening at the top, authentically designed to let the smoke out. Dad said it could be closed tight against any rain, but it seemed to me a design flaw.

"We are here to help," Val said. "Really. Just point us in the right direction."

"Chairs," Jim said. "We need to get some chairs over here." Leave it to someone from a big family to not be afraid to ask for help.

DAD HAD PLANNED FOR SATURDAY NIGHT around the bonfire. It was by the garden, in the middle of the loop made by the drive, where Dad and Jackie had wed. Teepees flanked all around, reflecting the flames reaching for the summer night sky.

Jim and I were in charge of Entertainment, and Dad had set us up with a podium and a mike, and we had Family Jeopardy in order to get to know our families better.

The light from the fire lit the faces out of the dark as we learned each other's histories, heard each other's stories.

Who knew that the Smiths had a cannery in Circleville, Ohio, the Pumpkin Show capital? And that Jackie's father had been at Notre Dame the same time Mom's dad had been at Law School there, serving as manager for the Four Horsemen. Small world.

It was late, so late when Jim and I finally climbed into bed.

"Your dad wants us in charge of the next reunion," Jim said.

"God, may that not be for five years," I said. "I don't think I'll have the energy before then." I'm not sure I was awake to finish the end of my sentence, I didn't remember anything until I heard doors slamming in the middle of the night, something thrown on the floor. Voices, toddlers crying. Rain.

"There're mattress pads in the closet," I said, waking from dark depths of slumber. I stumbled into my walk in and grabbed what I could. Half awake still and I pulled the awkward stack of blown up mattresses downstairs. Families, everyone's heads and blankets already soaked, stood stranded, looking for any open space, in the great room, in the office, by the upstairs game table, by the birding chair, even on the hardwood floor in the dining room.

"Blankets," I said, mostly to direct myself, and I ran back up, to dig out what I could find. Hands reached, and the pile was gone before I made it through the foyer. Back upstairs to find another stash, anything dry, especially for the families who'd come with toddlers in tow, who'd been relegated to the out-of-doors, on blown up mattresses, in teepees, grand in design yet suffering a minor, fatal, flaw.

FOR THE REUNION, AUNT SUE HAD CAME up from Massillon with her two younger boys—the ones who used to beat me up when I was young. They were charming now, and handsome, and they hugged me instead of hurt me.

"How are you doing?" I asked. Uncle Jimmy had passed, my last living link to a likeness of Mom.

"Well," she said, screwing up her face in thought, "I just got back from a weekend with the girls—my girlfriends, you know—and I've got a golf trip coming up." She folded her hands in her lap, content with all she'd planned.

I'd been expecting the sadness, the melancholy Dad had wallowed in for so long after Mom was gone. "I guess it's been awhile, now, since he passed?"

"Two years, that's right."

Unbelievable.

"I've finally gone through all his things. You know, I have a bunch of old family papers I'd bet you'd like, since you've taken over as the family historian."

I hadn't done anything since we'd moved to Minnesota. But when the girls started their Mother's Morning Out Program down in North Carolina, I'd gone to the Church of Latter Day Saints and patiently gone through eighteen microfiche, looking for a marriage record in Italy and one in Sweden. I'd sent away to Vital Statistics in three states and countless counties, looking for death records, looking for birth certificates. I'd called churches and cemeteries, looking for dates. I did all this without questioning whether it was my family history I was researching, at least until I ran into some of Mom's distant relatives and told them I'd done the family tree. Did they wonder about my other roots, the ones that had once been hidden from me? Did they think I didn't have a right to them? But this was the side of the family, I'd found, where women had babies a month after their marriage, and children's fathers by blood were uncles by marriage. The kind of family this child born of unintended pregnancy could claim heritage to.

Uncle Jimmy somehow had ended up with the family Bible, not Mom. But we'd had it once at my house because Gramma Verne had written down some of the dates that had been in it and tucked it among Mom's papers. It would have saved so much of my money and time if she'd written down all the earlier generations, too, but life is like that. We don't pay attention to what's in front of us, at least not until we realize it's missing.

The family tree hadn't been my idea, not at first. After Mom had died, Dad had asked for one. "I want it to go back four generations," he said. "Both sides. Mom's got that somewhere. You just have to find it."

But she'd only had one side going back four generations. That left three other branches, two of which had been lopped off years ago when Grandma Jo, his mother, had died and I thought she'd be around forever to answer my simple questions. I spent two years looking to fill in all that information. Now, with Aunt Sue's find, I'd gained a chance to ask the dead what I hadn't before.

"What did you find?" Not expecting anything I hadn't turned up already.

"Oh, I've got a bunch of old stuff," Aunt Sue tossed out. "Even have the marriage certificate of Josh Stewart and Julia Ryan."

"You're kidding."

"That might have saved you some time, if you'd had it?"

"A bit, yeah." The Sound-Exes I'd culled through, the states I had to narrow down from, the hours looking. The thrill of finally having a copy arrive in the mail. I'd whooped all the way down our Cary driveway. I said to my aunt, "You didn't know, though, what you had."

"No idea." She laughed, a toothy grin. "You keep it. It's important to you."

"You know to come to me if you have any questions," I said, wagging my finger at them.

"You were always the smart one," my cousin David said, grinning shyly.

Not so smart if it took me three years to cobble together a tree that could have been filled out by looking through a box in Aunt Sue's attic.

The tree I'd started working on years ago looked different now. So much had been grafted on, now, with Val and my birthfather David's families, and with Jim's. Val hadn't been able to give me hers yet. A relative had done one up and then there was an argument, and she burned all the research she'd done. If I had it, though, I don't know what I'd do with it.

I have a tree from David's side, but without the stories behind the people, the years of stories told around tables, ones ingrained as part of my childhood and grafted into my temperament, somehow the connection to that history is lost. Nor has shared some of these stories, which are too amazing to ever forget—like how the Hall family can trace their ancestry back to William the Conquerer. This I had to tell the girls, to make sure they knew and would remember this history that's theirs.

But I feel less of a connection to that heritage than I do to Mom's and Dad's, and yet if there's anything I could claim a right to, it surely would be that. Maybe part of it is that it's so unbelievable to this history major, to be connected to such an important part of history. Some of Nor's family research even revealed a distant relationship to Elizabeth Cady Stanton, who I'd researched for my honors thesis at Cornell. Would I have approached my subject differently had I known? Would I believe I owned a part of what had happened? I am sure I would have because when I hit reply to all, that I was filled with amazement and wonder, there were no email affirmations. Maybe they just don't do that in that family. Maybe it's their family experience, of course we are a part of the fabric of our culture, of course one of our family members had Frank Baum visiting when he came up with the idea for Oz.

Amazing to say I could be a part of that, even if I don't feel it's totally true. I've adopted Mom's and Dad's tree of life as my own. Truth be told, though, I don't see it so much as a family tree so much anymore. I have a family web, an interconnection, that looks as if it might be so easily broken, but the lines are strong, so strong, and as fine as silk.

∞ 20 ∞

A Family by Marriage

V al asked the question nonchalantly, as if it could be just as easily answered. "So, are you going to come for Chris' wedding?"

This was the part of the call I was dreading. I hadn't talked to Val since the reunion in August, when she'd come to our rescue. After we'd set up the tables, she mentioned that Chris would be married at the end of the year. In four months. And now, just two months to go and she's asking me if I'd come. A mother's asking: voice telling it's expected.

But the last time, the only time, I'd seen Chris was that Thanksgiving, three years before. I'd be someone he'd want in his wedding?

There were other considerations, too. If the wedding was a couple hours away in the car, no problem. But they'd be married back in Cleveland, a thirteen-hour car ride. A thousand dollars easy by plane.

"I don't know, Val," I began in my I-am-about-to-break-some-bad-news-to-you voice.

She must have heard it coming, because she cut me off. "Well, it's really important that you be there. Chris wants you there."

Now? Weren't the bridesmaid dresses ordered months in advance?

"But I haven't heard from him," I said. I wanted to add, ever. "You were the one who told me about the wedding." She was the one who'd wanted him to call.

"He's been meaning to call."

Right.

"Not to ask a huge role from you, but he'd like it if you did a reading."

"Shouldn't he be the one asking me?"

"Oh, he will," Val said. "He will."

As I'm talking to her, I'm walking, walking, walking around the dining room table, a loop out into the living room. "My concern, Val," I began, "is that the wedding is about the couple, about the two families joining together. I show up, and I haven't met these people before, I haven't met anyone else in your family before except your kids, and instead of the wedding . . ." My voice trailed off. I wasn't sure how to put it. "I don't want to upstage the bride, Val."

"You won't," Val said. So earnest. "You won't."

TWO HOURS LATER, THE PHONE RANG AGAIN. Caller ID said only: MICHIGAN.

"Who the hell is that?" Jim asked.

"That's Chris," I said. "Are you sure it's okay?"

Jim shrugged. "If it's important to you."

A vacation that wouldn't quite feel like a vacation, a trip to visit family that wouldn't feel like home.

The phone was ringing.

"My crazy folks," I said, apologetically. Patchwork now; growing up I had it so Disney. Mom and Dad and sister in suburbia before, but now Dad was on a second marriage and living in Florida, and here I was juggling Val and her family and David's family, too. Jim's side was so simple. Large family, nine siblings. But only one set of parents, all sisters and brother belonging to them.

I picked up, hoping Michigan hadn't gone to voicemail. "Hello," I said.

"Is your mom there?" The man said on the line, his voice gentle.

I laughed. "Chris, it's me."

"I'm so sorry."

"No, no, no worries," I said. "I get that all the time. How are you?"

We played catch up then, the way you do with a distant cousin you've lost touch with. A delicate dance of words balanced on the tenuous threads of a relationship. The things you know but shouldn't about someone with whom you don't feel a connection. How long his mother tried to have a baby again before she had him, how his father coached him all through Little League, how his college turned out much more conservative than his mother ever realized, how he got his first job up in Michigan and his fiancée at first wanted him down in Cleveland near home, instead. All this and all I'd done was show him around my father's house a couple of years before.

"You know," he said. "I'm getting married right after Christmas."

"So I heard."

"I would love it if you did a reading."

"Val told me you'd be calling about that."

"So would you?"

"To be frank, Chris," I said, realizing I was speeding around the dining room table again as quickly as I could to get through these most difficult steps of this verbal dance. "I don't want to be barging in on your day, on Lori's day."

"This is something that Lori wants too," Chris said. "She's right here. Do you want to talk with her?"

I almost tripped over a dining room chair. I tried to push it back to the table but it stuck on the carpet, and I had to lift it up to move it. "Absolutely," I said, daring to add: "I just worry Val has put you in the awkward position of having to ask me." Not like me to be blunt, as blunt as Jim could be, but this was no time to mince words. "I can play the heavy, say it was me who said no."

"No, no, we want you there. Here, I'll give you to Lori."

"Hi, Kate," the bride-to-be said. She was gushing, if I didn't know better. Very politely, but nonetheless gushing. I felt old, older. It'd been so long ago that I'd danced her dance. Two states and two kids ago.

190

"I understand congratulations are in order." I knew there was something you're supposed to tell the bride, and something you're supposed to tell the groom, and I could never remember. Actually, I thought I was just supposed to wish her much happiness.

"Kate, we would love it if you did a reading for us."

"Lori, I'd be very pleased to do that, but I don't want to detract from the specialness of your day."

"No, it would mean the world if you were there."

There were only so many times I could go round and round, with the same issues, the same concerns. I'd taken the same song and dance through all these people, all these would-be partners. "I'd be glad to come, then."

I couldn't help but feel we were all doing what was expected of us. The good children, fulfilling parental wishes. Funny thing about parents, though: sometimes they do know what's best for you.

MINNESOTA WINTERS CALL FOR PATIENCE. Nothing runs on time, nothing is expected to, and yet we all keep running. Ten inches of snow overnight, and we do not cancel school. We are too hardy for that and besides, we have the snow plows to sweep it all away. Buses may come a half hour late, but come they will, and school attendance is not taken until the last of the buses arrive.

Airports, however, have quirky birds. Sometimes flights will cancel, and sometimes they'll plow right through. The day of Chris and Lori's rehearsal, the day we were to fly to Cleveland, a storm came through, the kind where flights were canceled.

I called Val to deliver the news. Never even occurred to me to call Chris instead. "We're scheduled to fly out tomorrow, to arrive four hours before the wedding," I said. "We should make it, no problem. I just won't be able to make the rehearsal."

"That's okay, we can work with that."

Next day, sitting on the tarmac, with Julia next to me and Jen next to Jim, I nervously kept checking my watch. We were delayed another two hours—more snow—and time was tick ticking away.

"So you've talked to Michele?" Jim asked from across the aisle.

I nodded nervously, curtly. My friend and her husband, Mark, would be waiting for us, to take the girls right to her house. We'd join them at the end of the night. Nice to have friends you can rely on like family.

Julia curled up in her seat and leaned against me. I had the reading in my lap, the standard wedding verse: 2 Corinthians. "Love is patient, love is kind." I read it until I had it memorized. "Not jealous." I read it until I understood it. "Does not keep score." I whispered the words aloud until the words were a part of me. "And the greatest of these is Love."

But Love would mean nothing if we didn't get to the church on time.

We were not patient, nor kind, pushing our way through to the front of the plane, running down the halls, down the escalator, Jim hurrying along with Julia in one arm, pulling a bag with the other and me pushing Jen in the stroller, a diaper bag looped across the handle and another bag bouncing against my back.

Michele and Mark were waiting at the bottom of the escalator by baggage claim, walking toward us. Mark with his head shaved and Michele's hair so short, I wondered if I could call them hippies still. "You made it!" Michele exclaimed, the wide smile I'd known since seventh grade.

"Not yet," Jim said, setting Julia down and shaking out his arm.

"You will," she said, taking Julia's hand.

"Say good-night," Jim said to me. "We still need to get through the car rental line."

"I've got to tell them what to do with the kids," I said, with forehead wrinkles.

Jim looked at his watch.

Mark gestured to his two tow-headed kids holding onto their legs. "We should be able to figure it out."

I bent down and kissed my honeys on their cheeks. "Bye, sweeties," I said. "Be good."

Jim kissed them, too. "See you when we see you," he said to Mark and Michele. "C'mon," he said, and we were off and running to get the rental.

Nothing is simple: we had to hop a bus and take it to the fourth stop. I called Val from the bus. "We've landed," I said, my knees jiggling. The closer we were, the more nervous I got. "We're getting the car."

"It's going to be close," Val said.

"We're in good shape," I said. "We'll be there." I wasn't half as sure as I sounded. The bus was pulling up to our stop, and Jim and I were standing. We snatched up our bags, ready to go. I was in such a panic I stumbled down the bus steps, caught myself against the bar. A bruise would surely form, but we were out and going, going.

"Meet you in line," Jim said, tossing me a garment bag out of his carry-on. I held it around the middle, bunched in my hand. Around the corner, the ladies' room. Gray, all gray, tiny toilet stalls, and sticky floors.

And I had a formal gown to step into. Powder, lots of powder, to dust off the sweat down my back. The urgency of that change remains with me, and I am right there again, in that restroom, and I am wiping off all that powder on my jeans before I shimmy into my hose, standing on top of my tennis shoes so I don't have to put my bare feet on the floor. Someone else goes into the stall next to me, sits. I brush the powder off, always the powder, and pull the dress out of the garment bag. Whoever's next to me now, they have a stomach issue. I try not to breathe, try to feel like I am freshening myself up. I press myself close to the door without touching it to struggle into the grey lace top. And I bunch up the grey shantung skirt, all the way up, before stepping in, holding my breath that the hem won't touch the floor. There. Into the heels, stuff everything in the bag. God I hope I don't smell, oooh, a spritz of perfume, better. Yank open the door, bag next to me as I wash my hands and run a brush through my hair. The other woman comes out of the stall and barely runs her hand through the water. She gives me a once over. How many people do you see in a formal gown in a rent-a-car bathroom? I slap on eye make-up and blush, concealer for those ever-present dark circles, lipstick because it's a formal occasion. She leaves the restroom and I make a face at the closed door. I have to grab a paper towel to open the door, and I drop it in the garbage as I pull the garment bag through.

I am changed.

"Boy, you clean up nice and fast," I said as I sidled up next to Jim. He already had his credit card out for the attendant.

"You, too," he said. "Was your bathroom as gross as mine?"

"Probably, if not worse," I said. "Of course, ladies do a better job of getting everything in the pot."

Jim signed a form and slid it across the counter.

"Your keys," said the attendant.

"Thanks," said Jim, and we booked for the door.

"How far is it?"

"Question is: how much traffic will there be?" he said, and we swung our bags in the back of a white sedan.

I had the time to look at my watch again. Mom's watch, the one Dad gave for her fiftieth birthday. An hour and a half before the wedding. Ouch.

Across town, through traffic, the distance was interminable. "East side," I said, after looking at the map. Figures, opposite side from the airport. I called Val but only got her voicemail. It was too close to the wedding time. "We're almost there," I said, as we exited the highway, taking the off ramp at a speed that made me lean against the door and know I definitely got a bruise trying not to fall off the bus. We turned onto Sixty-Fifth, and into the stop and go, abrupt with each braking in our rush. I flipped on the air, turned it onto my face.

"You okay?"

I nodded. I did not have time to get sick.

The streets were familiar. I'd lived on this side of town when I clerked in Cleveland after law school. There was this guy from Iowa—Steve. He said he would look me up when he visited Chicago, where I would take the bar. He had a good friend there from high school he planned on visiting. "He's good people," Steve said. I did not know then he was talking about my future husband. Or that Steve would be my firstborn's godfather.

These streets of Cleveland I'd also traveled as a girl, when my mother drove Gramma Verne up to Cleveland Clinic for her heart, which we thought would kill her, and for her cancer, which did.

Down Sixty-Fifth, finally. A sharp turn into a parking lot. "Here, you get out," Jim said. Less than thirty minutes before the wedding. Just made it.

I ran up the steps, into the darkened vestibule, and came to a dead stop. Where was I supposed to meet everyone?

Doors opened to the historic church, wooden pews with torchlights adorned with twisted garland lining the aisle, leading to the altar, under a semicircular apse arching high overhead. Behind the altar, an ornately carved tabernacle, behind which were five arched niches, large enough to house these statues of saints—Jesus, Mary, Joseph and Stanislaus, for whom the church was named. There was another, but I didn't recognize him. Mary was in the center, flanked by angels, and above them five stained-glass windows stretched to the dome above the apse. Maybe that was not Mary, but rather Jesus in the center, wearing her color blue. Years later I would learn the dome over the apse threw the priest's voice back to the people at a time when priests faced away from the congregation to say their prayers, before the mid-1960s. In Catholic speak, pre-Vatican II.

A phrase came to mind, a corny one, but I believed it as I stood in that darkened vestibule: Verily, this was a holy place. I took it all in, even the church ceiling, sky blue with gilded accents, and I was mesmerized by the awesome beauty, having forgotten what a place of worship can look like. The church we'd been attending, which has since been renovated, has been described as 1950s outstate cabin décor, though the people and the pastor more than made up for what the ambiance once lacked.

"Katie! You made it!"

I turned and there stood Val and Joe, as if they'd been there all the time.

"It's just beautiful," I said. We hugged hello, like old friends. Or family.

The door opened from the outside, and December air blew in along with Jim. He gave Val a hug, Joe a handshake.

"The bathroom's down the stairs," Val began as I took off my coat.

Oh, God, I am meeting all these people and I do smell.

"Oh," Val said, "you've changed! You look lovely. Where did you change?"

"You don't want to know," I said.

195

"Rent-a-car bathrooms," Jim said. "Need we say more?"

Val laughed, a relieved happy laugh.

"So where do I need to go?" I asked.

She shuffled me to the priest, who walked me through what to do—when to come up to the podium, where to sit in the sanctuary, how to wait for the other readers and not turn to go back to the ornately carved Lector's chairs, but wait, wait to walk back down into the congregation. Val stood at the bottom of the steps, watching, a funny little smile upon her face.

I stood at that ambo and looked out at the pews, flanked on both sides by pointed arches running the length of the church. Some had begun milling at the back of the church, a few already seated in the pews.

"How far back will the people go?" I asked.

"Pretty far back," Val said. "All of Lori's family is in town. And you know how big my family is."

"Everyone's here?"

"Everyone but Jan and Lil. They're out in California."

That still left eight siblings, spouses, and children. Not to mention friends. I hadn't had to play the cocktail game in a while, matching names and faces, making meaningful small talk, all I'd signed up for when I'd agreed to come.

Yes, this would be quite the night.

DON'T TURN BACK TO THE LECTOR'S CHAIRS, I repeated to myself. Wait for the others to walk down. But I could still envision my gray skirt spinning beneath me, making me worry I'd do it again, just as I had during my brief brief practice, before I knew I wasn't supposed to turn back.

I was seated next to Jim near the front of the church, near the other lectors. A well-worn page lay in my lap. I was mouthing the words once again.

"It's just a reading," Jim said. "Relax. You're not the reason everyone's here today."

I bit my tongue, ready to differ. But that would be gross. After all, I was not that important, I was not the reason we'd gathered that evening.

"It's like they told me at lector training," he said. "Don't let the reader get in the way of the reading."

We held each other's gazes for a long moment, until he placed his hand over mine.

"You'll do fine," he said.

The organ changed tunes. Time for the processions to begin. Val first, on the arm of an usher, her face shining pure with joy. Her dress I wanted to remember always: a perfect cut, with a fitted bodice, shimmering jacket, a skirt that graced the floor, skimming along the aisle. Lori's mom next, a lovely lady. What Lori would be in twenty some years.

Another change of melody; the organ and then the trumpet solitaire, the slow procession up the nave. A glowing bride, oh, she was beautiful, handsome groom waiting at the crux. There, that's Chris. Would I have recognized him now if I passed him on the street? I don't know, I don't know, maybe I'd think he was familiar. But could I place him? Allisyn I could, I was pretty sure at least. She looked great, so great, in her bridesmaid dress. Her gown draped crimson against her ivory skin, her blonde hair swept up and off her face. Yes, I would know her if I passed her on the street.

Odd things to wonder at your half brother's wedding, but perhaps it was better than worrying that my reading was the only chance I'd have for sure to talk to all the family there. I wanted so desperately to reach out to them all, to let them know everything had turned out okay for me and for Val, but these words I'd been given were the only way I could say I was there for love and appreciation of all Val had done for me.

I was there for family.

The other reader rose up out of the congregation and walked up the short flight to the sanctuary, and so I followed, sitting next to her in the second chair for lectors. The mass was familiar, the structure what I'd come to know through the years. Jim's uncle, Father Bob, had once told me how comforting it was to know as he offered up his prayers, there were so many others across the world doing the same. One with God, one as a people. I was seated up in the sanctuary, I was one of many.

And, by some plan of God, there was a reason I was there that day.

I arose and walked to the ambo, and I lifted my head to speak. The words were there for me on the lectern, but I knew what I had to say that night, words first given by the grace of God. I had an idea how to deliver the lines. I'd taken drama in high school. Our final was a monologue, and I nailed it, I swear. I'd become the character, a nineteenth-century maiden beseeching understanding, not sympathy. I left the class stunned and silent when I clambered down off the stage, back to my seat. "Any critiques?" the teacher asked, but no one had any, not even Dave Lindburgh.

"Don't let your voice screech," the teacher said. "When women are nervous, up on stage, your voice gets tight, screechy. That's my only critique for what you did today."

So up on that podium, I kept my voice low, kept the words earnest. I was not the reason we were there that day, but I wanted them to know the meaning of those words. Those, too, would be my gift, for them to always remember.

The greatest of these, I told them, is Love.

ॐ 21 ॐ

A Family Reception

Jim and I lingered for a while after the ceremony.

"I suppose I should introduce myself to the bride," I said.

"I don't know you're going to get a word in, not here," Jim said. The people had long ago filed out, row by row. The photographer was starting to stage people around the bride and groom. "Let's head out to the reception. You'll be able to catch them there."

I caught Val's eye as we headed down the aisle, coats draped over our arms. I gave her a thumbs up, then a little wave. "See you over there," I said.

She nodded absently and waved us on.

In the years to come, Val would never forgive herself for that.

"I didn't get a picture of you with them," she'd lament, whenever we talked about the wedding. "I hate that. I'd even told the photographer I wanted that picture." But me stepping up to the front of the church with the rest of the wedding party didn't occur to either of us at the time. Maybe because I hadn't grown up with them, maybe because I hadn't been there the night before. I'd arrived too early for Val in her life, too late on the scene that day. Maybe it was simply because I wore grey, and the bridesmaids wore crimson, and we'd had it ingrained in us, like Sesame Street, to understand which one just didn't belong.

"NOW WHAT?"

We were standing in the lobby of the Cleveland Marriott. The wedding party had begun; there were people in the ballroom, there was a line before the bar. Laughter spun like silk, woven in chords of music dancing through the night.

We'd walked in on a family function, and we did not know the family. Strange thing was, the family knew us. At least, they knew of us. That I'd stood alone up at the ambo helped single me out. I didn't notice, but Jim could tell people were whispering about us. Look, you know who she is, don't you?

"Kate, I am so glad to meet you," a woman came up to me and took my hands. She was shorter than I, heavier probably than she'd like. Eyebrows arched and eyes sparkling. "I'm Arlene, Val's sister."

It took all my effort not to poke Jim. This was the woman who would have raised me if Val hadn't placed me for adoption. This was the woman who'd wanted to show up on my doorstep, unannounced, when Val finally told her sisters that she'd found me. All this I had to hold in, not tell him until she'd finally walk away. "I am so glad to finally meet you," I said instead.

"Val has us sitting together, so we'll have lots of time to catch up," she said. She was a nurse, she said. She and her husband were living down in Texas, but she was trying to move back up to Ohio. "To be with family," she said.

"Well, it's home," I said.

Another woman approached, shorter than Arlene. Or was it that her hair wasn't teased so high for the occasion? "I'm Gloria, Val's oldest sister," she said.

Funny thing with so many kids, you get a broad spectrum of genes. Like in Jim's family, a few of the siblings look so much alike, while a couple don't look anything like the rest. Jim's sister Judy used to take her younger, tow-headed sister Sally into the back bedroom and point to a strongbox up on a high shelf. "See, those are your adoption papers," she'd tell little Sally, the only blonde in that black Irish family.

"Can you believe how mean I was?" Judy will ask now.

I can. I know what the Bebba told my sister.

So Arlene got all one parent's genes, and Gloria and Val shared another's. And neither set looked like me.

As Jim pointed out, it still didn't keep people from gesturing my way, pointing, whispering, nodding. "We're the freak show," he said under his breath when we were alone.

"No," I said. "We're just stuck in the *Twilight Zone*." It was surreal, meeting the people who would have been aunts, who when you were little would have been the ones who got you the wrong color sweater for Christmas and you'd still have to wear it next time you saw them, who'd send you home with the cookies you wished your mother would bake, whose houses you'd know as well as your own, because that's where you'd alternate the holidays and where you'd go when your mother just felt like a visit.

Not far from me the crowd opened up, and there stood the bride. A couple was just leaving her. "Looks like now's my chance to meet my half-sister-in-law," I said. The term felt weird in my mouth, like a magician's trick gone bad.

The bride was beautiful, slim, doe-eyed, and suddenly free for me to meet.

"Thank you so much, Lori, for inviting me to be a part of your wedding." Strange words of introduction, said at the reception, but they seemed fitting at the time.

"I'm so glad you're here," she said, reaching with her arms as if in supplication, to give me a hug.

"Oh, Chris, hello to you, too," I said. Another hug. "I was just telling Lori here that I'm so glad for the chance to meet everyone," I said, sincerely.

"You did an amazing job on the reading," Lori said.

"Oh," I said, "It's just a reading."

"No, seriously," Chris said. "The way you said it, it was like I could finally understand what it all meant."

I smiled. I passed this final, too. "Thank you." This was what Val had hoped for, this connection we'd feel for each other. A genuineness we'd hear in each other's voices whenever Val handed him the phone when his family was with her.

"Allisyn's looking for you," Chris said. "Have you seen her yet?"

"No, but I've been wanting to say hi."

"I think she's by the back bar."

I found Jim on the way, so we stopped for a breather. "How's it going?" he asked.

"Okay," I said, not convincingly. "It's kind of overwhelming."

I saw Allisyn at the other end of the hall. She was standing with a couple of the ushers. Her laugh was loud, her movements exaggerated. She swayed as she talked, her hand finding the sleeve of the usher closest to her as she talked.

"You can't interrupt her now," Jim said.

"Allisyn?" I said, loud enough for her to hear if she wanted to, soft enough to ignore if she didn't.

She turned as I'd said it. "Oh, hi!"

The boys next to her dropped back. "We'll catch you later."

She reached out her hand to them, whether releasing or holding onto whatever connection had been made, I don't know.

Jim said hi, but excused himself to the restroom. "I'll let you girls catch up," he said.

"You look great," I told her, and I meant it.

Allisyn grinned and blushed, eyes sparkling with the prospects of the night.

"So," I said, "Seattle's treating you well?"

She nodded. It was not what she was here to talk about.

I felt like the aunt who lived away, who pinched cheeks and offered kudos for growing. We hadn't talked directly since the Thanksgiving I'd met her, though Val always gave updates when we talked. We'd sporadically exchanged Christmas gifts, this year because we'd see each other at the wedding. I had the feeling Val did the shopping.

I admit, I felt a pang of jealousy at that. How I wish I still had a mother to be there when I was at a loss for what to do.

There were the usual questions, about her apartment and how the job search was going. About her dog, a beagle, Janie. How Janie had handled the move from Cleveland out to the coast.

The questions came easier for me this time than they had at that Thanksgiving, but I didn't yet feel the ease with her as I just did with Chris. Val would ask in a couple of years if I would go to Allisyn's wedding in Vegas, too, but she didn't push so I didn't go. If I had, would the marriage have lasted? At least I would've shown more support for her, something a Catholic presider asked wedding guests to provide.

And, without knowing her more, I tried to give Allisyn what I could that dark December evening.

Allisyn sometimes struggles still (as we all sometimes do), and I'm reluctant to ask what I can do, just as I'd been when she was a student struggling at Kent. Struggling alone is Swedish, convincing yourself you don't need any help, convincing another won't want any. Celebrations, on the other hand, are Irish. For all to share—with each other.

That's how Val found us, chatting together, part of the celebration. "Look at you," Val cried, happiness resonating in her voice that Allisyn and I had sought each other out without her prodding. More than that, though. More than the joy that her son married that day, too. For here was the child she'd never been able to claim out loud, for all to see and know and perhaps even love as she did.

Finally, she'd later tell me, she could begin to believe she was whole.

VAL PASSED ME AROUND FOR INTRODUCTIONS that night. I met the faces to pair with the names she'd often mentioned over the phone—her friend Annie, her boss, Jennifer. Her siblings, their children. Before we walked back into the reception hall, I had Val run through the birth order of all ten of her siblings. As she introduced me to them, one at a time, I tried to remember where they fit in and where she'd told me they lived. I somehow even managed to remember what they did.

At the table, Arlene tested me.

"Gloria, Arlene, Mary Anne, Carole, Val, Jan, there's the gap, then Margaret, Pam, Bob, Greg, and Lil," I said. It was what big families did, at least Jim's did too; the faster you could run through the siblings, in order, the more you really cared. Never mind that the mother would start with the oldest when asking someone to do something and run through all the names until she got to the child she meant. I even do it for my small family, only I start with the dog and then Julia on up. Maybe it's just a way to make me feel better about having a terrible memory. Maybe I shouldn't be telling that.

This, though, I'll readily confess: I could run those names off so easily that night, but now I have to look them up, to be able to do it still. I did remember they had a gap, too, a couple of years where the mother just couldn't have another, she's so worn out. Jim's family had the bottom four; he's the second oldest of that group. And in Val's family, with one more, it was the bottom five.

I do not remember meeting all of them. I only remember that those faces, one after another, did not look like mine.

During dinner, Arlene could tell something was bothering me. Then again, you know me and my poker face.

"You know, it's funny," I said openly. No reason to keep secrets from a family that held such a doozy for so many years. "As an adopted child, you have this idea that if you walk down the street one day, you might see someone who might look like you, and you would know you were related, just from that. But here, here are all these people, and I don't see a strong family resemblance. I just don't."

Her face fell as quickly as the soufflé I once tried to make. "Oh, Arlene," I said. We apparently had the same poker face genes. "I don't question at all who Val is to me. I knew right away, when she listed the background info, the non-identifying information on my—" I hesitated, then wondered why I was hesitating. This was who they were. "My parents."

"You know who you look like," Arlene said. "She looks like Kathy, don't you think, Gloria?" It was a mission, then, for Arlene, to badger her husband to put down his fork and go find my supposed look alike among the guests.

Mission accomplished. Ed came back with a woman, tall with cropped hair. She had almond eyes, wide arching eyebrows, and a pointed chin.

Arlene took over. "Kate," she said. "I'd like you to meet Kathy."

I scrabbled out of my chair, standing up with my hand out to greet her. Jim was already standing next to me, his hand extended, too. She took it, but like so many others that night, they didn't take advantage of their chance to get to know him as well.

But back then I was busy thinking, Yes, definitely, if I saw her on the street, I would have wondered, before.

And finally I knew.

"So nice to meet you," I said, wondering how she could get away with a cropped cut and I never could. My face was too long, short hair always made my head look like a hot dog. But even with the hair, hers short, mine long, anyone could plainly see she could be the one, she could be my long lost relative.

Finally, I thought. After all these years.

I found out later, much later, that Val didn't see the resemblance.

"IT WAS A LOVELY WEDDING," I TOLD VAL when I got home. "I'm so glad I could be a part of it."

"Everyone loved meeting you," she said. Not because it was a social nicety to say, but because she meant it. Genuine and sincere, as I've come to know her.

Jim, on the other hand, had to point out that, of course, everyone liked meeting me, given the story behind who I was. Didn't I notice the whispering? Didn't I see the pointing? I like to think he was more self-conscious than I was, that we didn't detract from Chris and Lori's special occasion.

And there was another one, maybe not quite so special, coming up. It was my turn to raise the issue with Val. No way Val would bring it up, not with the stink I had raised before. Never mind what my mother had taught me about proper etiquette.

"You know, Val," I said. "If you want to send me a card or something for my birthday, I wouldn't mind. Not at all."

"I was hoping you'd say something," Val said. "It really was getting ridiculous, Kate. That presents were okay for your girls, for Jim even."

"No, I know."

"But you wouldn't mind now?" This was where this came from, the double checking that drove Jim crazy sometimes. "I mean," Val said, "you really wouldn't mind a present either—that would be okay?"

Who was I to turn down a present? I don't think it had anything to do with greed (well, maybe) or that she'd worn down my resistance over the years (maybe that, too). But I knew the spirit in which it was offered, the same spirit that could offer up a part of herself, and give that most precious gift away just to keep it safe.

And the only way I knew how to say how much that meant to me was to offer that gift right back. Maybe I, too, could give over a part of myself.

❧ 22 ☙

Trimmed in Rickrack

al's turn to get a gift. Her birthday, Valentine's Day, and I had something in mind to give her, more than the gift I'd sent in the mail.

"I've been thinking," I told her over the phone. "We need something, some name, for the girls to call you."

"Yes," she said, the syllable ripe with anticipation.

"Because it's weird for them to still call you Miss Val," I said. "That's not fair. It's like you're a stranger." Like someone a mom and dad would warn a child about. We'd established even in our first telephone call that I should call her Val. It never occurred to me I should have a different name for her. But she'd come to mean so much to my girls.

She'd earned a name, as much as my mother had in changing our diapers.

"Friends that are close, the girls call them 'Aunt So and So,'" I said. Like Christin. And Michele. "But that wouldn't be right. You're not an aunt, certainly."

"No."

"So I was wondering," I said, "if there's something the girls should call you."

It'd become such a dilemma. "Grandma" wasn't something I'd suggest, either. That was reserved for Grandma Teresa. Jackie was just Jackie, probably more a function of her not quite ready to be called a grandmother when we first asked her what she wanted to be called. Confused the bejesus out of Julia. For a while she was even calling Grandma Teresa "Jackie." Not because they looked alike, but because that's what she thought grandmothers were called. And I'd used "Gramma" for Mom's mom and the more correct "Grandma" for Dad's (couldn't use incorrect grammar for the schoolmarm, no matter how much we loved her), but these names were from a time when there was no question who was what and where up in my family tree. This time, this face, seemed to call for a new name. A variation. Something I could give her that wouldn't take away from Mom. Or Teresa. Or Jackie.

It would be a way for me to start giving over, to start giving back.

"Would something like 'Nana' work, do you think?" I asked. "Like, Nana Val? Would that be okay?"

"Oh," Val said, "that would be wonderful." Her voice sank into the cushioned syllables of her last word, leaving me to wonder if I'd given too much in the offer. Growing up, the name Nana had not meant Grandmother to me, but maybe it could for my girls.

For this, I did not think I needed to heed my mother's warnings about not being able to go back. Those admonitions had been for me, not my children. And Val had found me through Mom's obituary. This must have been what Mom had wanted, too. When Mom could not be with me, she'd sent Val my way.

Someone trained as a lawyer, trained to see where things might go wrong, should have known that rationalizations such as these will inevitably lead to complications.

THE WORD "NANA" FLOWED EASILY OFF MY PEN when I addressed envelopes for the girls' thank-you cards after a birthday. The word felt right, coming from the girls when I handed them the receiver, didn't sound at all jarring as when someone called Val my mom. Maybe, like for Nor and her family, only because I'd never been cautioned that these connections could be construed as familial disloyalty. Whatever the reason, I felt I could ask Nana Val to come up for Jen's First Communion. I'm not sure that I expected her to say yes. It was, after all, a thirteen-hour drive each way. I couldn't even offer a bedroom for them; I had two other sets of grandparents and a pair of god-parents to offer the room first.

But I didn't know the power of regret, what it could make you do without question later in life. I should have known: Of course she said yes.

"YOU'RE HAVING WHO OVER?" the ladies in my book club wanted to know.

Book club, still a constant in my life. And again, something I had lined up before we moved in—this time, through my realtor, Marty Siegel. Talk about full service.

"Whatever you need," he'd said. "Whatever group or cause you want to get involved in, just ask. I want to you to feel at home here, from the start."

First things first. "A babysitter—one I can trust. And a book club."

We were stuck at a light, which seemed odd on an entrance ramp, but that's how Minneapolis deals with managing traffic flow on their high-ways.

He turned to me, a smile spreading the distance between being sur-prised at and pleased with himself. "I can do that," he said. "I can do both. My goddaughter lives around the corner from your new house. And I know a woman who's in a book club. She'd love to have you."

Later, I learned he'd asked for a *mitzvah* from a woman who'd strung him along for three years, looking for a house, before Katy finally built one— with the husband she met and fell in love with during the time she was house hunting. Funny the ways friends are brought together.

The women in my book club shared everything together, from jobs to pregnancies suffered and lost. I felt safe telling them the story about Val.

They had been the first I'd told outside my family, outside my childhood friends. But with Val coming over, and being a part of my daughter's ceremony within our church community, I figured I needed to start sharing her story. Who she was, why she was with us.

"Well, there's a story to tell," Katy said. "You should write a book, that's what you should do."

"No," I said, not willing to admit I had already started writing. Snippets and pieces while the girls were at school. Took a year before I'd confessed what I was doing to my husband. What I was doing was rough, not well-formed.

The other women in book club were Minnesota nice, encouraging. "You really should," they said. And, "Why not?"

"No," I said. "Not yet." What more could I say? I didn't know how my story was going to end. More than that, I was afraid to confess that I'd begun to write. No task is as terrifying and as awe-inspiring as doing what we want most out of life.

SO MANY PROJECTS TO DO BEFORE EVERYONE came for First Communion. Most important, of course, were the Mother's Day gifts. For all the big holidays, Halloween and Thanksgiving included of course, I pored over magazines and searched the web for just the right craft for the kids to give their grandparents. We'd shop at Michaels' and pick up supplies, and then I'd herd the girls down into the basement and spread newspapers over the craft table. That's when the real work began, with popsicle sticks and glitter and Elmer's glue, with finger-paint and dot paint and tiny cylinders of poster paints all connected in a row and the tray of watercolors with a lid that wouldn't break off until at least the second time we used it, and forget trying to use the wisp of a brush included, laying in place along the edge. That's what broke the lid, usually, in the first place. Within ten minutes we'd all have paint all down our fronts and hopefully all of it ended up on our paint shirts and didn't get on our real clothes, not even on our cuffs, but we weren't always so lucky.

The only mathematical certainty in doing art projects with the girls was that clean up time was inversely related to how much time the project took.

We went to Michael's at least three times for supplies for this mother of a project. And it was: the girls helped me pick out all the usual suspects—paint and glitter and even those sheets of pink and yellow foam. But this project required new and dangerous parts, too, like dowels and florist bricks and even some rickrack.

Rickrack scared me. Any time I had to head over to the fabric side of a craft store, I get a little nervous. A lot nervous. I shouldn't, I certainly spent a lot of time around sewing projects when I was little. Mom sewed us Halloween costumes and even some bat wings for our first tap dance recital. She sewed a Betsy Ross outfit for herself and a Minuteman outfit for Dad for a 1976 Bicentennial party. She sewed us dresses when we were little, but somewhere around me starting junior high she stopped. I'm not sure why. Maybe it was simply because she started working for Dad, doing the books for the concrete ready mix mixer company he'd started up, or maybe and more plausibly because I was too cool then for something not purchased at the Limited.

But when I was little, before nursery school even, I loved whenever Mom said she'd sew me a new outfit. She would take us to the sewing store, where she'd pore through the books, page after vinyl page, while Aimee and I flipped though the packets in the bins, and by the time Aimee grew bored and climbed underneath the bins to hide, I would be lost in the possibilities each new outfit held. The drawings I loved most, the slim models in gorgeous, well fitting clothes, with windswept hair, a go-go-booted foot raised. Kicky, very kicky.

Mom had promised she would make matching dresses for me and my sister. She showed me the pattern, a sleeveless dress with the flower growing all the way up the front. "It'll look different," she said. "We'll use this gingham fabric, and I'll size it, so the flower will stay pretty."

"It's perfect," I said, but I was looking at the picture.

I got to hold the pattern on my lap all the way home, but the bolts of fabric were carefully laid in the trunk of our Skylark. The engine hadn't

211

yet sputtered off when I was in the house, packet clutched to my chest. I ran down to the laundry room and thudded the pattern onto the folding table. Mom took forever to come down. She told me I had to wait for her to open up the envelope and she would—not me—carefully pull the tissue paper patterns out and spread them out upon the folding table.

"Are you done yet?" I'd ask her, as she cut up the paper and placed them on the fabric. She showed me how you had to lay the pattern just so, so the lines on the gingham stayed perfect squares and didn't become diagonals, and she pinned it in place.

"Are you done yet?" I asked, as she cut out the fabric and pinned it together—backwards. I sat on the bench while she threaded the bobbins, while she laid the wrong-side-out fabric under the needle. I stood in the doorway, a better view, while she pumped the pedal, and I leaned my cheek against the doorjamb as the fabric raced along straight and then slowed around curves and corners.

"Are you done yet? I asked, as she laid out the cut out fabric petals underneath the floppy collar she'd worked on while I was napping. She folded the last of the pattern neatly and reached above the dryer for her filing system for her patterns.

I was confused. She did this as she finished with a dress, but this one didn't look anything like the one I remembered on the envelope.

She found the right pattern out of the box and tucked all the cut papers neatly back in the envelope.

"Here, let me see," I said, reaching for the packet. I looked from the pattern, a sunny yellow dress, to the black and white criss-cross pattern that lay before me. "It looks different," I said.

"I told you it would," she said patiently as she slid the packet back in the box, properly alphabetized. She tucked it back above the dryer, then unrolled the rickrack, the wavy line for the stem. Back at the sewing machine, she sewed that rickrack on all the way from the hem on up to the collar.

I should have been so excited when Mom said, "It's done," but she was holding up a dress that did not look anything like what the pattern said it would be.

"Where's all the yellow?"

"I told you, honey, it was going to look different." She held it up to my shoulders and let it rest there.

I fingered the daisy on the front. That was the part that was perfect. "It's too short," I said.

"You always wear shorts underneath anyway," she said, but she frowned as she held up the dress against my shoulder and touched the hem against my leg. "You and your sister will look so cute in these together."

"It feels like wallpaper," Aimee said up in her room, when Mom finally made her try it on. No way she'd ever be excited about a dress, not like me.

"It's the sizing," Mom said. "That's what keeps the flower looking fresh."

Aimee made a face.

"You two will look so cute together. It'll be perfect for pictures."

I held out the bottom edge of my dress, keeping my eye on that flower, and sidled next to my sister. Aimee shouldered me away.

I looked up to my mother for a rendering of justice as I ran my fingers along the bottom of the hem.

It was too short already, even for a four-year-old, even though Mom left enough room to let it down a couple of times.

And, now that I thought about it, it did feel like wallpaper.

OUR CHURCH ALLOWED ROOM FOR SIX in a pew, including Jenny, for her First Communion. That's their way of telling you to ask the godparents to sit with you, because there's no way you can favor one set of grandparents over the other during a sacrament, not if you're Catholic.

Catholics are also territorial, just as much as Protestants, but they won't admit it. Husbands get out of the way and head to church an hour and a half before Christmas masses, just to lay coats down, to mark off their spaces. I've come out of the children's mass and run into people milling about in the narthex, ready to rush in and take a seat for the following mass.

The worst part is, the people who only show up for Christmas and Easter throw a wrench in the weekly seating assignments every family so neatly work out over the years. For sacraments, when family comes in from out of town and then assigned to a mass different from when they normally attend—well, it's enough to throw the most regular folk off kilter.

Like us Vogls.

"I'll go save a spot for folks," Jim said, as I was fussing with securing Jenny's veil on her head.

He left before she said her next, "Ow."

"I don't know why this is being so fussy," I said, half-apologizing. Maybe the head bobbing in excitement didn't help. I had to readjust at the church.

"I've got to line up, Mommy."

"One more bobby pin."

"No, I don't need it, I've got to—ow!" She was pulling away, trying to go line up, like she was supposed to. Her father's daughter, I swear. She's a better person than I.

She was among the first in line. Mr. Erickson nodded at me. "Go on," the big bear of a man said. "She's fine. We'll see you in there."

"Okay," I said, but I wasn't entirely sure that headpiece would stay in place, not with her hair all smoothed back in that bun.

I hurried back into the church, smoothing the front of my pink Jackie O suit. All I was missing was a pink pillbox hat.

I saw Jim's oldest sister and her husband, Bob Pence, next to all the grandparents. For once, the Pences were early.

I should talk.

Dad was ready with the camera, Jackie was talking with the woman behind her. Bill and Teresa were settling in their pew, centering themselves for prayer.

I slid in the pew, next to Jim. "I didn't see Val and Joe."

Jim craned his neck around. "Maybe they're not here yet," he said.

But she didn't drive thirteen hours to miss the sacrament. I eased my way past Julia, my heels tapping across the church floor into the Narthex. A man with a camera slung around his neck stood at the door, rocking on his toes, trying to find his family in one of the row upon rows. A mother pulled a preschooler to the restroom, one last potty stop before the marathon mass. Families came together and parted in the gathering space, and I wandered through them all, looking for Val.

I saw her before she saw me. I saw worry lined in her face, that she could be here and yet not where she should be. Her opened silk jacket fluttering behind her in that lone rush through the narthex.

"Val," I said. "You're fine." There was still time, time to settle in.

She stopped, and her face relaxed into a smile. "I'm glad I caught you," she said, and we hugged hello.

"It's about to start," I said, master of the obvious.

A woman I knew from bible study touched her hand on my arm. "Big day," she said.

God, introductions. I hadn't told my friend Susan about Val and her visit. I'd laid the groundwork for the people I'd know I'd run into, told them ahead of time Val's story. But I hadn't expected to see Susan. I couldn't very well tell all the sordid details now, could I? And yet of all my friends, this one would most understand. She would soon adopt two children from Guatamala and not have any qualms about calling her children's birthmothers "mothers," too. I told myself this was because they were thousands of miles away, that there was and never would be an immediate threat she could show up on her doorstep. Little did she know who had shown up on mine.

"Susan, this is Val, Jenny's grandmother."

Susan looked at me, questioning. "Your mother, then?"

"Well," I said. I should have known Susan, of all people, was too smart to let my politically nuanced statement stand alone. "Yes," I said. The mass was starting and I didn't want to go into the long explanation. A truth and a lie, one for the woman next to me and one for a man—my father—already inside the holy space.

The feeling, like the morning after a one night stand with someone you thought you'd really liked. (Not that I would know what that was like, Dad.) And Val was grinning, so happy for the moment I'd given her, and we said our good-byes at the door to the worship space, all of us quitting each other for our respective places. Val up in the choir loft, me in the front.

And as I slunk down the aisle as the music started, I resolved never ever to do that again. I kneeled and crossed myself before sliding into our reserved pew, next to Jim and Juls and Jen's godparents. Girls in white and boys in suits stood at the back door to the church, awaiting their cue, and then as two great long lines, walking in pairs up the aisle, came the procession of second graders. One by one the communion dresses paraded by, with cameras flashing. At the right moment, Jim leaned around me, half standing to get a shot of Jen smirking as she walked by. She didn't seem to notice her veil was hanging by a lone set of criss-crossed bobby pins.

I prayed the pins would hold, I prayed Julia would behave the whole mass through. I prayed it was the right thing to invite Val and Joe, to have them here along with Jim's and my folks.

Mostly, I think, my prayers were answered. Jen's veil didn't come completely off. Julia must have made it through because she's still alive.

Pictures afterward and we didn't discover until we got the packet that Jen was going through the I-don't-know-how-to-smile-for-the-camera phase, the one where instead of grinning she curled her upper lip above her gumline. Yes, just about as attractive as that sounds.

We did manage to catch a couple of natural smiles at home, as Jen stood among her grandmothers. She'd just given each of them one the flowerpots we'd made, the green-painted dowels as stems, with tulips glued on made of pink and yellow foam cut into the shape of our hands—left and right of both Jen and Julia and even one of me, decorated with stripes of rickrack and scattered jewels.

As Jim made everyone stand close for a picture, Val turned the pot around in her own hands. "Isn't this clever?" she said. "What are you giving us gifts for?" She'd brought something for Jen for her First Communion, and something for Julia, whose birthday would be that Thursday.

Until then, all I'd done for Val was a card on Mother's Day. And here, this present, was much more thoughtful than that plaque over my mother's bed. My only regret was that I couldn't even remember what I'd done for Mom the only Mother's Day she had as a grandmother, just weeks after Jen was born.

I hope at least I sent a card.

The year of Jen's First Communion, I'd known way back in the aisle at Michaels, back when I was buying supplies, that there was no way I could make something for Teresa and Jackie and not one for Val. The biggest decisions somehow turn on the smallest of reasons. This time, out of fairness.

"It's for Mother's Day," I said, and I motioned for her to smile, Jim was about to click the camera.

Six people, and it only took one shot. You could see in Jen's uplifted chin how proud she was in that moment of the present she made that Teresa and Jackie and Val all cooed over. But I think, of them all, Val's smile was the happiest.

As for me, I was still grappling with all I'd done for this project. And I don't just mean the plant. This family of mine—I'd pieced together all the cut-outs into a beautiful whole, the possibilities I'd wondered about for so long. And now, having put together what I'd made, and what I was made of, I couldn't help feeling a bit stiff, and exposed.

Mother's Day with rickrack flower project.

∾ 23 ∾

By Any Other Name

I'm getting out of the big house," Dad told me. He and Jackie had settled into the Florida condo. "If there's anything you want, come get it."

"What do you mean?"

"You need to clear out the china. And whatever else."

"So, when are you talking about? Two weeks or two months?"

"When it works for you. I might have Danny or someone clear out all
the personal stuff and sell it furnished. I've got no place to put anything. None
of it fits down here at the condo. So, go. Take what you want. I'm serious."

A month later, I finally figured out Dad was really serious, and so I
had Jim pull the back bench out of the minivan and I took the girls up to
Ohio for one last trip to Papa's big house. We pulled through the gates, and
I knew the buzzer went off in the empty house.

"Papa!" Jenny called as we walked in the French doors, and I had to
remind her once again he would not be there.

We walked into a wall of heat.

No A/C? Let it just be off, let it just be off. God help me if the house
needed something fixed now. How much I depend on Jim to do anything, to
do everything.

And when I was twenty I'd told myself I wouldn't ever be that kind of wife.

I took the girls through the house, to remind them what was there and to survey what I should pack. The house seemed so lonely. The salmon carpet had bleached in spots in the wheelchair-accessible bedroom Dad had built for his mother, the spot above the fireplace still bare, never filled after Dad sent me the Italian painting for Jen's first birthday. The built-in cherry entertainment cabinet in the conservatory off the back had blackened from the sun, a burn in the Corian from a metal sculpture that had superheated over summers there without Dad, without airconditioning. Dad had rearranged the furniture since the reunion so everything now looked out of place.

"It's hot, mommy," Jenny said, and I sat with them to rest, but the grease spots on the armchair coverings were not cooling. Dead wasps once again on the carpets in my room and in the apartment above the garage.

I pulled out my old Barbie airplane and let the girls play in their own world while I packed up my old one. I started with the encyclopedias holding all the children's stories I'd loved so much, and yet I left those family pictures hanging on the wall. God, that kills me. I thought Dad was going to come back for those. And I still haven't found the story that haunted me, the one about Peter Pan. Not the Neverland version, but the one where he leaves home and his mother promises to always leave the window open for him. He goes away and comes back, goes away and comes back, and each time the window is still open but he doesn't go in. When he finally decides, yes, this is the time I go in and tell her I am home to stay, the window is shut, and his mother is there in the rocking chair, cooing over another baby.

That's a dark tale, whether you're adopted or not. Maybe it's a good thing I was never able to share it with my children.

Later that afternoon, the buzzer announced a visitor. Val came knocking two minutes later, a stack of boxes in the trunk of her car. She offered to help. I'd no idea just how much she would. "There's a U-Haul place right by my house," she said. "What do you need me to do? I can help pack, I'm really good at that."

"No, I think I need to be the one to go through things and decide what to take," I said. "What I need you to do is take care of the girls. Play with them, entertain them. Look after them."

"Do you want me to keep them here?"

A granting finally, what she'd always wanted but had never imagined could be. Always careful never to overstep bounds. I just never realized how clearly I'd marked out those lines. All I knew was now we stood in an empty, overheated house, with a pool that had never been opened that year. No children's toys, only expensive knick-knacks all at Julia's curious eye level. "You take them where you want," I said. "Your place, if you know some fun park to go to. Wherever. Your call. I just need to get through all this stuff."

"Really?"

"It would really help me out."

"Cool." She had plans for them. A park she'd taken her kids to, a friend who owned a horse barn. Later, I'd see pictures of the girls on horses and for the first time, I couldn't recall the animals, the barn.

"That's when Val took us around. You were busy," Jen said.

It would take me a while to piece it together: it was during the days I spent in that hot hot house, pulling out the family albums, Mom's baby albums and her school scrapbooks, one of Dad's army days (Mom must have put that one together), and the ones documenting honors: one for Dad's Aunt Theresa's Teacher of the Year Award, one for his skinny grandma's National Victory Garden Award. His Grandma Catherine made the men from Washington go to Norway, Michigan, for the publicity. She was a widow by then, she wasn't about to make that long journey by herself. She'd made one long trek when she was a newlywed, from the mountains of Turino, Italy all the way to the Upper Peninsula of Michigan. She would not travel like that again.

Later, Mrs. Gilbert would wonder why I hadn't taken some of the *Architectural Digest*-type lamps that graced the big house. But I filled my van with what I could, the most valuable first. Those family albums, and then Mom's china, both patterns. My favorite was the rose Limoges that Mom found at an estate sale with Aunt Mary, the ones we used for Thanksgiving dinners with Ray and Rachel. And the simplicity of the silver-edged bone china Mom and Dad had received as wedding presents, including the candy dishes Aunt Mary had given.

I was careful to leave the Waterford Dad and Jackie had just received for their own wedding. Dad had said, "Take it, just take it. Where am I going to put it down here?" But I knew better than to take something from a bride.

Val brought the girls back for dinners, and Joe brought us take-out from Applebee's.

"It's cooled down some," Val said, acknowledging the house was no longer god awful uncomfortable as we set the table.

"It's freezing in the basement. I shut the door to the downstairs. It's just going to take time to level off."

"Why don't you just sleep downstairs? The girls love the log cabin room."

"Mice," I whispered so the girls wouldn't hear.

I know, I know. If there's mice downstairs, they're just as likely to be upstairs, too. But I saw them down by the Africa room, I didn't see any indication of them up in mine. At least not until I'd gone through all the boxes in the attic off my closet. But those mouse droppings could just have well been from the attic from our old house, not here.

Amazing how easy it is to cull through things with the benefit of twenty years' distance. Though I still found it hard to part with my jeans purse from junior high, the one with the red mushroom patch on it. I had letters from my friend Michele in there, and even some triangular folded notes from Carrie, the friend to whom Aimee had first confessed we were adopted.

Two days later, and I ran out of boxes. And while I was picking up more, I had a good excuse to stop by and check out Val's new home.

A sweet 1830s farmhouse, tucked just outside Hudson. My Girl Scout troop had skated in Hudson, one of many of Ohio's small towns with Federalist architecture. As only a bookish, romantic little girl could, I'd decided—all on the basis of driving through for that field trip—I'd definitely want to live there when I grew up.

Or Vermont.

Or Colorado.

Not necessarily in that order, but those were the places I loved the most, I'd decided.

So Val's farmhouse was set on acres and acres of land, a place for a proper garden. A hundred-year-old oak spread its branches between the garage and the porch, shade for a bench and a potting shed. The girls were playing hide and seek there, but weren't so busy they couldn't come give me a hug—Jen while she was counting, and Julia as she was running in and out of places to hide. Val pulled me in for a tour, first onto the screened porch and right into the kitchen, quaint with shale shingles and barn-door cupboards.

Old homes have character as no new construction can. The eight-inch molding, the uneven floors, the shape of the rooms, the rustic beams on the ceiling. It's all there, it's all character. "I love it," I said, and I did.

"Don't you?" Val said. "Here, let me show you." She brought me through to the dining room. Some wallpaper was peeling just above the threshold, and I had to stop. The paper was vintage, and there were three more layers at least beneath.

"Have you seen this?" I asked. "There's a history lesson in there."

"I know, I love it."

"Me, too."

A closet in the dining room, the leaded glass windows. Stairs up, I had to duck my head. A step down into a large bedroom. Dolls on shelves, china dolls, the type some women collect.

Not my mother, not Peri. But Val. Like I had in my bedroom growing up and have since stuffed in Jen's closet. It's a part of me, a part I've kept hidden.

"My bedroom's over here," Val said. Painted red, with a cubby for a desk. And pictures, pictures everywhere. Of Chris' wedding. Of Allisyn. Of me and the girls, right in and among them. The ones of Jen as a baby, all that I'd sent that first time. And over the past seven years, Jen as a toddler, Juls as a baby. Family pictures, among her family.

"It's very homey here," I said. It's a thing to get used to, seeing your family among another's. It's like having another set of in-laws, maybe is the best way to describe it.

Only they are family, my family, in their own right.

Back down in the kitchen, we could see the girls playing out in the garden. And a spring bouquet adorned her table, a flower pot with foam tulips inside, traced from three different sized hands. Decorated with jewels and markers and, of course, rickrack.

THANK GOODNESS FOR SECOND CHANCES. Having a second child allows one to do everything all over again.

For me, it was a chance to do things right. At least for Julia's First Communion.

This time, I'd invite Jim's cousins and his aunt.

This time, I'd invite Nor.

Over the course of the second First Communion weekend, I would have twenty-four people for dinner on Friday, eighteen on Saturday, and nine for Sunday brunch.

So if you find this section moves too quickly, it's because it did. Time flies—*tempus fugit*—when you're having fun, or if you're hosting it.

What I remember from Friday night, with Jim's cousins and his aunt: we'd finished our basement the year before, and we shuffled everyone downstairs by the bar where Jim would serve drinks while I staged the dinner upstairs. I had notes, trust me, as to when the potatoes would go in and when to fill the glasses with ice. One of my jaunts downstairs to actually be social, and Jim's aunt had to pull me aside.

"This is the same carpet I have?" she asked.

"I believe it is," I said. I'd picked it out before I'd seen her new carpeting, but I'd noticed when Jim and I were at her place for Christmas the year before.

"But you don't have any seams showing."

"We had really good subs," I said. Her house is a gorgeous contemporary in an exclusive area north of St. Paul, a town that's requested Google to remove its streets from the website. To have her compliment anything in my house, even something as mundane as carpet installation was, well, something I should get into print.

Saturday, May Day, First Communion Day. Only eighteen people to host that night, and first we had to get through the ceremony. My first communicant's veil was secure, of that I'd made sure. The only wild card with Julia was if she'd remain reverent throughout the ceremony. I shouldn't have worried. In all of her pictures, she holds her hands clasped in prayer, caught in the spirit of the moment.

I should have been keeping an eye on my husband. While I was talking with the sisters who'd come, Margie and Annie and Julia's godmother Sally, Jim was busy getting a picture of Julia up on the altar, holding hands with the boy she'd sworn to marry since kindergarten. Three years was a long time for a relationship when you're only eight.

Jim was in high picture-taking gear that night. We took pictures of everyone, all together, formal and candid, group and alone. Must have just bought a new camera that year.

Val and Joe of course came, too. This time I didn't feel like I had to worry about tending after her. She'd be fine, I knew. She'd done this before. She'd help where she could. She and Joe would blend in with the family, with Dad and Jackie and Bill and Teresa and all the rest.

I received more compliments on the food that night. "Two nights in a row, gourmet dinners," Margie said. As the oldest, and one of the ones still in Jim's hometown of Cedar Rapids, she gets stuck hosting many family events. Thanksgiving, especially, ever since that pressed turkey fiasco, as Jim calls it. Considering everything Margie has hosted, her compliment meant a lot.

The other compliment I remember was one from Teresa, telling Julia how beautiful she looked. "I know it's not possible," my mother-in-law said, her voice quiet, between us, "but little Julia looks so much like her Grandpa Jim. A spitting image."

I couldn't help but look between Juls and my dad. I couldn't see the similarity, but surely she had his attitude: the glass was always at least half full. And wouldn't you know, it was usually her favorite drink.

My mind was whirring with the transitive property, the times I'd run into old friends of my mom, how Margie Smith said without hesitation that Julia was a little me. "Oh, yes, she looks just like you when you were little, I remember."

My friend Susan puts it this way: God brings families together in many different ways. Susan was the one I introduced Val to just before Jen's First Communion, the one who's adopted children from Columbia. Like them, for me, adoption was the way my family was meant to be brought together.

And by family I mean all of us.

SUNDAY, EVERYONE IS UP AND OUT. Jim's folks left by seven. His sisters and their families, who stayed at a nearby hotel, didn't even stop by before they left. They'd said their good-byes the night before. That left Dad and Jackie, and Val and Joe. So, for brunch, I'd invited Nor. Only nine for Sunday brunch, so I could relax and enjoy my way through it.

When Nor showed up on my doorstep, tall and lanky with her hair up and John Lennon glasses, it was the first time she met both Dad and Val. Three years later and Dad wouldn't remember meeting her until I reminded him it was over Julia's First Communion weekend.

"That's right," he said. "She's the hippie."

First time I'd ever thought of her like that, but sure, it probably fit. She told us about how she'd been commissioned to write a piece for some group or other, so she'd prepared something on Lady Godiva, and she'd planned on wearing long gloves again. I can't remember what she said about the rest of what she'd wear, but she said she was working on a getting a horse.

Dad told her he could help her with that.

I brought out the Eggs Benedict, and we ate in the dining room for the third time in three days. But I did not use mom's china, I used everyday dishes. Didn't mean anything except I'd done enough domestic work by then.

Nor sat across from Dad at the table and talked about the May Day Festival in Powderhorn Park, where they march giant, building-sized puppets

225

in a street parade down to the park lake. "At the end, they banish winter with the singing of 'You Are my Sunshine,'" Nor said.

She would not know that counted among my favorite memories, Mom and Dad singing that Gene Autry tune in harmony. I used it as a lullaby for Jen, banishing night monsters with the song. But now I still can't get through it without my voice catching.

I thought the parade sounded fascinating, Jim thought it sounded crowded. I pushed until Jim quietly reminded me that Dad's ankle made it hard to get around, especially on uneven, grassy surfaces.

Curses, foiled by practicality again.

That weekend, we did not celebrate a holiday together, but we celebrated a sacrament. I sat in wonder at what I'd brought together. The woman who'd given me over, the man who'd taken me in, the woman who'd taken over for a brother dead too soon. We did not dwell on childhoods gained or loved ones lost. We enjoyed the moment for what it was, brought together in the present, no matter what had happened and who'd done what in the past.

SIX MONTHS LATER AND I WAS STANDING at the photo counter at Costco. Jim had handed me the memory card and reminded me which photo to use. I'd picked out the decorative frame, the holiday quote: From Our House to Yours. Perfect. Christmas cards without any Christmas sentiment, but you know why I'm sending it.

To wish you good cheer.

It's Jim's belief that Christmas cards are something that should be mass mailed, that should not require time-consuming personalization on each letter. "Have the greeting printed on the card, so I can just mail them out," he tells me.

So that's what I do. And then I write out a personal note for each of mine. I still hate it that he gets his done in an afternoon, and it takes me three days.

That Christmas, we'd decided to send out a picture of Julia's Communion weekend. We had some good shots, and we'd had one of Bill and

Teresa and Dad and Jackie and Val and Joe. It seemed a good family card to send out. I think Jim liked it especially, since it had almost as many people in it as the one his parents send out every year, one of Bill and Teresa and their ten kids, never mind that the kids range in age from fifty-one down to thirty-four.

Well, I tried to fit my life story in these little boxes for the personal message on the card. You try to fit "Grandparents Bill and Teresa and Papa and Jackie at Julia's First Communion, together with Kate's birthmother Val." It just doesn't fit in the three lines, the thirty-five boxes. But I can tell you what did.

"Grandparents join us for Julia's First Communion." What the hell, why not, the girls do call her Nana. I dropped it in the box, and by noon the next day, it would be officially in print.

The guilt hit me as I pulled out of the parking lot.

I called Dad first, from the car. "Dad, I have to tell you about our Christmas card this year," I began.

"Oh, hell, I don't care," he said.

I called Val next. "I just did something and I hope it's okay," I told her.

"Oh, Kate," she said. "That's fine. That's just fine."

But her voice told me it was more than fine.

Thirty-eight years it took to get back where she'd always wanted to be.

As I say, better late than never.

➷ 24 ☙

Readers Wanted

For three years, I hid all evidence of my darkest secret from my husband—even with my poker face (or shall I say, my lack thereof). I got involved after our younger daughter had begun kindergarten. Didn't mean anything at first. It was something I could walk away from. I'd go months without, back then.

Look at me, it's hard for me to even keep the secret from you. The night I told Jim I kept it in only until the appetizers arrived, only because until then I was busy taking in our evening out, a wine bar and everything. The sensation of a new silk skirt around my legs as we walked back to a white linen draped booth in a side room. It'd been a long time since I wore anything other than jeans.

It'd been a long time since we flirted, too. Curse of having small children. I tucked my hair behind my ears, I batted my eyes. I sipped my wine, my fingers curving around the fullness of the glass. Running up and down the length of the narrow stem.

Yes, I'm pretty sure I giggled, too.

"Okay, I've something to confess," I said, shifting in my booth.

Once languid, Jim's eyes were now sharp and focused, and I regret my choice of words even now. I am not so good with the putting together the words thing, to paraphrase a certain lion in Madagascar, especially after a glass of wine, especially when I haven't written it all down first, crossed it out and rewritten it twelve hundred times. I wished I hadn't waited to tell, wished my mind was sharper and not wine dulled.

"Nothing like that," I said. "It's just that," I said, "I've started writing." I looked up at him from my wineglass. My fingers were suddenly nervous, dancing upon the round base.

"Oh?"

"I've been writing a lot, actually," I said.

The Oceannaire is well lit, for a nice restaurant. No hiding in the shadows there. I did what I could; I tucked my hands underneath my legs.

"I've pretty much written a story," I said.

He smiled, relief and pride. "So, a children's story?"

"No," I said, annoyed at the suggestion. As if children's literature was somehow a lesser genre than adult fiction. This was, obviously, before I'd come to understand the genius behind the creation of *Harry Potter*.

"It's for grown-ups."

Jim spread his elbows out. "What's it about?"

How to distill what I'd been working on for three years into a single sentence. There were nuances in the story, a complex intertwining of characters, a sad, inevitable resolution. How in the world could I put all that into a few measly words?

"It's about a woman, searching for her runaway daughter. Starts out that the girl is totally rebellious and they fight all the time, and the mom thinks she's finally got her straightened out but, no, the girl has taken off with this boy who's in a whole mess of trouble, can't please his father."

Jim sat back in the booth and I realized I'd already lost him. I hadn't captured the essence of the story for him. "There's some of my sister in it," I said.

"The girl?"

"No, actually. The boy."

Jim laughed, took a drink.

"And the woman, she goes looking for her daughter, and she won't stop until she brings her home. But this woman, she's so controlling—she got issues of her own, which is why the daughter puts up a fight and no way does she want to go back with the helicopter mom." I was on a roll, running through all the issues without any coherence, all the intricacies meshed together and it made no sense even to me, even though I loved so much how it all fit together on the page.

"And this is the part that's really interesting," I said, as if saying it would convince Jim, even though his eyes glazed over after my third incoherent sentence. "The reason Nancy—that's my main character—is so messed up is because she's not married to the guy she really loved. And the reason—get this—is because he was one of the ones killed at Kent State."

Jim looked like he's about to say something, but I plowed ahead.

"It's about twenty minutes from where I grew up. My babysitter went there, years after it happened."

I sat back, finally, in the booth. And since I'd poured out my story, it somehow seemed flat, as if opened too early, exposed too much, with all the fizz gone.

"So," said Jim. He was clearly not sure where to take the conversation from there.

"I sent it to Mark," I said. My friend Michele's husband. "He runs that small press on the side, remember? And he loved it. Absolutely loved it. So I think it's got real potential." At least I was earnest, in all my naïveté.

"What's your next step?"

"I look for an agent. They take it to a publishing house."

"You know it's a long shot."

I cocked my head. Where was the unconditional spousal support? "For most people."

"I'm just saying," he said, only he didn't. "Have you talked to anyone who's gone through this process? Like what's her name? Nora?"

"Nor," I said. "Not yet." I ran my fingers along the wine stem again. I would forgive him for not asking to read the manuscript yet. Nor would read it. She'd put me in touch with her agent. See how wonderfully easy everything could fall into place?

I WAS BEING AN OPTIMIST IN MORE WAYS than one. We'd had such a lovely brunch with Nor the year before at Julia's First Communion. But that had been the first time I'd seen her since we'd moved up to Minnesota. We lived close, but we were worlds apart. With my writing, I was hoping to change that, as much as that scared me. To move ahead with what I wanted to do in life, I needed to get over being intimidated by people who'd care to help me.

But God, my birthfather's family was such a formidable bunch. The first winter we were in town, Nor had brought her parents over when they were visiting. Her father, still as horribly tall as I remembered and again with the funny beard, was barely in the door when he found a chair and plopped down, copper wire in hand. Without hardly a word of hello, that lion of a man fashioned a wire angel ornament right there in my front room. "For your tree," he said.

What, didn't he have time to make it before he came? It wouldn't dawn on me until the next year, as I pulled the angel out of my ornament box, that each year I could also pull out the memory of him creating it.

I think I make myself slow in front of these people.

Carrell, for whom I'd been originally named, was a quiet woman Nor fussed over the whole evening. "Mother, you can sit here," Nor offered, standing next to a chair. "Mother, do you need anything?"

For the love of God, I was being derelict in my duties as hostess.

But as Nor passed me, a present in hand for the girls, she said in a stage whisper, "She's quite fragile, now, you know."

That was all Nor said that evening of her mother's condition. For most of the rest of the night, Nor read *Eloise at Christmastime* to Jen and Julia, crowded in her lap. She wrapped her arms around each, clearly cherishing the girls and her moments with them. I was not so much in the moment. Flighty with worry over what to busy myself with and what to say in Homer's imposing presence and Carrell's bird-like tentativeness.

I gave a book to them: To Our Children's Children.

"Why, look at this," Homer said.

Though I never did get used to being on a first-name basis with Dr. Hall. And Grandfather wasn't something either of us proffered.

"What is it?" Jenny said, leaning back to see from Nor's lap.

"I think it's your mother's way of telling us she wants to learn more about us," he said.

But could I think of anything to ask him? Should have studied the book beforehand. At least I thought to ask for a photo before they left, a picture of the patchwork of four generations gathered in my home.

It was important to me because it had been important to my mother. She'd long treasured a photograph taken on her front lawn when she was but three months old, cradled in her great-grandmother's arms. Behind the seated pair stood her mother and grandmother. And behind them all stood the towering apple tree my mother would, for the next seven years, be told not to climb and she would, breaking an arm as if to prove it hurt that her mother had been right. And all that was ahead of them still in this picture: the women are smiling, the matriarch with silent laughter facing not at the camera, with knowledge of the joke and its teller lost forever to time.

Mom had tried to pose a similar photo when her grandmother came to visit when I was a toddler. She positioned the toile loveseat against the brick wall in the living room, seating Gramma Verne and Great Grandma Edith and Mom and I all in a row. But I was two and not cooperative, climbing all over the white haired women and not keeping my dress pulled down. I know that because I've seen the succession of color prints, none as iconic as that black and white from a generation before. No chance for a four generations photo for my girls, with Gramma Verne and Mom long gone.

That is, until now.

"I know we don't have David," I said, as if apologizing for his absence, "but I can't tell you how much I would love it if we could all get in this shot, with Nor, too, if you don't mind?"

I sat next to Dr. Hall—Homer—on our couch, and Nor next to her mother. We each took a girl on our laps, and Jim snapped a picture.

Nor had barely stood when she said, "You ready, Mother?"

But the evening's just starting, I thought. I was finally coming up with something to say, some questions to ask. I walked them to the door, lost by their leaving. "Good-bye," I barely had time to say.

Nor and her parents with me and the girls.

It would be years before I would learn just what Nor meant about Carrell being fragile. How she'd been that way off and on for years, how the siblings learned to cover for her episodic depressions.

No, I didn't yet know their vulnerabilities, I only saw their intellectual might. And I would be undaunted in asking for help with my writing. I would dig Nor's number out of an opened priority mail envelope I kept in my night-stand, and I would call. Manila envelope, engraved letters on watermarked linen. How professional, I thought. How like the writer I yearned to be.

I dialed the number at the top of the letterhead, half hoping she wouldn't be home. This would be the first time I'd shared something with Nor that I hadn't with Val. And not even Dad. The feeling I had as they rushed out the door that winter's night threatened to bury me once again. Had that just been a duty visit, something to be fulfilled?

What was I doing? No way should I be making this call. I should just hang up.

"Hello?"

Drat. She was home. "Nor? This is Kate St. Vincent Vogl," I said. "David's . . ." I wasn't sure how much detail I needed to give, to remind her.

233

"Yes, Kate, how are you?" She sounded truly happy to hear me.

This could be easier than I thought.

She asked about the girls. I told her our plans for the summer, and then eased into the reason for my call. "You know, I've started writing," I said.

"Really?" she asked. She sounded as genuine as Val. Thrilled. "What kind?"

"A story."

"Oh, like a children's book?"

What's with me and the children's book thing?

"No, a grown-up story," I said.

"So you've been taking classes at the Loft?" she asked.

I'd never heard of the place until two weeks before. I'd just told my book club, and Katy mentioned it. I was annoyed at the suggestion. Not just because it sounded more uptown than I thought I could ever be comfortable with, but because I'd already spent three years of my life writing this book. I knew how to write, I'd done it.

"I've heard of it," I said to Nor. "But no, I haven't had the chance to check it out yet."

"You should," Nor said. "It's wonderful, the biggest literary center in the country. I taught some of the first classes there, you know."

Figures. I am so behind. "Maybe I'll look into it some," I said. "But my friend's husband has an independent press, and he loved it. So I thought maybe I would want to contact some agents?"

"Yes, I suppose you could do that for your next step."

She didn't mention the need to rewrite the damn thing fourteen times first. Then find an editor and rewrite it a few more.

Then look for an agent.

"And I was wondering, did you use an agent for your book?"

I'd tried getting a copy of her *Moon and the Virgin*. She'd sold over thirty thousand decades before, but now it was out of print. I didn't know then the dismal percentage of books selling more than a thousand copies, much less than those selling over a hundred.

"I did, I guess, but, Kate, that was years ago. I don't even know if she's still in the business. Even if she is, it was non-fiction, not fiction at all.

And now, of course, they're all even more specialized than that. I'm afraid I'm not much help."

All my resolve, out the door. Did she not want to? In truth, she was being honest, but I couldn't see that for the obscuring veil of my insecurity. It seemed to come out of my closet every time I wanted desperately to belong.

It helped, sometimes, when my optimism got the best of me. "Can I send you a sample?" I asked. She'd change her mind, she would, if she'd just read what I wrote.

WELL, NOR LIKED IT—AT LEAST SHE WAS KIND and said she did. Didn't give me an agent to contact, though. It would take me another year to realize why. Agents really do only take on the genre they specialize in. Some handle mysteries, other romances. Others poetry and memoir for others still. She'd told me the truth; I'd just been too stubborn or insecure to listen. A few months later I submitted twenty pages to the Loft, and it earned me a place in an advanced fiction class.

Among my classmates were a playwright trying to write—of all things—a children's novel, as well as another Loft instructor looking to perfect a piece for an application to NYU's writing program. "Michael Cunningham teaches there," she said in awe. The next year I would have a beautiful rejection letter from his agent. "Well-written," the agent said. "I just don't know how to market it."

Took me two more years to figure out I should totally restructure the thing.

Maybe even make it a young adult novel.

I THOUGHT I'D ONLY NEED TO TAKE ONE CLASS at the Loft to perfect the manuscript for agents. Class critiques would cover the first hundred pages. And the instructor offered to read fifty pages on top of that, at the end. That would get half the novel edited, I thought.

And, oh, I had such grand delusions with that first chapter I'd submitted to the class. They'd love it, I was sure. Won't know how to add anything to make it better. The characters, nothing like them since Hemingway. The writing, by God, sheer Fitzgerald reincarnated.

No one wanted to start in with their comments. Who could dare?

"Well, I might as well go," the Loft instructor/student next to me said. "Your characters are flat."

I can't help but picture Flat Stanley, a two dimensional character in our three dimensional world.

"There's nothing to them," she said. "No emotion, no reaction."

But they're there, I can see them, I think. I feel their pain, their anguish. I want to protest, but I don't. Not allowed. We just have to sit there and take it until the end of the critique, when we can ask questions, clarify the comments. Suddenly, I was Kafka, unfairly on trial.

No, different book altogether. I've awoken from my delusions as a cockroach.

The playwright was next. "Reads like backstory," he said. Backstory? What was that? "You're telling us the story before the story. Just jump right into it."

That's when I realized I was in over my head. In that class, I was doomed to keep rewriting the first chapter. Over and over.

It was, I suppose, a useful exercise. But I needed—I wanted—the rest of the work critiqued, too. And I was wary now of this instructor who would keep me on this treadmill of those first twenty pages.

Six weeks into the class, and Mark, my friend Michele's husband, had read the first three chapters, but that was all. I needed a good solid review from someone else I could trust to read it quickly and read it well. I turned to my most erstwhile critic, one I trusted above all others. "Could you read this?" I asked my husband. "Tell me what you think?"

He'd just come home from a twelve-hour day and was flipping through the mail. I don't think he'd taken off his coat. He didn't even look at me when he said, "I don't think our marriage could survive that kind of pressure."

No faith!

"I can take it," I said.

"I can't even play golf with you anymore," he said. "And that's a game you've barely invested yourself in."

"You're the one who doesn't want to play me. I don't mind it at all, really."

"See?" he said, taking off his coat. "I haven't even looked at what you've written and we're fighting. Please let's not go there."

So quickly my options had narrowed. Not Nor, not my Loft class, not even Jim. My dad I didn't even consider: he hated reading so much that for years I wondered if he even could. Didn't occur to me there were professionals out there, who would do it but for a fee.

Especially since there was one other person I could ask. I just had to get over the embarrassment of admitting what I'd done, as if writing was a weakness, something not to talk about except with others sharing a similar affliction. I knew she would do it, she'd done so much more.

"I would love to read what you've written," Val said. "Yes, email it, that's fine. I'll start reading it tonight."

So I sent Val that early, awful draft. The one I'd written before I believed that first Loft instructor. Yes, you will need to rewrite it again and again. And twice more after that. Not just tweaking the words here and there, varying sentences and phrasing. No, complete rewrites. Start the story from scratch, and do it again, once more.

Val read the version with my first, early ending, before the boy found out what his father had done to betray him. (See, it was a tragic ending.)

It was the version with thoughts pounded out and fit together, jigsaw style, as the girls learned to put together words of their own at school. The version with the scenes I lived but my characters didn't.

I emailed the whole thing, chapter by chapter, to Val that night.

And I don't think I slept a wink until she told me what she thought of it. You know what I mean, if you've ever submitted your writing. For me it starts the moment I send it. I know it's unrealistic, to think that someone is waiting on the other end, ready to hang on my every word, but once it's out there, my worry begins.

I made myself wait two whole long days before I flipped through what I'd sent Val. I tried to imagine what she'd think as she read the scenes where the girl fought with her mother, or where another character realized he had to break the law in order to do right by his daughter. This time as I read it, I saw all the typos I didn't catch the other twelve hundred times I proofed it.

I made the changes and forwarded them to her.

After I sent it, I noticed forty more stupid things. Verb/noun agreements. Sentence structure. Should I send more corrections?

Should I? No, I decided.

But should I?

A few days passed, and I had not heard from Val. Was she reading it? Did she like it, really like it? Or did I still have a load of backstory, weighting down the action?

I don't know what's worse, seeing the changes that need to be made or being so afraid to look at my piece again, to see the awful mistakes that maybe, just maybe, I missed all these times. So I paced and I paced, anxious as a cat searching for a place to give birth. There, that's a phrase I could use for that other story I was thinking of starting.

A week. I could call. Just to see what's up. Maybe she might have a few things to say about what she'd read. Maybe not. Granted, there'd been weeks and even months that went by before we'd talk to each other. Though I had remembered this year to call her on Thanksgiving. I'd congratulated myself on remembering as I heard the smile spread across her voice. So she hadn't been the only one to call out of the blue, so far.

I could call. I could. So I did.

"How are you?" she said. There, that smile again. Worth it all in itself.

"Just calling to say hi."

"I got a chance to read a little bit of what you sent."

"You did?" How nonchalant could I be? At least try to be?

"You know, I liked it," she said. "I did. You have a way of capturing things, little moments."

There, take that, Loft instructor/student.

"How far did you get?"

Just so you know, it's never far enough. Not unless you're at this part of the memoir already and it's the day after you started this book.

"I'm in the middle of the second chapter, I think," she said, and then must have realized she should have known where she was. "Yes, that's it. I like it, I do," she said. For more than a moment I worried if it was more to convince herself than me.

"Well, let me know how it goes," I said.

I realized after I hung up the phone that it mattered to me what she thought. She would know in her gut what was right, what was wrong in a story, of that I was sure. She might not know at first to use "flat" to describe a character she can't picture in her mind, to use "backstory" instead of saying it needs more action. She would tell me where I went right. That I knew. And with that, I'd be able to find my way.

Val and me with the girls.

❧ 25 ❧

Rewrite and Rebirth

When people asked me what I was up to, I dared to tell them about my writing. Funny how a little confession would spark another. I found out a stockbroker on our parish council had been working on a book of his own. Another Girl Scout leader wrote fractured fairy tales, had actually gone to a writer's conference out in San Francisco.

"You should go," she said.

No way could I rationalize that, not without making some money on my writing first.

"But what comes first?" she wanted to know. "The chicken or the egg?"

For me, all I had was a big goose egg so far. Just some lovely rejection letters, collecting in my file. Well-written, just not right for our list. Well-written, but too concerned with the domestic.

I could hear that playwright from my novel writing class again: Reads like backstory, Kate.

I started rewriting the stupid thing one more time. I brought my laptop up to the lake, kept on my schedule of rewriting a chapter a week. When

Jim woke up early to fish, I curled up with my laptop and worked on Chapter Eight.

Nor asked me and my girls over to her cabin. She called it a cabin, anyway. There were actually two houses on her property on the bluffs overlooking the St. Croix, an older one in the shape of an octagon and one built just a couple years ago, Frank Lloyd Wright style.

Interesting what didn't happen for that visit: Nor did not take us in the new cabin that first visit, and I would not tell Val about going until afterwards. Now I'm sure there's no meaning to where we lunched or didn't that first time. But as for me not telling Val, I was guilty of doing something I was reluctant to share with her. One of these days, I resolved, I would try and grow past such guilt. No reason for it. It's like how you treat your children, I suppose. And fairly does not always mean equally, especially when one lives just an hour away, and the other thirteen.

At Nor's river place, we settled in on the deck and let the early June rays warm us. Her younger sister Welling was in town. She's just eight years my senior, halfway between Nor and me. Welling, a redhead, with a son between my girls' age. Beautiful thing about kids: give them a pool, or any chance to play, and they can be friends whether or not they really have anything in common.

What was nice was that they did. Julia hit it off with him. They liked the same things. Like splashing in a pool.

Turned out Welling and I had some things in common, too. She was working on a book of her own, so we had a chance to talk shop. As much as I could, anyway.

"So how often are you writing?" she wanted to know. We didn't face each other, but sat side by side on the deck as we watched our kids in the water.

"Two, three hours a day."

"Every day?" she asked. She rolled her eyes. "I just don't have that kind of discipline."

Finally, a point for me. Let me come clean here, though: she's a professor of International Law. She was writing a textbook, for God's sake. I don't think I could go more than an hour a day on that, either.

241

"You have a place you like to go to write?" she asked.

"Why would I go someplace when everything I have is right on my couch in my living room?"

"I'll tell you, I need noise," Welling said. "I have to go to a coffee shop, get settled right in the middle of everything, and then I can get going. I have trouble concentrating if I don't see other people working. Role models," she said. "I need role models."

I don't know about anyone else, but I can't say I ever imagined my law books might have been written by a professor in a Starbucks or a Caribou. A book-strewn office, maybe. But not a coffee shop. Even more interesting: that the people gathered there would inspire writing about international law. Now that's a law book I'd want to read.

"Oh, God, I need quiet," I said. "Earplugs are my friend."

Nor came in and out of our conversation, making sure we were settled, making sure the house was taken care of, making sure the kids had what they needed. The love of the writing, the love of symbolism, an undercurrent of caring for family and others and in discovering what that meant wherever life led. Finally, I was beginning to understand. I shouldn't worry so much about not following what she would say. I knew it already. I went home from that visit and sat down in front of my screen and wrote and wrote and wrote.

These are the things, I've found, that can get a writer inspired.

WRITE WHAT YOU KNOW, I'VE LEARNED. It gives your writing depth and reality.

Write what you don't know. Your writing will take off with imagination.

"Interesting you talk about Kent State in here," Val said, when she got to that part in the book.

"I went to school with a guy whose dog was killed in the crossfire."

"I never heard that."

"Well, amidst the rest of the tragedy," I said, leaving the rest unsaid.

"I say that mostly because Joe was at school there at the time."

"He went to Kent?"

"Yes."

"And he was there the day of the shooting?"

I could not believe my luck. Of all coincidences.

"Yes, yes he was."

My voice grew quiet, hushed. "Was he there when the shots were fired?"

"Not right then, but right after," Val said. "Here, you want to ask him?"

Of all things to fall in my lap. The instructor had said we needed facts about what the characters wore, what cars they drove, what music they liked. I didn't have any of that. Until now.

"Val's sister was there, too. You can ask her about it, if you want," Joe said.

Val got back on the phone. "Now that I think about it," she said. "Jan's a lot like your main character here. She never got into any of that protest stuff, even though that's what everybody did. Just wasn't her style."

A chance for me to interview my character? I couldn't stand it. "Okay," I said. I would talk to a complete stranger for this.

I HAD TO WAIT TWO WHOLE DAYS FOR VAL to let me know she'd contacted her sister.

"Hi, this is Kate," I said. I was shaking so much I thought the phone might jump out of my hand.

"Hi," Jan said. "Val said you'd be calling."

What a relief that the whole explaining-who-I-am part was already taken care of.

"Nice to meet you," I said. "Over the phone here." She was one of two sisters who hadn't made it to Chris' wedding.

"Val's told me so much about you," she said.

"Well, and she's shared so much about you, too," I said, but all I could remember was that she was a teacher. I couldn't remember where she lived, didn't dare ask.

243

We talked the niceties, as strangers or family will, before talking about what matters. "So," I finally said. "I guess Val mentioned I was working on a book?"

"She did, as a matter of fact," Jan said. "That's so interesting."

"Thanks," I said. Interesting/good or interesting/you are such a loser and my sisters and I are so going to talk about this? "There's a part of the story that talks about Kent during the shootings, and I understand you were there then?"

"Well, I was in class at the time of the shooting."

Sort of like my character Nancy. She was going into a building for class when it started.

"When you got out, did you walk right in the midst of it?" I asked. "What was that like?"

"I didn't see anybody," she said. "I mean, it wasn't like I walked out in the middle of pandemonium, or anything."

Shoot. Maybe I should change that scene, then.

"We heard something'd happened, so we wanted to know what was going on. So we went to the side of the hill, and we sat down."

"This was on Bunker Hill? You sat down on Bunker Hill?"

This was the place from which the National Guard had just shot thirteen students. And what she was describing was so different from the interviews I'd read about in so many books and magazines from the time.

"Yeah," she said, like it was no big deal. "We felt like onlookers or something. It didn't feel like we were part of this terrible thing. It was our campus, it was our home. So we weren't in a panic, or anything. We went up the hill, and we sat down. To watch."

She paused a long moment. "And we were sitting there, just sitting there, with the guardsmen looking at us, which was fine," Jan said. "But then they raised their guns, and I decided it was time to get out of there."

How she said it made me think of a soldier raising his rifle in a military exercise, perpendicular to the ground, and then resting weapon against shoulder, barrel pointing away and into the sky. But the guardsmen that day were not wearing military dress; they were in fatigues, with gas masks, on no sleep coming from watching over a trucker's strike in Cleveland the night before.

"Wait," I said. "What do you mean, they raised their guns?"

"They raised them up, pointing them at us."

"Like they were going to shoot?" This was something no one had mentioned, not in any of the materials I'd seen. Not *Time* or *Newsweek*, not books by Michener nor Eszterhas. Could it be a confabulation? Something she'd created in her mind over the years? No, it was something she and Joe had talked about that day and in the years to come.

Think of the significance. Thirteen college students had been carted off to the hospital, four mortally wounded, and here's the Guard, taking aim once again at a crowd of students—this group just sitting on the ground.

There was more she had to share, enough to make me wonder if I should change my story, and by how much. She was not Nancy, I had to remind myself. And yet she had so much to tell me about my character's experiences. How she ironed her hair. How she carried her books, what slacks she could wear for her class that day, because of the dress codes.

Dress code? For college?

All her answers, and each brought more questions, along with the weight of knowing I had yet another rewrite coming my way.

I couldn't wait to tell Val all I learned. "You'll never guess," I said.

Funny thing was, the person I'd learned it all from was her sister. That's how I thought of Jan: as Val's sister. Not my biological aunt.

I can't say why I didn't think of Val's sisters that way when I talked with them or got a Christmas card from them. And yet for Nor I did. Maybe it's because David was gone already, so there was no way he could be a threat to my father and his relation to me. Maybe it was just that Val had such a big family, I had to look at them in relation to the one I knew, just to keep track of them.

Maybe.

And maybe I've got issues of my own.

ANOTHER REWRITE CALLED FOR ANOTHER AUDIENCE. My book club, God love them, was willing. I made copies at Kinko's, and the ladies insisted on writing me checks to cover the cost. "And you have to sign my copy," everyone said. "So we can sell it on eBay when you're a famous writer."

I hosted that month. Hosts for book club were always responsible for coming up with a bio on the author and questions for discussion. I couldn't say if it was easier or harder to come up with either. Should I talk about the work as if it were a real book? Or should I ask for their critiques?

I was so nervous I prepared a main dish and two sides and about three desserts and set it all up in our lower level, music and lights and candles and everything.

Sara was the first to show. "I thought we were cutting back on what we were serving," she said.

We had decided that. We'd had a big discussion just the meeting before about how things were getting out of control and how it was too much work for the hosts, how it was too much to eat for the guests, too.

"You know, you're right," I said.

"I shouldn't have eaten dinner," she said.

"I should have just made a cake and not worried about the rest, I guess."

Katy and Jean showed up next. "Look at all this food," Katy said. "You got another book club coming after us?"

"I have another dessert upstairs," I said. "You have to try some."

"Stop, just stop."

By the time the women called me over to sit down, relax, I was trembling all over. Katy had already emailed me how much she loved it. I knew they'd be kind. But still, I worried. It's your baby, when you write a book. You want readers to love it, to love you. Because no matter what writers say you know there's an awful lot of their own reality in whatever characters they dream up. Those characters have to come from somewhere.

"So, who's read this?" Katy wanted to know. "Are we your first?"

"Well, my writer's group have read it twice, through my first and second rewrites. And I showed it to Val. She's read it both times, too."

246

"Val being?"

"My birthmother. You remember." I'd told them her story when she was came up for her visits, for the girls' first communions.

"You're kidding me. She's read it?" Katy asked. "No, wait, she's read it *twice?*"

All eyes on me. I was afraid to nod my head, but it was true.

"So, was there that much of a difference?"

"A huge difference, I think," I said, rushing into my answer. This was the easy part of what she could have asked. She could have asked what it meant for me to share it with her. Could have asked what it meant that she'd liked it so much. "She read that first draft, when I didn't know what I was doing at all, just piecing together different scenes, didn't really have a coherent story as a whole."

The group fell silent. Could have been they were thinking about what it would be like to have your birthmother read the very thing you created, that you hadn't yet shared with anyone else. Could have been they didn't think I'd moved the story beyond those awful first drafts.

Katy eyed me carefully. "How much do you talk to her now?"

"Not much." I said. "More now, I guess." A lot, really, when I would send her a revised chapter. If I didn't hear from her within a few days, I'd call, see how far she'd read.

"I didn't realize you were in that much contact with her."

"We didn't use to," I said. "We'd go months without hearing from each other." I was calling once a week, now. Pretty much. "I guess we talk a couple times a month now."

"Oh." Katy eyed me, as I imagined her parents would when they were evaluating an animal for show on their farm. "So are you ever going to write about Val?" Katy asked. "Because that's the one you need to write."

Jean and Sara and the others nodded in agreement. "You do," they said. "That's the one."

I looked down at the tiny notebook I clutched in my lap. In it were questions I'd scribbled in preparation for this moment. Before the end of the night, we would talk through them all, and my friends would say how much they enjoyed my book—once they got into it. Past the backstory, I suppose. Katy would say how she got goosebumps when the boy found out what his father had done, and everyone else would lean forward and said yes, yes, just like they do when there's a good part in a book we've read.

I did not know all this yet. All I knew was there were issues still, with this book. And there were issues still with my writing.

"No," I said to their suggestion I write about Val, surprising myself with the firmness with which I spoke.

But for once I didn't care what the others thought. No way was I ready to write about Val yet. I couldn't introduce her properly still, and couldn't call her sister an aunt, for God's sake. How could I be ready to write about our relationship? Especially when, like in Madagascar, I hadn't gotten the putting together the words piece yet. "Not ready yet," I said. "When it's time."

ॐ 26 ॐ

No Place Like Home

I call my dad on Sunday nights. It was a tradition we started in college. It was a time when I actually had to find a phone, in my room at the bottom, way bottom, of the Hill or in a phone booth at the Straight, the student union. It was, in all my freshman self-centeredness, a pain.

"How about I just call when the mood hits me? I might end up calling more," I argued.

"How about I just send you money when the mood hits me?" Dad answered.

It did not at all sound like it might end up being more.

So, even after he stopped paying my bills, which happened to be after I graduated from law school, I still called every Sunday night.

And it was a Sunday night just after the girls started school when Dad handed the phone to Jackie. She was laughing, as if embarrassed to say something. "Well," she said. "I guess it's time for another family reunion."

I panicked. Was it our turn to stay in a teepee?

"Everyone's headed to the 2006 Pumpkin Show," she said. "We'd love it if you could join us."

As if we could take our kids out of school for a pumpkin festival. But it turned out the show fell over Fall Break weekend, in the middle of October.

"Darn," Jim said. "I've got school that weekend." Yet another good reason to be getting an M.B.A.

Unlike Jim, I looked forward to the trip, to getting together with Dad and Jackie. I could even visit Val and Michele first. It'd been four years since I moved the vanful of albums out of the big house, two years since I saw Val—too long, according to her. Plus, I was still feeling guilty for not inviting her to Jim's surprise fortieth. I hadn't invited Dad, it hadn't occurred to me to invite Val. Not until I'd told her how it all went. Lame, I know. But I wanted to make it up to her, somehow.

I'd only mentioned flying into Cleveland, when Dad asked why I didn't just bring Val down to Circleville.

"For the Pumpkin Fest?"

"Pumpkin Show," Jackie called from the background.

"Right," I said.

"Why not?" he said.

I don't know, something about not wanting to share any holidays— but fall breaks must not count. Bonus.

WE'D ALREADY LOST MOST OF OUR LEAVES in Minnesota by mid-October, but down in Ohio, leaves were still golding all along the roads. My favorite time of year, and I'd get to see it twice.

It would be a busy weekend: Two nights at Val's, then a drive down past Columbus to stay with Dad and Jackie in a park cabin. And Val had arranged with her sisters a brunch for me and the girls.

"Everyone can't wait to see you," Val said.

Drat, I should have looked for the list of her sisters, my cheat sheet reminding me their names and birth order. Now how was I going to remember?

Leaves scattered brown and red and gold upon the ground at Val's farmhouse. Since I was there last, they'd put a lot of work into it, painting and planting and grading the drive. "The house looks great," I said.

"Wait 'til you see the inside," she said.

She'd set up a Halloween Town on her kitchen table, little houses with orange lights. And Reese's sprinkling the road.

"Are these for us?" Jen asked. Somehow Nana Val knew Reese's were her favorite.

"All for you."

"This is the best place ever."

And I'd promised I wouldn't let Grandma Teresa know she said that.

I HAD ME TIME, TOO, THAT WEEKEND. Time to visit alone with Michele and another friend from high school. Of course, I'd drag my girls along, since Michele's daughters were so close in age to mine. On our way, I made a point of stopping at Ray and Rachel's, who continued to welcome Dad and now Jackie to their Thanksgiving spread.

"How's your writing?" Rachel asked me. "Any action on the book?"

"Just some lovely rejections, so far. Lately I've been thinking of writing a memoir," I said. "Not that my life is so important. But one about Val finding me."

"Something to keep that brain of yours working," she said, in that breathy, cracked voice of hers. "You always did like to tell stories."

"Really?" Funny, I never knew others were watching. How like a kid is that?

"Oh, you used to get lost in yourself for hours."

I guess some things never change. "So," I said. Anything to change the subject. "Tell me, what you're doing now that you're retired. Everything?"

"Oh, Katie, I'm so busy I don't have time to sleep," she said. "I'm getting ready to go down to Argentina. We'll be gone all winter, and you won't believe what has to get done in the meantime. Here, let me get you some hats. You need some hats."

Really, just as random as it sounds, but this must have been what made my mother laugh when she and Rachel and Aunt Mary were all sorority sisters up at Michigan State. Rachel went into a closet and pulled out a beret and a bowler and a Kentucky Derby hat and an Easter one. "Would you like this pillbox?" She set it on my head. "No, not quite right. This one," and she put a black tea hat on me. "Girls, you need hats, too."

She'd been volunteering at the Medina nursing home. There was a woman there who was a milliner, who was selling all her wares. From the looks of them, the hats had been ones she'd made over the span of her career, nothing recent.

"We need a picture," Rachel said, as we stood outside her door for our good-byes. Afterwards, she sent us off, wearing hats from another time, another woman's place.

OF COURSE WE WORE THE HATS TO MICHELE'S. It was fitting: this was my friend who'd stopped at Kmart on the way to her wedding reception and had everyone march the aisles. "We're looking for a blue light special," she announced, and found plastic sharks for all eighteen in her wedding party. The trinket was somehow a fitting accessory for the scarlet dresses of the bridesmaids, the gray tuxes of the groomsmen. Ohio State colors, right down to the red socks each of the ushers wore.

"Do you like my hat?" I asked Michele.

She must have read *Go, Dog, Go!* a few times to her kids, too. "I do like your hat, I do!" she said. "Come in, you goof."

Everything in Michele's house was floating, as my mother would put it. Controlled chaos, and some days it was not so controlled. When Marko was born, Michele served everything on paper plates for at least three weeks, she couldn't handle organizing clean dishes back in the cupboards. Sometimes even for hippies, being ADD trumps living green. No matter what shape her house was in, I loved it. It was a block down from her parents' home, a street with sidewalks where the kids rode their bikes and played kickball. In the back she kept a rabbit hutch and sometimes even a rabbit. They had a screened-in porch that overlooked a pond, and I was there in time to see sheltering leaves flamed red and orange and gold over her backyard.

"Leslie's on her way," she said. "Have you had lunch?"

We had our own mini-reunion, the three of us. The children did the things children do when visiting a friend of their parents, checking out each other's toys and games and comparing notes on parental controls. We sat in the kitchen, on benches around the table. From where I sat I could see the door to the garage. On it there was an Uncle Sam poster that said: I want YOU to kill for MY Oil Profits. And: Preemptive War Is TERRORISM. A bulletin board next to the door was plastered with signs (My Country Is the World and My Religion Is to Do Good) and buttons (All you need Is Love—in a Beatles font). The Hippies Use Side Door sign might have been vintage. No wonder her husband Mark loved my book about Kent. The board was balanced, though, with loads of pictures of her grinning girls and her little boy, and even a Napoleon Dynamite picture. By balance I didn't mean the inclusion of any flattering pictures of George Bush.

Not long after, Leslie rang the doorbell. Her little boy burst through the doorway, taking off with Michele's kindergartener. And in Leslie's arms snuggled a tow-headed toddler. Cherubic defined, with round cheeks and eyes that spoke words she couldn't yet form—telling me in no uncertain terms she'd not let me hold her, she was there with her mommy, and her mommy was the only one she'd abide.

It was killing me. She was adorable, runny nose and all. But I loved babies, loved to hold them, especially now that mine weren't anymore.

So we were back in the kitchen and I was trying to get a toddler to smile at me when Michele jumped in with, "Katie is writing a memoir about her birthmother." She said, "She's staying with her this weekend."

"Are you?" Leslie asked, trying to get a Kleenex under her daughter's nose, but the girl turned away every time Leslie got close. "You keep in touch?"

Such a loaded question. How I answer depends on who I'm talking to and where they fall if anywhere on the adoption triad, whether adoptee or adoptive parent or birthparent. I'll tell them the truth, but I try and tell it from their point of view. Leslie might be an adoptive parent, but she had also been my friend for over twenty years. "It'd be different if Mom was still alive," I said truthfully. "It'd be a lot harder."

She nodded, carefully folding the tissue and tucking it under her plate at the table.

"You hear anything from your daughter's birthmother?" I asked.

"This first year I have," she said. "We've emailed, and I sent pictures. Hard to pick the right ones, though, you know? Nothing too cute, nothing sad." Nothing to foster regret. "Just—what's representative." A high chair shot maybe, with food on her face.

"But now you've had her awhile," I prompted. Surely Leslie would want to stop cultivating that connection at some point.

But she gave me a look as if she didn't understand.

"Didn't her Facebook say she'd moved?" Michele said, setting out the salads.

"Yes, " Leslie said, pulling out the Kleenex again. "So if I send them, I'm not sure she's in a place anymore where she can get pictures of someone else's child."

Physically or emotionally.

Maybe, she thought, the birthmother just wanted to move on, forget that part of her life. Or else maybe she was with a new boyfriend or back with her parents, who knew nothing of the child.

So Leslie would hold off. Not to withhold anything, but to look out for the girl. To be a mother to the birthmother as much as the child.

My friend caught her toddler with one arm, and gently swiped a yellow line of snot from her daughter's lip. "I should set aside some pictures still, I guess," she said.

And isn't that just a mother's best intentions.

VAL HAD WAITED UP FOR US. I don't know if it was out of politeness as a hostess or out of worry like a mother, but she was up.

Truth be told, it was great to fill her in on the day. Together, we put the kids to bed, and by then, Val was ready to crash too. "I'm sorry, I just can't stay up any longer," she said.

Joe was stretched out on the chair in the TV room. "I'm up forever, I'll be watching this game. You can stay up with me if you want," he said.

I flopped down on the couch. "If you don't mind," I said. I'm such the night owl. My best work in college was from ten to two, and I don't mean over the lunch hour. Having kids definitely puts a wrench in keeping those hours, though.

Joe and I talked for quite a while as the TiVO'd football teams made their drives up and down the field. He forgot to fast forward through commercials as he told me what it was like as principal for a charter school for urban kids, ones that have dropped out and are given a second chance. Murders and jail time are not uncommon in their circles. A bad day at the office took on a whole new meaning.

We'd talked through the end of the game, in and out of a couple of conversations before Joe said, "I'm glad you're here."

"I'm glad I'm here, too."

"No, I mean it. I'm glad you're a part of Val's life. You know, I wasn't too excited about her getting in contact with you at first."

I knew. I couldn't blame him, though. If Jim had told me after we were married that, by the way, he'd had a child from a previous relationship and he wanted to finally meet that child, I think I would have needed some time alone to figure out if we still had any trust left in that relationship. But Joe went along for the ride, and here he was telling me he was glad where it had brought him.

"I'm glad we all got this chance," I said, pulling a fleece blanket I had made for Val for Christmas a couple years before off the arm of the sofa. I curled my feet up on the couch and spread the blanket over me, making myself at home.

The next day Val and I packed up her car for our trip down to Deer Creek State Park, some twenty minutes from the Pumpkin Show. The girls sat in the back, Nintendo DS duly apportioned to the winner of rock paper scissors. They'd set the timers on their watches so each would get an equal turn.

Val had me at the wheel, which was awful because I am the world's worst driver. I'm worse now I know my biological father was killed driving. I try to be careful. I'm just not that good. I have spatial issues. I can't tell where the outside boundaries of the car are. I think my eyesight must have been worsening when I should have been developing that sense, so I never mastered that ability.

But then Jen has the same problem, and she has perfect vision. So much for that theory.

Driving along, I realized we were taking 71 South, right past Dad's old shop, two miles from our old house. "Do you want to swing by and see where I used to live?"

"Sure."

A Bob Evans Restaurant now sits on the lot where the old shop, ST Equipment, once stood. It'd been a converted gas station, with three desks when you walked in, and then through the door to the left was the shop and all the concrete mixer parts: gaskets and solenoids and even some drums, all those parts filled the shelves and the floor all the way to the door in the back.

I took the familiar exit off of the highway, but once I was heading west I lost all my landmarks. A lot can change along a road in twenty years. I almost missed the turn—the sign for Rustic Hills was much, much smaller than I ever remembered.

I told her who lived where. We passed the old house of my friend Debbie who'd also been adopted, whose twin (or someone who just looks and sounds exactly like her) worked at the Cub Foods near me in Minnesota. We passed Jungle Larry's house. He used to do local TV shows with animals, a crocodile hunter minus crocs and certainly no stinging rays. We passed the country club, where I always came in second to Jennifer Thompson in swim races. We turned up River Styx, past the bus stop where Mom once picked me up to tell me Gramma died. We climbed the long hill I'd walk up when I was in high school. I always walked backwards up the hill, keeping an eye on where I'd been. Somehow it was easier.

"We'll just drive by the old house," I said. "We won't stop, unless it's for sale."

Of all things, a For Sale sign stood in my old front yard. I swear.

We pulled in the driveway and knocked on the door. No one was home. "Let's call the realtor," I said. "Get a showing."

Val had forgotten her cell, so I handed her mine. "It went directly to voicemail," she said.

"See if we can get in on the way back."

In the meantime, I walked her around the split-level home. We peeked in windows. The dining room was right off the front porch, that's where we started our Thanksgivings with Ray and Rachel. Gramma's room was the window down to the left, Mom and Dad's was right above that.

"My room's in the back," I said. "Here, let's go around."

By the fence lay a rock that said if it's wet, it's raining. Jen looked up at me. "It's so obvious it's funny," she said. "This was here when you grew up?"

No. Some things do change. We went through the gate back by the pool. I stood on the patio, one they'd redone beautifully in brick, and looked up at the little window above the laundry room. "That was my bedroom," I said. "It was all done up in pink." Girly girl.

The big picture window was Mom's, so when she woke up she could look out over the pool and across the woods to the lake. Maybe looking out over possibilities was just something Dad wanted to give her when he put it in.

I took Val back around to the front of the house, and we walked down to the end of the driveway. When Mom and Dad had the house built, they set it halfway back on the acre lot, instead of right up front, as the rest of the houses on the street. Dad was in the concrete business, so he put in a long concrete drive. When it was poured, we stood with Dad at the edge by the street, and he lifted Aimee and I up, one at a time, and onto the wet cement so we'd leave our footprints in it.

I'd wanted to show Val the imprint of my foot when all she had of me was her imagination. But the end piece of concrete was missing. Dad must have brought the memento to the farm when they'd moved. Who knew where it was now.

"Your feet wouldn't fit in mine anymore, anyway," I said to Jen. Hers were already bigger than my grown-up feet.

"What about mine?" Julia asked.

"Yours either," I said. She was already a seven, bigger than what Aimee's were, and I remember how much bigger Aimee was than I, growing up.

Subdued now, we walked back up the drive to the car. Someone had pulled all the arborvitae lining the drive, and it looked so bare without them. "There were bushes here," I said. "On this side, they were always so much bigger. Aimee used to toss her vitamins there on her way to the bus."

Val's car was parked under the basketball hoop. No net now, only the rusted rim. Everything looked so much older, so worn. Gold leaves hung in all the trees through to the street, as if suspended for but a few more moments, a few more days. Only skeletons of the trees would stand the winter.

"I'm still just getting a message," Val said, cell phone in hand.

"We've got to get going," I said. "We'll never make it when I said we would."

Of course, that would be nothing new.

It was a good two hour drive south, past Columbus. We thought we'd arrived when we hit the park entrance, but it was still a few slow miles in before we reached the sign for the lodge. We wound our way along the road, past fields and a golf course and signs for horseback riding.

It was worth the wait. Manicured gardens, flowers lining a brick path leading to a sprawling brick and cedar resort, flag flying by the door.

"Man, this is awesome," Julia said from the back.

"Man, this is awesome," I said, once inside. A fieldstone fireplace warmed the lounge, and windows overlooked Deer Lake, which was ringed in flame colored leaves. To the far right of the lobby was the entrance to Rafter's. I asked for a Jim St. Vincent, my eyes on the showcased view beyond the restaurant's terraced seating.

"Kate," I heard. There, silhouetted against the mid-afternoon sun stood Dad, napkin in hand. A table right by the window, of course. The girls ran ahead to give him a hug, and I was close behind. I was forty years old and I still got that warm, homey feeling when I saw him. That visit to my childhood home taught me it wasn't the physical place—that was just a shell for the love kept inside. It's the feeling you got coming home after a sleepover, or back from college. That feeling of being able to let your guard down, that you're safe and back with those who'll loved you, no matter what. Now I loved the home my husband and I have made, but there's something about that childhood feeling of being home that was pure and true and better than anything else in the whole wide world.

And here, with Dad, was that homemade feeling all over again.

He was greeting Val, and I missed the exchange, I swear. I was busy giving Jackie a hug. I could picture, him though, tucking in his chin and giving Val a sheepish grin before sticking out his hand. "Good to see you again, Val," I heard him say.

I imagine Val clasping his hand with both of hers. "You, too."

"I don't mean to rush you, but you've only got two minutes before they shut down the kitchen."

Leave it to me, to be late even for a lunch such as this.

"What's good?" I asked, motioning the girls to sit.

"Everything," Jackie said. "The sandwiches, they're divine. How was your trip?"

"You won't believe what we did on the way down."

"Get caught in traffic?" Dad asked. My usual excuse. He was on to me.

I told him about the old house, that it was on the market. That we were trying to get a showing on the way back.

"Get out," Jackie said in amazement.

"Does it still have that corrugated roofing on the porch?" Dad asked.

"It doesn't look so hot now."

"It didn't look so hot when it was new," Dad said.

I'd never considered he didn't love everything about the house he'd lived in for twenty-five years. He's not sentimental that way, though, when it comes to things. He won't wax nostalgic for the old house, just for the times he'd once shared with Mom.

Like me, though, he does get nostalgic for the things of his childhood. He's told me more than once about a little three-legged milking stool his grandfather made for him. Each time he tells the story, he mentions the drawer underneath, for a cloth. I can picture the look of delight on a little boy's face, his chin tucked in and his smile wide, when his grandfather pulls open a drawer underneath a stool and whips out that scrap of combed cotton for the boy to wipe his hands clean. Maybe the boy remembers his grandpa's warm Italian smile under that oversized handlebar mustache.

I suspect Dad, too, misses that feeling he'd get coming home. Especially the feeling of being big enough to help his grandpa, the one who forged his days down in Vulcan's Michigan iron mine.

When Grandpa Benzo died of black lung in his sixties, my dad remembered only that he lost him too soon. He's told me more than once that his grandfather died and left his grandma to raise those six kids all by herself. Funny how Dad so earnestly believes this, even though Dad could never had known that grandfather if he'd died so young. I even have the death certificate from when I was researching the family tree, and still every time Dad tells the story, his grandfather is gone too soon, and his grandmother is left alone to do it all. For Dad, it's not so much what happens that matters. It's what resonates for him. And he knows what it's like to be left too soon in the middle of a suddenly too empty home. Unlike me, he hadn't had any extra branches of the family tree to give extra support.

❧ 27 ❧

Family Reunion

Saturday we'd planned for brunch with Val's sisters, though Dad declined. "Hell, I don't even want to see Jackie's family," he said, though Jackie was right there.

Yes, sometimes, Jim's a lot like my father.

And so it was just Val and I and the girls who made the hour's drive up to the north side of Columbus. Val was my navigator, just as Mom used to be for Dad. Val directed me into a sunny subdivision, stately homes perched up on a hill, then onto a street lined with lovely brick townhomes, a lot like the golf-course community Dad's sister lives in outside of Chicago. I parked in the only open space on the other side of the cul-de-sac and we pulled the hostess gifts out of the car. Jen and Juls carried them to the door. Should we ring the bell? Were we guests or family?

"Just go inside," Val nodded to me.

Inside, it was light and airy, white walls that looked designer white, not afraid-to-use-color white.

Carole came out of the kitchen. Her eyes lit up, and she greeted me with a hug. She's my mother-in-law's height, small, with coiffed curls and eyes that maybe just maybe could be similar to mine. "I'm so glad you came," she said, holding on tight.

"I'm glad to be here," I said.

Arlene stood behind Carole, as if impatient for her turn at a hug. She lifted a binder clipped packet of paper in the air. "We all can't wait to discuss this," she said.

I looked to Val. "We're talking about my book?"

"Of course we are!" she said. "Didn't I tell you?"

Eek! A test and I wasn't prepared for it. Then again, I wrote the damn thing. You'd think I could do a decent job of remembering it.

"Is Jan here?" I asked. What would she think? My mind whirled, trying to remember all I'd added from what that sister had told me about Kent that day. How stiff would the story seem for someone who'd been there? And God, what would she think of that stiff character going through all she'd experienced?

"Yes, she's here and she can't wait to meet you."

Should I just apologize for everything right away when I meet her? No time to think, Carole had finished hugging my girls with a flourish and was directing us in her brunch protocol.

"First thing," Carole said, "you have to pick out your cup."

I must have given a blank look. The gears in my head were still spinning.

"For your tea," she said. "Everybody has their own special cup. Your girls, too. Come on," and she led us to the back of her condo to a garden room. On a baker's rack against the wall sat a collection of tea cups, china of all different patterns: floral and Art Deco, bone and translucent, scalloped and Henley.

Julia and Jen each pointed to one right away, as certain of their decisions as their father could be. As for me, I had to look over each, sorry for the ones I would not choose. "That one," I said, and pointed to a rose pattern with gold trim, not unlike the set Mom had bought antiquing with Aunt Mary.

"The girls might want to check out the garden," Carole said. "There's some fairy houses out there." A little sidewalk led up to a couple of miniature homes. A fairy perched on a mushroom outside the door of one, on the rooftop of another.

"You collect fairies?" I asked. I noticed them now, sitting on shelves, pictures in frames, sculptures.

"I love them," Carole said. "Any kind."

When we saw a collection for sale at a craft fair the next year, Jen wanted to get one for "the fairy lady." Maybe because of how fondly she remembers that day, maybe because that kind of gesture is what I've taught her to make.

"There are cousins downstairs," Carole said. "Make yourself at home."

The girls disappeared down the stairs. I know they had fun, since I didn't see them again the whole time we were there. Julia told me later the others introduced themselves as "cousins you didn't know you had." There was candy in dishes all around the room, and Julia ate so much she was sick. It was the best brunch ever, she said.

We'd sent the kids through the line first, and I couldn't wait to follow. There were egg bakes and fruit and pastries filling the counters. I had to mound my plate strategically, it all looked so good. And how could I not try all the family favorites?

The sisters had started taking seats around the table. I looked for a spot next to Val, but Carole shooed me away. "She's not allowed to hog you today," she said. "You sit there instead." The head of the table.

At least that's how I remember it, sitting alone, away from Val at that table, but Val remembers it differently: That we sat together, nudging each other at the things that were said.

Arlene, as far as I remember, had managed to nab a seat to my right. And Mary Anne and Margaret, sisters I had not met at the wedding, sat to my left.

Lots of catching up to do, finding out who these people were who were a part of Val's family, a part of my blood. Margaret, a horse lover, had Arabians out in California. She was in sales, nutritional supplements. Mary Anne had a radio station.

Val sat at the other end, down by Jan, who waved at me. Her hair was short now, swept back, and she was neatly dressed in a tan pantsuit. More a professional than a teacher. Not at all yet just like the dark-haired Nancy stand in I'd imagined. Did she feel as if I betrayed her, by putting some of what she'd done to paper? No, she was smiling. It was okay, I had to tell myself.

On Val's other side was Pam, who'd come in wearing an Ohio State Marching Band jacket. Not hers—her husband was the one who'd played tuba. She never went to college, I later learned, though she home-schooled her three girls. What a mother is determined to try to master when her kids aren't getting what she wants them to.

The sisters-in-law of Val's brothers, the only blondes in the group, sat between OSU Pam and horse-loving Margaret. The oldest sister, Gloria, was by Arlene, and then Carole's daughter, Kathy, the one who looked like me, then Carole. Turned out Carole was a credit underwriter for a bank, like the clients I had while in-house at First Union.

Keeping all those sisters straight was a challenge. I called Carole "Gloria" when I walked in the door.

So far she didn't seem to be holding it against me.

I don't know how I mistook one for the other. As I broke bread with those sisters, I tried to get them straight in my head again, as I had at Chris's wedding. Not just to memorize the name this time, but also the face and what she did, what she held dear.

The sisters were ready to talk about my book.

"It's so good, I can't wait until it's published."

Yeah, me, too.

Jan read the part of her exodus off campus after the Kent State Shooting. "You captured it," she said, sounding like Val did on the phone. Jan's eyes were expressive, honest. "It brought so many memories back to me."

"I never knew it happened like that," Mary Anne said. "It's all true?"

"Nancy, of course, I made up," I said, "but everything else is well documented—the riots on Friday night, the burning of the ROTC building, the bayoneting of those students the night before."

"I had a hard time believing that part is true."

"Poor training on the Guard's part," I said.

"Boy, that sounds familiar today, doesn't it?" Margaret said, to no one in particular. So I knew where she stood on the Iraq War, though most of the sisters were otherwise still Bush supporters then.

"They weren't trained for crowd control," I said, "and they handled it poorly. Didn't help they were given the wrong weapons. I mean, really, the M-1s were from World War II, meant to shoot an enemy two miles away. That's what they had to work with, to hold back a crowd of unarmed students." Okay, I could remember some of the supporting details. I was giddy with the attention. I was low on blood sugar, like the daughter in the story.

"So, Aunt Arlene," I said, knowing that would get her attention. "Could you pass the butter?"

She turned to me first, her eyes full of love. I could not for all the world have said anything kinder to her, and I knew I could never take it back.

In that instant, I wished I could. She was the one who'd almost showed up on my doorstep, until Val talked her off that ledge. I knew what would be coming: they'd all be sending me emails and letters signed "Aunt," these women I'd just recently met.

It's just too weird for me. Maybe I'm just too old to call anyone else aunt, anyone other than Aunt Sue, Aunt Joan, or even Aunt Mary, the ones I grew up with. On the other hand, I've no problem calling our daughters cousins. My girls already have twenty-two others, what's another twenty or so more?

Aunt-Not-Aunt Arlene handed me a plate of decorative butter pats. "For you," she said, her words honeyed, the kind you can't get off your knife.

"Thanks," I said, feeling everyone's eyes upon me and looking to Val for help. In that moment I realized it was no coincidence, this labor of love I'd written about a woman her age who'd lost the one thing most important to her, how she'd track down her daughter at all costs, even if it meant losing her career. Even if it meant losing her husband. My fiction was no fiction, it was an ode to Val, a tribute. Nancy was me, or a more uptight version of me, if that's possible, but the struggles she faced—those were Val's. No wonder I wanted so much to make that character real. My face burned red, and I hoped no one else could see the transparency in my words. Or, maybe, that's really what we were all there to discuss that day.

Val patted her manuscript, as if to remind everyone, including me: Back to the story, the fiction, with pages tattered and worn—and loved—as those who lived it.

"It was amazing how well you captured her fights with her parents," Val said.

The sisters all nodded. They knew about fights with parents.

"It was like you'd been there, you'd heard it."

Maybe I could imagine.

I'd told Val once she didn't have it as bad as it could have been with her father. I'd read a newspaper article, one that connected domestic abuse with unintended pregnancies. It had concluded that over eighty percent of abused girls would have an unwanted child, and it argued that if we could stem abuse, we could dramatically lower the number of abortions and welfare dependents, not to mention profound unhappiness.

I had brought up the article because I'd been amazed how strong the connection was, and then I realized just who I was talking to. "But I guess it's not like your situation," I said, embarrassed to suggest her life could be distilled into cold statistics. There had to be something more.

"What do you mean?" she asked, words sharp, on edge.

"I mean—" I didn't know what I meant. I had no idea what she'd been through, but I couldn't imagine the worst, couldn't imagine anyone I knew having gone through it. "It's not like yours rose to the level of abuse mentioned in this article," I said. "Like real abuse. Physical, like."

"No, Kate, it was real abuse. It was physical." Her voice was low and weighted with meaning. "Count me in with the worst of those numbers," she might as well have said. "I went through years of therapy," she admitted aloud. "My sisters didn't go through what I did with my dad, but they weren't as verbal as I was. He took it all out on me, and it was bad. It was really, really bad."

So bad all that mattered for her firstborn was to get that child away from him.

That bad.

LATER THAT AFTERNOON WE WENT to the Pumpkin Show. I use the term "we" loosely. Dad begged off for that, too. "My ankle," he said. "Too hard for me to get around." It was true, with his arthritis. But the real reason he didn't go is that, like my Jim, it's just not his thing. Jen either; she stayed back with Papa, her father's and her grandfather's daughter.

So I drove Jackie and Val and Julia to Circleville for the Pumpkin Show. Cars were parked along the road miles out. We'd no idea what a big deal this was. Jackie told us stories, like the ones I'd told Val as we swept past old familiar neighborhoods. The yellow Victorian her mother grew up in, how a famous Vaudevillian singer grew up next door. So many of our stories relate back to our mothers and what they did or didn't or couldn't do for us. Jackie directed us into the town's hardware store. Her brother knew the owner. We would watch the parade from inside, so we didn't have to deal with all this "riff raff," as Jackie put it.

Better, too, because a chill had settled in the damp fall air, the kind that sucks the warmth right from you, no matter how many layers you put over the oversized Pumpkin Show 2006 shirt Dad made for you and everyone in the family.

Jackie led us to the store, lettering on the window and a recessed door. Her face lit up as she stepped inside. "Hey," she called out.

Grouped in front of the store window, seated on chairs and standing around, were nieces and nephews, faces I recognized from the teepee reunion. "Jackie," her brother said to her, arms outstretched. "Hello," he said to us.

I introduced Val as Julia's grandmother, and it went over without question. Julia found more cousins she didn't know she had. So easy to make friends when you're family. Steve led us back, past shelves of nails and screws and nuts and bolts, back to the workroom for some beer—true Pumpkin Show form.

After, Jackie was itching to go see pumpkins.

"It's why we're here, isn't it?"

Into the late afternoon gray, we dared the crowds—more than two hundred thousand, according to the evening news. We were jostled past pumpkin bar stands and pumpkin juice vendors and pumpkin memorabilia. Val took Juls for a treat while Jackie and I stopped inside vendor tents for presents for those who could not be with us. I found a set of pumpkin cards for Jen.

"She needs something from the fair," I said.

"The Pumpkin Show," Jackie corrected.

"Right."

We met back by the pumpkin displays. Pumpkins painted with scenes, pumpkins coaxed into different shapes, even people's likenesses. Large pumpkins—six, seven, eight hundred pounds. As tall as me.

"Can we do the Ferris Wheel?" Julia asked.

"That's a great idea," Jackie said.

We all squeezed into one seat, hoped for warmth, and the ride lifted us up into the air. We could see the town and all its Victorian buildings. A mural, a tribute to a hundred years of the Pumpkin Show, was in progress on the building behind us. Midway games and a Rotary booth in one direction, crafts toward the other, food and drink booths dotted all around. Jackie told us the story about her mother and the vaudevillian actor again, but I just figured amidst all the excitement she forgot what she'd told us before. We didn't yet know she'd already begun her struggle against the thievery of Alzheimer's. As the Ferris Wheel lifted us above a town Jackie had already once described to us, we felt the chill of rain hanging in the air.

"Can we go home after this?" Julia asked, peering out over the safety bar. She'd clutched her arms around herself, still cold with her fleece and tucked between Val and Jackie. We were soon back at the cabin, where Dad had cozied with Jen, just shooting the breeze by the fire.

We'd found what we came for. Jackie had come to relive what she'd shared with her family. I'd too come for the past. But not only had I planned to rediscover the comfort of home, I came so my girls could enjoy the comfort of a newfound source of unconditional love. Maybe some of that for me, too. And so Jackie had been right; the Pumpkin Show did feature all the wonders of this life.

JOE CAME DOWN FROM CLEVELAND after conferences to join us for dinner. Our seating was at six, but we'd be there at least until nine. Dad would not be rushed to turn the table over for another party. He's the party, one you won't want to end. There's a reason, after all, he went into sales.

Dinner was everything I remembered of dinners with Dad, and now with Jackie, too. Easy conversation, flowing in and out of the silly and the sublime. Dad would alternate the jokester, then devil's advocate, digging in to see what we thought, what we didn't realize we thought, of what was happening in the world and in our lives. Between appetizers and salad, six deer gathered down below on the banks of the lake, and the up lighting cast their flanks in a honeyed glow. Their eyes large and black and expressive, as if this family, too, knew we were watching them.

After dinner, Dad slapped my hand when I reached for the tab. "You get your turn when these kids bring their own to visit," he said. Like my friend's brother said when I tried to pay for dinner after he'd taken us skiing. Pay it forward, he and his wife entreated. Give back. And more importantly, teach.

"What about me?" Val said, credit card in hand. "I get to pitch in, too, then."

Dad eyed her carefully, with the look he gave when I was in high school and needed correcting. She'd paid her debt already, giving everything she'd had to give.

"No," my father said. "Not tonight."

WHEN WE GOT BACK TO THE CABIN, I shooed the girls to bed. "It's late, it's been a long day," I said. I was helping them dig through their suitcases for jammies when Dad peeked his head in our bunkroom door.

"I'm going to bed," he said, as he will at the end of a long day. Nine o'clock, and he was ready.

"But they're having a party over at Number Four," Jackie said from the living room. "Steve told us today at the Pumpkin Show."

"Honey, I don't give a damn," Dad said sweetly. He was past seventy and past his bedtime.

"Good night, Dad," I said, giving him a hug.

"You got everything you need?" he asked.

He'd set us up in this cabin, a bedroom for him and Jackie, the bunkroom for the girls and I, and a pull-out for Val and Joe. He and Jackie had stocked the fridge in the kitchenette with drinks and munchies and still had taken us all to dinner.

"Yes, we're fine," I said. "Thanks."

He gave the girls kisses, too, and he turned in for the night.

"Let's go," Jackie said, reaching for her coat. She had her own family to connect with. "Do you want to go?"

"Let me get the girls down first," I said.

"I can stay back with the girls," Joe offered. "There's a game I want to catch," he said to Val.

She rolled her eyes.

"So, a girls' night out," I said.

We crossed the cul-de-sac over to a moonlit path on the way to the Number Four cabin. The wood was pale and rough cut and new, rebuilt last year after a fire.

Jackie tapped lightly upon the door. "We're here," she sang, opening it.

"Come in, come in," someone called from the back. We passed through a hallway, past the modern kitchen, nicer than our cabin's. Through the tragedy of fire came something better.

Back in the great room, the family had gathered on a plaid sofa and in denim armchairs and in kitchen chairs pulled close by. The niece from D.C. stood for Jackie and another stood for Val to take their seats. Steve went to find more chairs in the kitchen, but Jackie was already so engrossed in conversation she didn't realize she could sit. Val hesitated, waiting for Jackie.

Steve swung a Shaker chair behind me, and another by the D.C. niece. "Sit," he commanded, and we all did.

The talk was easy and louder as time ticked by, though by all accounts it could have been awkward. We were not a family that all grew up together with summer picnics and Thanksgiving dinners. We came together one by one, over the years, and each time someone would pull a chair out for another to sit, and the circle would grow ever wider.

For this was family, however brought together—marriage or remarriage, birth or adoption.

"That's so cool you brought your mother along," D.C. niece said.

It still catches me off guard every time. Consider: What if people called a woman you met ten years before your mother? You'd have to think about it, too, trust me.

"Yes," I said. "I'm glad she's here."

"You've gotten to know her pretty well, then?"

"She's a grandmother to my girls that my mother could never be," I said. My pat answer, one I still use, delivered lightly but weighted with meaning within. Val has offered everything she is to us, and I've taken what I can. If I haven't gathered it all up, it's only because I'm still trying to take it all in. I've gotten better at it, over the years. "It's nice, too, having an answer to all those questions you have as a kid, you know?"

Val was right next to me, but she wasn't listening, she was animated in her own conversation with Jackie's brother-in-law.

"And she's good people," I said, as I'd once told my mother-in-law. "Who couldn't use more good people in their lives?"

NEXT DAY, AND WE WERE ALL BACK TO REALITY. Dad and Jackie left early, not much past dawn, to catch a plane back to Florida. Joe left next, to catch up on some work at home. Val and I cleared the cabin, while the girls supposedly helped.

"What do we do with all this food?" I asked. The fridge was stacked with fruit and juice and cheese and a cake Val had brought from home. "There's a frozen pizza up here, too. You have to take this."

We filled a couple bags and stuffed the car. I did one last check of the suite, my duty since I'd been Jen's age. Maybe I should start having her do this now. But it's hard to let go, to let someone else have control. How many times did Val anguish over whether two strangers would really be giving over all they had to her little Carrell? Strange still to think that's me.

The girls were lounging against the car when I shut the screen door for the last time. "Climb in. Let's go," I said.

It was a quiet ride back north. We'd talked all weekend and were facing a three-hour trek up to the airport and past my old house once more. I had Val leave another message with the realtor.

As we drove, our conversation flowed, a river of words meandering through a landscape we'd culled together. I began working through how to tell her I wanted to start a memoir about her finding me, but the opening wasn't quite there yet. The kids lulled off to sleep in the back, and Val and I soon found once again that certain frankness you can have when you know such intimate details about each other right from the start. There are secrets you'd share that you'd never share with a mother who'd raised you, secrets too difficult to share with a daughter known since birth.

"What kind of a person gives away their baby?" Val said, flinging the words out as if expecting them to come back and slap her in the face. Even after all we'd been sharing, such brutal self-questioning seemed to come out of nowhere. "I mean, really," she said. "It's so wrong, totally wrong. I should have never done it. I was awful, just awful, to do it."

Thirteen years I'd known her, a weekend of nothing but talking, and she lands this on me at the end. And what does she mean? That I shouldn't be who I am? Because if she hadn't given me up for adoption, I don't know who I'd be. Different memories, different mom. I don't even know if I'd have been able to have a relationship with a dad like I did.

"Don't say that," I said. "You're not awful. It was the right choice at the time."

"But it wasn't right," she said. "It was what others told me I had to do, and I did it. I should have stood up to them. I shouldn't have done it."

"Oh, God, Val." All the years of angst she'd been through, even after we met. The books I'd read on birthmothers, the pain they all felt, grieving a child lost who wasn't dead, and she'd felt it too, all along. It was, indeed, as bad as I'd read in that article so long before.

For all the fairy tale ending I'd convinced myself this was—this one out of the one hundred thousand adoptions that happen each and every year here in the United States—even my adoption triad had a tragedy weighting one corner, wounding the very one without whom I wouldn't exist.

It'd been there for me to see, from the start. I would go back and read the non-identifying info on Val again. I had checked it for facts, for heritage and hair coloring. I hadn't seen the pain. It was there on the page all along, right from the start. I hadn't registered before that it wasn't clear to the agency why Val made an adoption "plan." Especially since she felt "ambivalent and anxious" about her decision and found it "difficult" to separate from the baby. How could they call it a plan when it didn't "appear that the agency worker ever had contact with [the] father"?

It'd been there for me to see all along, only I'd chosen not to see it. Not until Val ripped open the wound inflicted by following her parent's wishes so long ago.

"It's not fair, it isn't," I said.

And all that weekend I'd felt so welcomed, so comfortable in the moment with Val and her family, and all that time she was agonizing over the could-have-beens. My childhood fantasy, her all-too-real heartbreak.

I should have realized.

"I don't know what life would have brought if you'd kept me," I said. "And it wasn't the right choice for you. But I think, I really do, it was the right choice for me, it made me who I am, and what I do, and I don't think I would have met Jim if things would have been different, and then we wouldn't have Jen or Julia, and then where would we be? There's no easy answer, there's not. But there's one thing you've got to know, I think it was incredibly courageous, what you did. I don't know I could have gone through with it. I might have just not told anyone, gone and found some back alley place, had an abortion." God forgive me, I'm Catholic and I'm adopted and I really believe I might have chosen Door Number 2, that other lifelong closeted grief.

By now I was crying in front of Val and driving and thank God both girls were sleeping through all this emotion. There would be time, I knew, to talk about the possibility of writing down all we'd lost and all we'd gained. Another time. She'd say yes, that I knew. Anything for me, for the child she'd already given everything she had.

"I don't blame you at all. I don't," I said. "You've got to know that. You can let that guilt go. For God's sake, let it go."

Val looked down in her lap, at her empty hands. "Maybe," she said.

THE REALTOR DIDN'T CALL US BACK UNTIL we were in line at Burger King. Val took the call, stepping out of the line and over to the door. She put a finger over her other ear and focused on the floor as she listened. "We'd love to see that house in Rustic Hills," she said. "Like at noon today?" She didn't say, because I have to drop them off at the airport. She paused, listening to the agent for a moment. The agent was telling her no, the house just went under contract.

"Tell her why," I said.

That's when Val turned, her back to me like she wanted to explain something but didn't want me to hear, needed to say something that needed to be said. "My daughter is only in town this weekend, it's the house she grew up in, we wanted to see it."

My daughter. She'd turned her back, like Aimee, before Mom caught her up in her bedroom.

My daughter. The girls hadn't even noticed what she'd called me, they were planning what they'd order.

I'll admit, even after all we'd shared those intense leaf-littered days: those two words grated on me. My daughter. Can't go back, can't ever go back.

But I said nothing, just turned to the clerk.

Who would want to explain something like this to a stranger? To be overheard by a restaurant full of people. And I was the one who'd insisted on explaining why it was so urgent we see it.

My daughter.

She's my birthmother, I try to make clear to those who'll call her my mother. But for Val, what am I, if not her daughter, too?

❧ 28 ❧

Other Sides of the Family

I sn't it amazing seeing David in Jen's expressions?"

I was sitting at Nor's new cabin overlooking the bluffs of the St. Croix last June. The Octagon, where we'd lunched the first time, still stood on the other side of the boardwalk bridge. As distinctive as the older place is, the new cabin is more so: It's beautiful, with cork floors and architecture reminiscent of Frank Lloyd Wright. There's only one piece of art in the place, a photograph of the woods, and what's odd is that the home is so well designed, so much a part of the landscape, you don't feel any lack of beauty in the place. And I've been in places where you feel the lack of beauty.

Nor was talking to her youngest sister Welling, who'd come for another visit with her son. I caught the rhetorical question and savored it in all its implications. I had to confess what that meant to me, to hear that from my birthfather's sisters, how important it'd been to find who I looked like.

"Oh, you definitely look like David," Nor said it this time, as we watched my girls playing stealth attack with water guns against their biological cousin and Deirdre's oldest son. (My head hurts trying to figure out how

Deirdre's kids are related to mine, so see what you can do with it.) "You've got to send me pictures of Jen and you from when you were little."

I knew what she'd be looking for in them.

"So, I've wanted to ask," Nor said, settling in on the couch across from Welling and I. "How's the memoir going?"

"You know, I have to apologize," I said. I'd sent her my first chapter, not realizing I included the summary in what I'd emailed off to her. And in that summary, I had some personal things about her. About her family. How could I be sharing all this? I was making them all as vulnerable on the page as I'd made myself. What would you think, if you'd read this about your dead brother, written by someone who'd never met him?

The black sheep in his family, he was a sculptor among professors and oceanographers and other multi-degreed intellectuals. I met his parents in the middle of Charlotte-Douglas International Airport and now get together about once a year with his sister, who lives in St. Paul. A Jungian psychotherapist, she writes experimental plays and practiced Tai Chi before it was offered at any McHealthClub. She's done everything I wanted to explore in college, but Dad refused to pay for any such frivolity. "No, you're nothing at all like any of us," my blood relative said after surveying me. "Must come from your birthmother's side."

What a way to share all that with someone. Talk about a Freudian slip. I tried to explain: "My synopsis . . ."

"Did I really say that to you?" Nor said. "I can't say I remember. Isn't that horrible?"

"No, no, you didn't," I said. Who was I, to be sharing all this? My story, it was her story, too. And so many others. "I double checked, looked at some emails I exchanged with Christin—with a friend of mine—when we all first met. It wasn't you," I said. "It was your father."

Nor tipped her head back and laughed. "Oh, I can see that. He scared me when I was a kid." Conjugating verbs of dead languages at dinner and all that.

Good to know I wasn't alone. I remembered all too well how I felt when I met her parents, when I couldn't translate a simple Latin phrase. Still can't.

"Hey, I had it even worse," Welling said. "The only kid left at the table and the sole focus of those awful interrogations." She smiled then, a coy little smile. The kind I used when I know something others don't. "At college, though, when I got into my major"—Ancient Greek, one of my other favorite courses I never dared float by Dad as a possible major—"I learned he really didn't know much Greek. Really."

Of all things. This, from a man who was so smart that as his mind began to fail at the end of his life, his children would have to convince the doctors that normal cognitive tests wouldn't work for him. The things we learn about people, the things we want to remember.

Nor said, "You know now how much I enjoy you and the girls, don't you?"

"And me, too," I said quickly. "Us, too."

And of course Welling, too. It's all good, and there's plenty to share, just like Dad said.

It's a dance, an intricate one, this joining of our families. No, we can't go back, but we can all go forward.

Back at home I sorted through Nor's pictures of her family once again. I can't see David's eyes in mine, and I don't see his smile when I flip between pictures of me and pictures of him. But I of all people should know the shortcomings of these still and unmoving pictures, the comfort of finding life once again behind the features of those we have lost. Oh, the comfort of having the chance to connect with them once again.

Best of all, to see those features react to the love you still have to give. A lovely feeling, like finding an odd-shaped piece that makes the rest of the puzzle fall into place.

A few months later, I would be at a fund raiser for youth literacy programs, and Nor would happen to be there, too. She'd arrived late, having been at a museum opening for a tour of Frida Kahlo's paintings. Nor was dressed for her first stop of the evening, gold lamé sarong wrapped around her waist, a headband with a tiny skull dangling from it. I sought her out across the room even as Dad's words chimed in my head: "Yes, Nor's the hippie, the hippie." Even among writers, my birthfather's sister stood out, dramatic and free. That I could never be, I'm too comfortable in my Talbot's dresses and my Eddie Bauer jeans, but Nor certainly has a kind of style I've always envied. It's just the way she is, the way she'll always be. And now I know it's a part of me.

People that night had talked about finding a home at the Loft, that center for writers that Nor had first told me about. And I knew what they meant as Nor draped her arm around me to introduce me to a friend. Nor's eyes raised to the heavens. Was she looking for direction from her brother David? "Let's see, introductions," she began, laughing, as if recalling a favorite family story. "My niece. Yes, this would be my niece," she said, squeezing my shoulder.

"That was nice of her, to call me that," I said later to a friend from book club who'd joined me that evening. My friend and I were hurrying back to my car, parked a block and a half away. It was the end of October in Minneapolis, and all I'd had was a wool paisley wrap for my shoulders, but I was warmed by the memory of Nor's arm across my shoulders and by her words.

"Well, you are," my friend Jean said.

Probably not right, for me not to be bothered by Nor's claim as I'd been with Val's sisters. Maybe it's just been a way for Nor and I to reach out to our dead. Maybe I'm just fickle. Whatever the reason, I can tell you that, just as with Val's sisters, I won't be calling her Aunt Nor anytime soon.

But the girls can, if they want.

LAST WEEKEND I MADE MY FAMILY DRESS UP—even insisted my thirteen-year-old put on a skirt—and come along to my mom's cousin's fiftieth wedding anniversary. "They're not cousin cousins," I said. "Might be once removed or something. I can't keep it straight."

In the eight years we've lived within forty-five minutes of them, I can probably still count on my one hand the number of times I've seen them. I've had them down to dinner when Dad and Jackie first came to town, and we went to Julie's wedding three years ago. It's hard enough to schedule a dinner with friends, I guess it shouldn't be any easier getting together with distant relatives like Harvey and Patsy, or with biological ones like Nor. Besides, we don't get to see some of Jim's sisters but once a year sometimes. Same thing—maybe.

Mom might have only had one brother, but her family considered even her second and third cousins close. I remembered when they'd come to visit, Patsy huffing from the exertion of walking all the way around the house, and we'd have drinks out on the porch, the one with the awful corrugated roof that was never fixed. And yes, we had porch furniture exactly like what Kitty and Red have on *That 70s Show*.

Mom's family's parties were more Irish than Swede, lots of drinks and singing. Even back when Mom was growing up, those Swedes in Norway, Michigan, would sing around the piano in Gramma Verne's home. And Dodo (pronounced DooDoo—really—it's short for Dorothy) would play until the varnish wore off the piano bench.

"That's hyperbole," I once said to Dodo at some cousin's wedding reception years ago.

"Oh, no, Katie," she said. "That's the truth."

On the way to Mom's cousins' reception, I picked up the Mapquest pages Jim had tucked between us. "It's right by the Girl Scout Store," I said.

"Hey, hey," Jim said, half teasing, half not. "Don't be messing with my directions." I'd love to help navigate like Mom used to do, I really would. But I can relate to the need to be in control, to know what's going to happen next. Maybe that was something Dad could let go of, when he was with Mom, something Jim and I just can't do.

Then again, maybe Mom was just a better map reader.

"Mom and Dad would have had their fiftieth back in July," I said out the window.

"You've said that."

"I'm just saying." I turned over the invite. It had a picture of the Johnsons on their wedding day on the back—a slimmer Patsy, Harvey with hair on top of his head, and a black mustache instead of white. These were the things I would have helped coordinate this year, had Mom still been around.

Jim pulled into the parking lot for the Church of Grace.

"We won't stay long," I said. We'd come just for the last hour of an open house, and it looked like it was winding down already. Church elders gathered around round tables. A laptop hooked up to a projector flashed pictures upon a screen. We must have come at the end of a continuous loop showing fishing trips with grandsons, birthday parties. Black and white and the early years would appear later during our visit.

I was pleased I recognized Harvey, even after all these years. We gave each other hugs, and he kindly guessed that the girls were in a higher grade than they were. Retirement was treating him well. The joy he shared with his family flashed above us on the screen. Birthday parties, hunting trips, ice fishing with children and grandchildren.

I recognized one of their daughters from across the room as she recognized me. Julie or Lisa? Julie or Lisa? "Julie," I said, and Harvey let us cross over so I could give her a hug. "I haven't seen you since your wedding, you look great," I said. "What's it been? Two years?"

"Three," she said.

We talked about her family, got caught up on the niceties. Hungrily I took in the spread. I don't mean the well-stocked cold cuts and sandwich bread and potato salad and pickles and other sides, but the effort she'd put forth for her mom. She'd done what I couldn't; she gave back something to the woman who'd given over so much. I wished I'd thought to do the same for mine before it was too late to do anything at all.

At least for Val I know to give more than a stupid plaque—though it can be hard sometimes to be more creative than that.

Julie talked about the pictures flashing on the screen as it looped through group shots, tow-headed kids grinning with Lisa's arms around them. "Such little blondies," I said. "Our family is all so dark. Irish blood took over."

Julie was nice and didn't say, "But you're adopted anyway." Instead she said, "There's a picture of us with Grandma Carlson."

"Oh, Anna," I said, pronouncing it with my great Aunt's Swedish accent: Uh-na. "That's right, that's how we're related." We go through it every time. My Gramma Verne was her mother's sister. We had an extra generation on my side, with her grandmother marrying late, and my great-grandmother marrying young. A miracle pregnancy: Gramma Verne arrived just a month later.

"Back then, pregnancies didn't last as long," Jim said.

Seems unexpected pregnancies run in my blood line, by nature and by nurture. Hopefully my daughters don't get that gene.

Julie led me to her mother, who was sitting at a table, a cane propped next to her. Not robustly healthy, but still here. Patsy didn't see us at first; she was busy talking with a couple of older friends.

She caught my eye and smiled, leaning with one hand on her cane and reached up with her other. "So glad you could make it," she said.

"Oh, I wouldn't have missed this," I said. "It's too big an event. Julie and I were just catching up."

A woman, a friend, hung close by our words. Patsy pulled her into our conversation. "Do you know who this is?" she said, gesturing with her cane.

The woman looked at me, her eyes bright but rheumy from age, and she shook her head.

"It's Peela's daughter," she said.

Peela's daughter.

I hadn't heard that expression in so so long.

Peela—my mom's nickname as she grew up, one of many of the goofy names among friends in their small hometown in the Upper Peninsula. I'd forgotten what that sounded like, what it was to be among those who'd considered her family.

And oh, I tell you, it felt like home.

๑ 29 ൭

Last Words

"Sometimes," Julia pouts at the end of a particularly difficult fight with Jen, "I wish it turned out she wasn't my sister. Like yours."

"Whoa," I say. "Aimee's just as much my sister as Jen is yours."

Julia ducks her head, and I realize I have spoken too loudly, too fiercely. She's touched a nerve, and she regrets it immediately.

I soften my tone, but I can't keep the words from coming. This she has to know: "Aimee and I are just as much sisters as you and Jen are. Papa and Grandma Peri and Aimee and I were just as much a family as we are. Knowing Nana Val now doesn't change any of that."

Julia doesn't say anything.

"Okay?" I ask. I lift up her chin. "Okay?"

Julia scowls. "You don't get what I mean."

"You don't get what I mean."

And she won't. She hasn't lived it.

Sometimes I wish it were simple again, back when Mom was alive and I had my little family I grew up in and my family with Jim.

But a song to be sweet needs more than one note. A band is richer, more interesting the more instruments that play. I'm glad Val made the

283

move to find me and helped me connect with David's family, too. For my daughters, for me.

Nice metaphors aside, though, I can't help but miss the alto who always sang a little flat.

IN FIRST GRADE FOR PARENT'S NIGHT we had to fill out a sheet about ourselves. Our favorite color (green), if we had any pets (a cat, three dogs, fourteen horses), how many brothers or sisters we had (one sister) and what we thought of them (she's too loud). We also had to write what we wanted to be when we grew up, and I put down either the first woman in space or a writer.

Sally Ride beat me to my first dream. But I was more interested in being the latter than in being an astronaut.

Funny how I knew being a writer was what I wanted to be, even before I knew of Fitzgerald or Hemingway, even though I didn't start writing until Julia started kindergarten. This was the story I wanted to tell, but I knew I wasn't ready for it yet. I started with fiction, with characters that would do what I wanted them to do, who would succeed or fail with my key strokes. It would be hard, I knew, to have to write about the people I love. To be honest about what happened when my little family of four fell apart and how we put it back together.

Like Steve Austin, I think we are better, stronger. Maybe not faster. But definitely bigger.

And yet, through all the joys of connecting with Val and Nor and their families, my mother's warning words remain. Now, finally, I know what she means, that we can't go back. Because the moments we had with her are gone. And I miss her so.

I have learned something, though. Of course, I've learned about Val and the kind of person she is, the kind of person David was. But as much as I've enjoyed this journey, I wasn't the one looking for a mother, like P.D. Eastman's baby bird. I wasn't looking, yet I was still missing a piece of myself. I'd been searching for it in family albums and by interviewing relatives, ones

I always knew I had and ones I had discovered. And like Dorothy in *The Wizard of Oz*, I've since learned everything I ever needed is with me already.

When my mother died, her life spread out before us. It happened in the waiting room by Intensive Care at Akron General. Dad was with Mom, and I was just coming back from the big house.

I'd left earlier that night to put Jenny to bed. Mom had crashed during dialysis, gone in to respiratory failure. She wasn't conscious, hadn't been for hours, and the doctors had told us to say good-bye, that it would be a matter of minutes, not hours.

But the minutes had ticked by and turned into one hour, then another. I had a baby with me, one who was used to naps on schedule, dinners on time. I could keep her happy for a while, hold her off, but when it was past nine and Mom still hadn't left us and Jenny was reaching that fussy point where Jim couldn't love her to a quiet, Dad turned to me and said quietly, "Katie, it's okay to go. Your daughter is the one who needs you now, not your mother."

I stood by my silent mother's side, and I kissed her good-bye. I was quiet as Jim drove back to the big house. With one hand I tried to massage to sleep a daughter too tired to try. I nursed Jenny in the wing chair in the guest room. Fitful at first, she finally settled as I soothed over her head, singing "You Are My Sunshine" through my tears. I lifted her into her crib, and I wanted nothing more than to curl into a fetal position myself on the bed when the phone rang and I stumbled back out to the great room. Jim was talking on the phone, tones quiet and short and small.

"She's gone?" I asked, resolved to the inevitable.

"She's up," he said eagerly. "Kate, she's conscious again, and talking. You have to go back."

I grabbed the keys and flew out the door. The snow was coming, down through the darkness, and the roads were wet on the way. I prayed she would hold on until I got there, hold on until I could tell her good-bye once more, so she could hear. We'd had two and a half years since her diagnosis, two and a half years to come to grips with this night, but denial kept me from ever facing that simple reality. Thirty percent survive, I kept telling myself. To my mother, who was third in her class at Michigan State with a biology degree, that had to be easy odds. She was always in the top one or two percent, she could be again.

I ran up to ICU, back to where I'd spent my day. "I'm here to see Perianne St. Vincent," I said.

"You have to wait," the nurse said. "She has someone with her."

Of course it was Dad. "But we all should be with her," I said.

"One at a time."

"Even when she's dying?"

"One at a time."

Good Lord. "Will you let them know I am here? They called me to come."

The nurse nodded and gestured to the waiting room door. I swear to God, if she dies while I am here and standing in this stupid waiting room—I pushed open the door. Nowhere to sit, this waiting room was full. I recognized Lil first, flipping through a magazine, waiting more than reading. But others were there, too, across the room, filling the chairs, all of Mom's friends: Ray and Rachel, Cal and Donna Wible, and the Gilberts, who had taken a seat by Aimee. And there were the Haddads, and the Smiths, and even the Glasses. Some had known Mom and Dad since college, like Rachel and Bruce. Some had played golf or tennis with Mom, like Donna and Sally and Lil. Some shared vacations and holidays, like the Gilberts and the Wibles and the Smiths. We'd shared picnics by the pool, dinners with the bishop, nights at the Gin Mill after a day on the slopes in Ellicottville.

And now, they'd come to be by her side, by our side, at the end. They were there, even though the doctors wouldn't let them go back to be with her. Only family, only one at a time. It was all she could handle.

But she knew they'd come. She knew because I told her.

"Jesus Christ, why are they all here?" Dad had swung open the door to the waiting room, to let me know I could go back.

"They're here for you."

"They don't need to be here for me."

"They're here for her," I said.

"But they can't see her."

"Well, they're here for themselves!" I said. "Because they want to be. To show how much she means to them."

"Jesus H. Christ," he said. The beginning of his withdrawal. But as I ducked out the door, he'd started with Ray, to thank him for being there.

Mom was lying on the bed, an oxygen mask still on her face. To ease her through. The tears started coming, I didn't want them to come but they were there.

"Mom, they're all out there," I said. "All your friends, did you know?"

She tried to say something.

I guessed at what she was saying. I told her who all was there.

Her lips moved again, she was trying to say something. A question?

"I'm sorry, Mom, what?"

Something, something.

Would she be asking where Jim and Jenny were? Had Dad told her she'd been out for so long? Did she know it was so late at night? That we'd thought we'd already lost her?

"Jim had to take Jenny home. He's with her at home." Oh, she might think they were back in North Carolina. "Back to the big house," I said. "That's where they are."

Mom reached out for my hand, and I took it. Her mouth formed the words, she spoke slowly, and I leaned in so I could hear.

I wished I'd been there when Aunt Mary had taught her to read lips, to guess what words were being spoken, to make sense of sounds you could not hear.

"You can count on me, Mom," I said. "I'll take care of Dad. And Jim. And Jenny. I'll tell her stories, so she won't ever forget."

287

I held tight to her hand as her lips moved again, trying to tell me what I couldn't hear before. These, the last words we'd share, and I'd no idea what was being said, what wisdom I should always hold close in my heart.

"I love you, too, Mom," was all I could say. "I love you, too."

"YOU KNOW WHAT SHE'D TELL YOU," Jim tried to comfort me later. Four days before Christmas, and we'd lost a most precious gift. "She'd say she loves you."

"Probably." That's what she told Dad. "I love you I love you I love you," he said she'd said, and she whispered the words soft and fast, as if she was getting the phrase out as many times as she could before God took away her last chance to say it.

I wished I'd heard what she'd told me, in those breathy words. No doubt it was better than Dad's father's last words: "Follow the money."

This Thanksgiving Jackie tried to give Dad grief over that, until I reminded her of her own mother's last words: "My nose is too short." Which at least was better than the last words heard by a child whose mother died in a car accident. ("Oh shit.") There's more not said in those last words, all the love and care and concern for those left behind. We know it's there, even if never uttered, never heard. That's what I hang onto.

Reading this will be the first time my father learns I do not know what my mother told me in the end. He's already read parts of this; I've sent him the first chapters.

"I couldn't read the first couple," he told me. "But I read the third."

And?

"I didn't know you struggled so much with telling me about Val."

So much more he doesn't know, so much I've struggled with not telling. He says he's not ready to read the rest. He'd rather just philosophize about the business end of it, about how I should be proud enough of what I do to walk away from a book deal if it's not enough money.

I wonder how many writers are brave enough actually do that.

Dad stops himself and says, "You tell your story, though." He says, "You tell it how you remember."

Or what I don't. Jim and I have run through all the possibilities of what Mom could have said. "She told you to look after your children," Jim suggested, at the time.

"I know. And my husband."

"And your dad. Especially your dad."

"I told her I would."

"See there?"

"And I told her I loved her."

"Well, then."

More than anything else in the whole wide world.

Aunt Mary tells me Mom's still with us, that she still shares our joys and all our sorrows. It's what angels do.

That's what mothers do; she's a part of me and always will be. But thirteen years have since passed, and Dad and I are still grappling with the whole eternal life question.

"Do I get to be with her right away when I die?" he asks me. He thinks because I work in a church I know the answer. "Or do I have to wait until Judgment Day?"

My priest says he didn't take that class in seminary. But time is a human construct, anyway, and means nothing in eternity.

Dad says that means he's here to heal, and the dead won't talk.

I don't know what to think. A part of me believes in the pearly gates, standing on the clouds, getting angel wings when bells ring, just like Clarence did at the end of that Jimmy Stewart movie. But a part of me thinks the spirit is just what we the living carry with us in our hearts.

So that's why I am telling you this. So I can share all that I carry in mine. Mom, mostly. But all the other mothers in my life, and what spirit they've given me. Val's good intentions, Aunt Mary and her prayers. My mother-in-law Teresa and her love of children. Gramma Verne and her love of a good time.

By the time it's Val's turn to go, I'll have spent more time with her on this earth than with Mom. And it will be just as hard to lose her, I'm sure. She'll be a part of me in a way I've yet to imagine. Not in place of, but in addition to.

And by then, maybe I'll have another story to tell.

In the meantime, every week I go to church and listen, to hear what Wisdom has to tell me. I believe she's there, as she was at Julia's baptism, when the songs from her funeral echoed once again through the church. And so each week I go to hear comfort in these words: Go, and may the Spirit be with you.

And with you, too.

IT'S TUESDAY, AND I'M RUNNING. Not in the usual sense, getting the kids from soccer to karate to piano, but really running. I surprised myself and broke out in a run at my daughter's school marathon a month ago. It's only been a month now, we'll see how long I can keep this up.

I usually walk instead. It's a pace I can think at. Running, I can't do anything but be in the moment. I suppose that's what I need at this point in my life, I'm so busy thinking about what I've got to get done that day, that week, and too busy berating myself for what I did or didn't do, it's nice to just be for a half hour a day.

It's the end of October again, and we've managed to steal another beautiful day. Warmer than usual, and the Crayola-blue sky against the caramel-colored leaves is all I can focus on as I pick up my pace at the end of my street, our dog, Happy, trotting beside me. I've started too late, I won't have time to do a full run before I meet Jen at the bus stop and walk her home. But when I loop back to her bus stop, she's not there, no one's there. I run home to catch up with her, bring Happy into the house on her leash, which can only confuse that small brain. But Jen's not home, either. A house is eerily quiet when a child's not home and she's supposed to be.

I know where she is, though. Back outside, back up the street, past the library. I can't go in because I have the dog, but I know Jen has stopped in. She got an email earlier that day that the book she'd been waiting for had come in. I loop back through a park. There's a pair of older women resting on a bench and I chug up the hill. I wave at them, and they wave back, and the incline isn't as bad as it looked from below.

Back out to the street, and when I turn the corner I see a girl laden with a backpack coming out from the library. I'm buoyed by the sight of my daughter, and I run along the other side of the street, convinced I can catch up to her. I wave at the cars coming out of Cub Foods, thanking them for letting me pass when I know they'd really rather go first.

Jen doesn't see me until I cross the other side of the intersection and catch up with her on the corner. She laughs when she sees me, even with a stack of books ready to tumble out of her arms. "Can you help?" she asks, but Happy wants to do what she can first.

"You stopped at the library," I say, taking the stack of Manwha, a Meg Cabot, and the sequel to the *Traveling Pants*.

"How could you tell," she says. She's laughs again, not the belly laugh she had as a baby, but still the kind that lights up her whole face. I am amazed every time how beautiful she is, that she is my daughter. I've seen the same look on Val's face when we've visited. I hope Val has learned what I have, too. That what we love will live within us. I trust this is what Val hung onto all those years without her baby Carrell.

Jen is saying something now, but she speaks so quickly and her words run together so I can't tell what she's saying.

I know where she gets that from.

"What?" I ask. "You saw an old lady in good shape with a dog that looked like Happy, and then you saw it was Happy?"

"No," she says. "An old lady in a green shirt."

"I liked it better the other way." I laugh.

We walk the block and a half home, and I make a mental note to ask the girls to sign a card for my sister while Jen talks about a game they played in French that day. She loves the class, loves that she's the fastest to come up with the answer. She is so much like me it drives her crazy.

"I think I inherited some French speaking skills, from you and Dad," she says.

"Well, it was a French major who married that Ojibwe," I say. "You've got it in your blood." It's not really true, they were Dad's paternal grandparents eight generations back, but I know we've at least adopted their spirit.

"So what else happened today?" I ask, but this middle schooler won't tell me much more now than when she was two and couldn't, when I picked her up from Mother's Morning Out, a picture of a bear with a round belly and stick legs clutched in her hand.

"Nothing," she says, but she smiles, keeping something to herself.

"You know I love you, don't you?" I say.

"Mom, you're weird," Jen says as we turn up the drive.

"And you get to grow up just like me," I tease, but I wish more for her, so much more. Just as my mother—my mothers—did for me.

"Well, God help me," she teases back, and she unhooks Happy's leash. We wait as the garage door rises. The golden leaves of the river birch shimmer in the wind, and a few sprinkle to the ground to join the purpled oak and sugar maple and yellowed elm leaves already there. This weekend Jim will blow them all to the back into a dark pile that will melt into the ground come spring, but for now October colors fleck our yard.

Jen heads inside for her snack, and Happy and I follow. Julia's bus won't come by for a while yet. We will be here when she comes through the door.